Prophetic A

RELIGION AND SOCIAL TRANSFORMATION
General Editors: Anthony B. Pinn and Stacey M. Floyd-Thomas

Prophetic Activism:
Progressive Religious Justice Movements in Contemporary America
Helene Slessarev-Jamir

Prophetic Activism

Progressive Religious Justice
Movements in Contemporary America

Helene Slessarev-Jamir

NEW YORK UNIVERSITY PRESS
New York and London

NEW YORK UNIVERSITY PRESS
New York and London
www.nyupress.org

References to Internet websites (URLs) were accurate at the time of writing.
Neither the author nor New York University Press is responsible for URLs
that may have expired or changed since the manuscript was prepared.

Library of Congress Cataloging-in-Publication Data

Slessarev-Jamir, Helene.
Prophetic activism : progressive religious justice movements
in contemporary America / Helene Slessarev-Jamir.
p. cm. — (Religion and social transformation)
Includes bibliographical references and index.
ISBN 978-0-8147-4123-8 (cl : alk. paper) — ISBN 978-0-8147-8385-6
(pb : alk. paper) — ISBN 978-0-8147-4124-5 (ebook : alk. paper)
1. Social justice—Religious aspects. 2. United States—Religion—1960-
3. Social justice—United States. I. Title.
BL2525.S572   2011
201'.70973—dc22   2010049594

New York University Press books are printed on acid-free paper,
and their binding materials are chosen for strength and durability.
We strive to use environmentally responsible suppliers and materials
to the greatest extent possible in publishing our books.

Manufactured in the United States of America
c   10 9 8 7 6 5 4 3 2 1
p   10 9 8 7 6 5 4 3 2 1

Contents

Acknowledgments

I initially conceived of writing a book on prophetic activism nearly ten years ago as a result of my personal participation and interactions with a number of the organizations featured in this book. However, I would never have been able to complete this project, had not so many organizations' executive directors and staff responded to my email requests for interviews, taken the time to talk with me, and in many cases also send me their materials. I am deeply thankful for their willingness to share their stories, and I only hope that I have authentically represented their organizations' work.

I especially thank Kathy Partridge, the director of Interfaith Funders who connected me to a number of key community organizing activists and to Ernesto Cortes who shared his expertise on congregation-based community organizing during several lengthy conversations. I owe my knowledge of Catholic social teaching to Msgr. Jack Egan, which he shared with me during the last years of his life. I am grateful to both Kim Bobo and Alexia Salvatierra for taking extended amounts of their time to talk about their work. I must acknowledge Harry Smith for all his hard work in making the arrangements for a week-long visit to the humanitarian organizations in southern Arizona that I and five Claremont School of Theology students made in January 2009. I thank my fellow members of the United Methodist Church's National Immigration Task Force and especially Bishop Minerva Carcaño for enabling me to gain a national overview of religious responses to immigration. Bill Mefford, the UMC's Washington lobbyist on immigration issues, provided crucial assistance in mapping out various religious organizations' legislative positions on immigration reform.

I was already familiar with congregational-based community organizing, worker justice, and immigrant rights activism. I had been an active participant in immigrant-rights work since 2006, first in Chicago and now in southern California. However, I had little previous experience with religious peacemaking. Therefore, I am especially indebted to several close friends who guided me in developing chapter 6 by sharing their experiences and contacts with me. These include Ellen Marshall, Glen Stassen, David Cortright, Jim Wallis, Rose Berger, Duane Shank, and David Gushee. Several of them also gave me opportunities to talk through my findings and conclusions along the way.

My friend and former colleague, Sandra Joireman, shared her impressions of religious global justice work as I started working on chapter 7. Both David Beckman and Bobby Shriver found time in their very busy schedules to give me firsthand accounts of their work with Bread for the World, the Jubilee campaign, DATA (debt, AIDS, trade, Africa), and the ONE organization.

I am very grateful for my colleagues at Claremont School of Theology who have given me multiple opportunities to give public lectures on topics related to this book. Since coming to CST, I have also been able to incorporate aspects of this research into new courses and as a result have grown through interactions with my students. I also want to thank my hardworking research assistants, Jacob Kang Brown, Vanessa Stotts, Ivy A. Melgar Cargile, and Andrew Jordan, who always responded to my requests for background material, data, and activist interviews. Finally, I am most grateful for my ever patient, loving husband, David Jamir, who not only encouraged me to write this book but also tolerated long months of my single-minded focus on completing this manuscript.

Acronyms/Abbreviations

ACORN	Association of Community Organizations for Reform Now
AFSCME	American Federation of State, County and Municipal Employees
BFW	Bread for the World
BUILD	Baltimoreans United in Leadership Development
CCHD	Campaign for Human Development
CIO	Congress of Industrial Organizations
CLUE	Clergy and Laity United for Economic Justice (ALSO, CLUE-LA, etc.)
COPS	Communities Organized for Public Service
CSO	Community Service Organization
CtW	Change to Win
DCP	Developing Communities Project
DRC	Democratic Republic of Congo
ECUSA	Episcopal Church USA
EFCA	Employee Free Choice Act
EITC	Earned Income Tax Credit
ELCA	Evangelical Lutheran Church of America
FIRM	Fair Immigration Reform Movement
FLOC	Farm Labor Organizing Committee
FOR	Fellowship of Reconciliation
HERE	Hotel Employees and Restaurant Employees
HIPC	Heavily Indebted Poor Countries

IAF	Industrial Areas Foundation
ICC	International Criminal Court
ICE	Immigration Customs and Enforcement
IDEPCSA	Instituto de Educacion Popular del Sur de California
IWJ	Interfaith Worker Justice
JWW	Jewish World Watch
LAANE	LA Alliance for a New Economy
MACC	Mexican American Cultural Center
MDG	Millennium Development Goals
NAFTA	North American Free Trade Agreement
NICWJ	National Interfaith Committee for Worker Justice
NLRB	National Labor Relations Board
NMD	No More Deaths
NNIRR	National Network for Immigrant and Refugee Rights
OCCCO	Orange County Congregation Community Organization
ODA	Office of Development Assistance
PEPFAR	President's Emergency Plan for AIDS Relief
PICO	People Improving Communities through Organizing National Network
RCNO	Regional Congregations and Neighborhood Organizations
SAPs	Structural Adjustment Policies
SCHIP	State Children's Health Insurance Program
SEIU	Service Employees International Union
UDHR	Universal Declaration of Human Rights
UFW	United Farm Workers Union
UNO	United Neighborhoods Organization
USCCB	U.S. Catholic Conference of Bishops
USWA	United Steelworkers of America
WFP	Witness for Peace
WIC	Women, Infants, and Children
WTO	World Trade Organization

An Introduction to
Prophetic Activism

All religious traditions have certain sacred holidays that embody their core narratives. Within Judaism, Passover commemorates the Israelites' flight from bondage into freedom, while within Christianity, Christmas celebrates the birth of Jesus. The weeks leading up to the Christmas holiday are an extremely busy time, yet in 2008 nearly 1,000 people gathered at Disneyland in southern California to take part in a *posada*. Posadas are Mexican celebrations of Jesus' birth in which people go from house to house in remembrance of Mary and Joseph's search for lodging in Bethlehem. This posada had been organized by Clergy and Laity United for Economic Justice (CLUE) in support of workers from the three Disneyland hotels and their children. The hotel workers were members of the Hotel Employees and Restaurant Employees union (HERE) who were in contract negotiations with the Disney Corporation.

During the posada, Christmas wish letters written by the workers' children were left for the managers of each of the hotels. The crowd stopped at the front entrance of one hotel to recite a liturgy written by the clergy active in CLUE, explaining why they were performing the posada at Disneyland. It read in part:

> We also are reminded that Christ entered the world in a manger, where animals eat. . . . In the Christian tradition, we see that our King was one that identified fully with the poor and the stranger to teach us of a kingdom marked by holiness, justice, love and peace. . . . Today, as it occurred many centuries ago, there are many people seeking lodging and hospitality, like our sister and brother workers of the Disneyland hotels. . . . We, as religious leaders, will accompany them in this modern day Posada as we stand in solidarity with the workers who are on this long journey.

The liturgy then invited the hotel managers to have a conversion of the heart because "Our workplace should also reflect God's justice by ensuring that those who are seen as 'lowly'—janitors, housekeepers, cooks—are lifted up and not sent away hungry."[1] Afterwards, everyone gathered in a nearby parking lot where the children were given gifts donated by various community and church groups while the adults drank delicious Mexican hot chocolate.

While CLUE reinterpreted the traditional religious meaning of a posada to become a call for Disneyland to treat its workers justly, the Jewish World Watch (JWW) has reinterpreted the Passover seder as a pedagogical tool that highlights the broader concept of all people's rights to freedom. The Jewish World Watch, which has sixty-four member synagogues in southern California, sees Passover and the Jewish High Holidays as important moments for educating its supporters on the genocides occurring in Darfur and the Congo. As one of Judaism's most sacred holidays, Passover serves as an ideal forum for Jews to explore present-day cases of genocide. Every year JWW distributes forty thousand pieces of educational material designed to be used at a seder, which normally takes place at a family's dining room table. At the seder the ritual seder plate contains six food items, which each symbolize the Passover story of suffering, liberation, and renewal. In 2008, JWW created a small fold-out companion brochure that connected each food item to discussion questions designed to provoke small group conversations around the table about the contemporary meaning of the seder in the context of ongoing genocide in Darfur. In this way, the seder guests were invited to participate in a very traditional Jewish method of study based on one-on-one conversations in which participants reflected on how they might be willing to respond in the face of contemporary genocide.

Both CLUE and JWW are creatively drawing upon sacred events in their religious traditions to remind adherents that they ought to commemorate their religious origins as outcasts by embracing the demands of today's outcasts for freedom and justice. These stories are two examples of an increasingly broad range of progressive religious justice organizing occurring in the United States, which is motivating growing numbers of people to act on behalf of justice for the marginalized. Yet, the extent of these forms of religious activism may come as a surprise to many Americans who have become far more accustomed to religion, especially Christianity, being used to support conservative political causes. Religion is becoming increasingly contested as it is mobilized to lend credibility to very divergent political agendas. This is especially true of Christianity since it is the faith embraced by the majority of the country's religious adherents. During George W. Bush's eight years as president, Christian conservatives gained unprecedented levels of political power by successfully championing what they portrayed as a "Christian" political agenda.

At its most extreme, conservative Christian rhetoric sought to project an image of the United States as a nation uniquely ordained by God to assume the mantle of the world's hegemonic superpower. Claims that the United States is invested with divine power have a long history, dating back to the nation's earliest days when British colonialists proclaimed their colony in the Americas to be the New Jerusalem, "the shining city on the hill." American exceptionalism gained renewed vigor in the early nineteenth century as Euro-Americans pushed into the far western reaches of the continent, displacing the indigenous people they encountered and eventually laying claim to the northern states of Mexico. This territorial appropriation was commonly viewed to be the United States' "God sanctioned mission to fulfill" its "Manifest Destiny."[2] Interestingly, this rhetoric reappeared in Sarah Palin's speeches during the 2008 presidential campaign and was no doubt an animating force behind the new conservative populism that emerged in response to Barack Obama's presidency. More than thirty-five years ago, the activist theologian William Stringfellow offered a prophetic critique of this worldview.

> To interpret the Bible for the convenience of America . . . represents a radical violence to both the character and content of the biblical message. It fosters a fatal vanity that America is a divinely favored nation and makes of it the credo of a civic religion which is directly threatened by, and hence, which is anxious and hostile toward the biblical Word. It arrogantly misappropriates the political images from the Bible and applies them to America, so that America is conceived as Zion: as *the* righteous nation, as a people of superior morality, as a country and society chosen and especially esteemed by God.[3]

There have been times in recent years when these triumphalist voices became so loud that it almost appeared as though they were the singular possible construction of the nexus between religion and politics. In reaction, there were calls, both in the United States and abroad, for a return to a purportedly older, liberal secular version of American politics in which all references to religion are banished from public political discourse. Many secularists would prefer that all mention of religion would once again be confined to the private sphere.

This book demonstrates that there is a third option: religion can be and is being used to frame a progressive politics that prophetically calls for justice, peace, and the healing of the world. Indeed, some of the most significant social movements of the twentieth century emerged from exactly such interpretations of ancient religious texts that pointed to the essential dignity and equality of all human beings as rooted in God's love for all humanity. From Gandhi's rereading of the sacred Hindu texts to Dr. Martin Luther King's use of the Sermon on the Mount to construct a nonviolent movement for racial change to the emergence of liberation theology within the Latin American context, religion has served as a powerful motivator for social change among the marginalized.

In offering a far-reaching analysis of contemporary social justice activism in the United States, which emerged out of progressive religious ideals, this book acts as a counternarrative to conservative Christians' narrow constructions of politics that became the embodiment of religious activism over the past twenty years. While conservative Christians strive to impose their singular set of religious ethics upon a religiously diverse American body politic, progressive religious activists' interpretations aim to broaden American politics by incorporating people who currently have no voice within the political process.

While conservative religious leaders also often use the word "prophetic" to describe their critiques of the societal status quo, I employ it throughout this book to reference a religious understanding of politics defined by its inclusiveness, its concern for the *other*, for those who are marginalized. Borrowing a phrase from Howard Thurman, the grandfather of African American theology, it is religion that speaks to those who live with their backs against the wall.[4] In the midst of the chaos and pain of the present, prophetic politics envisions an altered future in which human relationships to one another and the natural world are repaired. Within Judaism, this is known in Hebrew as *tikkun olam*, which means repairing the world. Prophetic approaches allow activists to ground their present actions, no matter how difficult or even life-threatening, in a vision of hope for a transformed future in which justice will be realized, right relations between nations restored, and peace ushered in.

The Contours of Prophetic Activism

Contemporary prophetic activism has grown in direct response to the steady reversal of both formal and substantive rights triggered by the shift from national to global capitalism and the accompanying rise to power of conservative free-market politics. In this country, conservatives gained national political power in part by vilifying the marginalized, including "welfare moms," young urban black and Latino men, gays and lesbians, undocumented immigrants, and Muslims. Prophetic activism has also expanded in response to the exigencies created by the globalization of capital and production that has contributed to the exacerbation of income inequalities in wealthy countries and the deepening impoverishment of the poorest nations. These conditions have in turn fueled regional violence, especially in parts of Africa and Latin America, as national leaders make use of paramilitaries to engage in acts of genocide against marginalized groups in their own countries. Moreover, the religious peace movement in the United States was reinvigorated in reaction to the aggressive nature of American empire in the wake of 9/11 that left the country mired in two wars.

Present-day practitioners of prophetic politics are characterized by a commitment to nonviolent social change. Their thinking has been heavily influenced by paradigms that emerged over the course of the twentieth century, beginning with Mahatma Gandhi's powerful example of building a spiritually grounded, nonviolent mass movement capable of driving the British out of India in 1947. This was followed by an equally powerful, spiritually grounded movement to end racial apartheid in the United States that succeeded in contextualizing Gandhi's concept of *satyagraha* or active nonviolence to the struggle for African American civil rights.[5] Both of these movements were grounded in the fresh reinterpretations of Hinduism and Protestant Christianity that affirmed the sacred and reciprocal quality of all human life, out of which flowed a call to do justice to the *other*. Similar processes of reinterpretation have occurred within Catholicism, Judaism, Buddhism, and Islam.

Another commonality of contemporary practitioners of prophetic organizing is their incorporation of aspects of liberation theology into their work. Having first emerged within Latin American Catholicism, elements of liberation theology's message have now been rearticulated within a variety of American contexts. It is particularly common among Christian activists who are engaging in solidarity work both within the boundaries of the United States and beyond. It is less common among organizations whose primary focus is influencing the national legislative arena. However, when used, it shapes organizations' moral call to action, and it articulates commitments to give voice to those who are marginalized, to empower those lacking rights to gain the capacity to act on their own behalf, and to stand in solidarity with people in developing countries who are suffering at the hands of regimes allied with the United States.

Although many of the activist organizations whose work is featured in this book remain grounded within the Christian prophetic tradition, in some cases, their self-understandings are expanding to embrace more diverse faith and spiritual practices. This is possible in part because this work exists independently, outside of the strictures imposed by direct denominational control that would be more likely to impose doctrinal limits on such work. Certainly, denominations do still connect and support prophetic activism, yet their priorities lie elsewhere. They tend to be more comfortable drafting position papers, doing educational work, holding press conferences, and engaging in legislative lobbying than directly engaging in prophetic activism. Independence gives present-day prophetic activists—and the organizations and networks they have created—the flexibility to respond to the ever-changing American political landscape, refocusing their religious lenses to respond to newly emerging issues and constituencies. None of the various organizations we examine in subsequent chapters are isolationists. Instead, they all work with a broad array of other religious organizations, secular advocates, and institutions including human rights organizations, legal advocates, unions, schools, health-care institutions, foundations, and even sports clubs. There is also a strong multireligious presence, especially within religious peacemaking, along with a growing Jewish presence in congregational community organizing, and in worker and immigrant rights work.

In this book's final chapter we discuss a set of global justice organizations that have been birthed since 9/11 and are not overtly religious, yet some members of their staff and volunteer supporters engage with the issues they champion out of their religious convictions. It is probably not a coincidence that two of these organizations have the youngest supporters and staffs of any organization featured in this book, given the Pew Charitable Trust's findings that eighteen- to twenty-nine-year-olds are considerably less religious than older adults.[6] Another one has developed a set of religious resource materials for use in four of the world's major religions, which they make available on their Web site. This pattern may well be the harbinger of an emerging trend: to be simultaneously secular *and* religious.

Prophetic activism is not a new phenomenon. It has manifested itself in this nation's long, colorful history of religious activism on behalf of the abolition of slavery, the creation of a national labor union movement, the prevention of war, and most significantly for our present era, on behalf of African Americans' civil rights. Many current activists are motivated to take action by a strong sense of connection to this historical legacy. So, for example, the Progressive Jewish Alliance organizes against sweatshops in Los Angeles, in part out of its sense of responsibility to Jews' own history of immigration to the United States in the early twentieth century. Not only had Jewish immigrants worked in the sweatshops, they also became the leaders of some of the unions that continue to organize immigrant garment workers today.[7] Yet, despite its long presence as an important current in American politics, present-day forms of prophetic activism have remained largely submerged, hidden from widespread public view. For example, while there was considerable media coverage during the 2008 presidential campaign of Barack Obama's work as a community organizer in the early 1980s, it was rarely if ever mentioned by the mainstream media that Developing Communities Project (DCP), the organization for which he worked, is a congregational-based community organization. In fact, it is affiliated with the Gamaliel Foundation, one of the four large national congregational-based organizing networks. Not only did this omission leave the impression that DCP was a secular organization, it also hid an important manifestation of President Obama's own religious identity.

Many of the contemporary prophetic organizations situate themselves as the descendants of earlier social movements and include participants who were personally involved in the civil rights movement, farmworker organizing, anti–Vietnam War mobilizations, the Nuclear Freeze campaign, and the Central American sanctuary movement to name just a few. As one issue faded, participants moved into new areas of activism. Many of the older organizations now have multiple generations of activists within their ranks, who respond and engage with issues very differently. Still others, faced with the aging of their most loyal members, are struggling to stay alive, let alone attract younger adults. Interestingly, certain organizations' concerns about membership decline are not unlike those facing the historic Protestant denominations with which they often share overlapping memberships.

The current flourishing of varied forms of prophetic activism is particularly significant because religious commitments create possibilities for people to act in ways that defy the dominant models of rational, self-interested actors found in most current theories of political behavior. Religiously constructed activism certainly has the capacity to sustain marginalized people in the face of great opposition. This brand of activism also has the power to create the ethical foundations for solidarity between the politically marginalized and those with privileged access to political power. By evoking humanity's scared bonds with one another, religious organizing can straddle the existing gulf between places of marginalization and places of privilege. Doing so opens up new spaces for broader social change campaigns. In fact, the last major period of progressive social reform that led to a large-scale expansion of formal and substantive citizenship rights during the mid 1960s was an outgrowth of exactly such broad alliances, albeit tenuous and short lived. Certainly one of the lessons of that earlier period of national reform is the central importance of strong grassroots activism integrally connected to effective advocacy within the national legislative and executive branches.

Prophetic activism is fundamentally concerned with the well-being of the marginalized both within the United States and within poor and violent regions in developing countries. A person's well-being is fundamentally determined by their access to basic human rights, which rest on a universal understanding of the dignity of all human beings.[8] Much of the activism highlighted in this book should be understood as a struggle for the attainment of basic human rights that are supposedly universally affirmed by the language of the United Nation's Declaration of Human Rights (UDHR). Thus, religious activism in support of workers' rights can be conceived of as a struggle for human rights since the declaration claims that access to work is a fundamental prerequisite of human well-being. Article 23 recognizes the right to work, along with the right to equal pay for equal work, and the right to form or join a trade union as fundamental human rights.[9]

Yet, in the United States and elsewhere, those rights are often flagrantly violated. In modern democratic societies, well-being is integrally tied to access to basic legal and substantive citizenship rights. Within the world's wealthy democracies, there are inherent citizenship rights that people acquire by virtue of their membership in a particular sovereign nation-state. These include *positive* rights such as the right to vote, the right to work, the right to fair remuneration for work, and the right to form associations, including labor unions, as well as *negative* ones that protect against unwarranted intrusions by the state. There are also varying sets of substantive rights that citizens have acquired through the exercise of their legal rights. Among these are such publicly provided benefits as access to free public education, health care, old-age pensions, disability, and unemployment benefits. Despite being one of modernity's first democracies, the extension of full citizenship rights has been a slow and painful process in the United States. After all, the nation was founded on the basis of a constitution that sanctioned African American slavery; it initially restricted voting to white men with property, and denied women's suffrage until 1921. Asians, who were completely excluded from citizenship, were even denied the right to own property. This denial of citizenship rights ultimately culminated in the imprisonment of Japanese Americans during World War II. Limitations on suffrage and ongoing practices of racial discrimination have led to the creation of a more limited set of substantive citizenship rights in the United States than in other economically advanced Western democracies. Even though the nation has slowly purged itself of the worst of its racist past, there are still millions of people living in the United States, many of them people of color, who lack the full complement of legal or substantive citizenship rights.

The Contours of Global Empire

This book situates contemporary prophetic activism within the context of today's global empire, which following the work of political scientists Michael Hardt and Antonio Negri, is conceived of not as any one singular nation-state but as unbounded, global capitalism taken as a whole.[10] I chose to use the word "empire" as a means of emphasizing the political consequences of economic globalization. Globalization is structuring many of the policy options being weighed by policymakers at all levels of governance, ranging from those managing international institutions down to national and local politicians. The internal and external policies of individual nation-states are now more interconnected than ever before. Simultaneously, religious activism has arisen in direct response to the negative repercussions of globalization upon many of the world's most vulnerable local populations.

Historically, empires were characterized by highly centralized systems of economic extraction where the flow of goods and tribute from the periphery to the center was enforced by the center's administrative and military control over the periphery. Today's much more diffuse form of empire is characterized by the existence of tightly intertwined global capital markets, which have spread their tentacles into virtually every corner of the world. The economically dominant nation-states embedded within this global empire collaborate within one another, while simultaneously vying for increased market advantages in an insistent race for global dominance.

While economic globalization has undoubtedly created tremendous wealth for a few and upward mobility for emerging middle classes in certain rapidly developing countries, it has plunged other parts of the world into deeper poverty. In the 1960s many newly independent nations pursued import substitution policies aimed at industrializing their economies. They did so by erecting high tariff walls to exclude foreign investment and manufactured goods so as to create the space for the growth of domestic manufacturing. By the late 1980s though, with the collapse of the Soviet bloc and the triumph of capitalism, "free trade" became the new mantra. Countries either willingly or through outside pressure, lowered their barriers to global trade. Capital began to flow freely across national borders, constantly in search of the highest profit margins, but it drained out of the weakest economies, especially in Africa and Central America. These regions were already beset by violent internal conflicts, weak governments, and increasing levels of unpayable international debt. In too many cases, undemocratic regimes had borrowed from the International Monetary Fund (IMF) and the World Bank to finance their militaries and the lifestyles of their political elite rather than investing in strengthening their domestic economies. Recognizing that these countries were at risk of defaulting on their debts, the international financial institutions began imposing a set of strict structural adjustment policies (SAPs) in exchange for refinancing their existing debt load. The SAPs forced countries to offer increased economic incentives to foreign investment, reorient their domestic production to the export market, and reduce public sector expenditures. By the 1990s, such policies were displacing local farmers, while shrinking public sector employment.[11] The rise of religious global justice activism is a direct consequence of the detrimental impact that these dramatic economic shifts have had on the world's poorest regions.

One of the most significant consequences of globalization has been the freeing of labor from its traditional moorings. Like capital, labor has also become far more mobile than it had been in the past. Not only did it unleash large-scale migration from rural areas into urban centers, it has also precipitated unprecedented global migration. At present it is estimated that there are roughly 200 million migrants scattered across the globe who financially support an equal number of family members back in their places of origin. Although some are refugees, the majority are labor migrants. For these millions, migration has become a family survival strategy as their traditional means of earning a livelihood have been replaced by the penetration of capital intensive production into less-developed economies. Yet, while the richer nation-states support policies that facilitate the free movement of global capital, they are moving in the opposite direction with regard to the free movement of workers. Even as poorer migrant-sending countries are loosening their definitions of citizenship to account for the bi-national lives of many of their citizens, rich countries are militarizing their borders and tightening citizenship requirements. As access to citizenship in richer countries is restricted, millions of labor migrants are at risk of becoming a permanent disenfranchised underclass. The consequence of these twin forces of massive migration accompanied by a tightening of access to citizenship is the creation of vast pools of people living in countries where they have no citizenship rights. It fact, the pressures of the contemporary globalized economy have quite possibly created the largest pool of noncitizens since the 1648 treaties of Westphalia established the European system of sovereign nation-states.

In the United States, the resultant surge in undocumented immigrants has become a political flashpoint, with conservative demagogues willing to depict the supposed "immigrant threat" as a major cause of the nation's economic woes and a drain on national resources. Congressional legislators from both political parties embraced demands for stricter border security and the elimination of undocumented labor. By 2010, however, the majority of religious activists and most national religious bodies had embraced a call for just comprehensive immigration reform that would open up an avenue through which the vast numbers of undocumented immigrants could regularize their status. In countless local communities, religious activists, acting out of their religious beliefs, were choosing to stand in solidarity with immigrants who were seeking to empower themselves in their local communities and workplaces.

Following the demise of communism, the United States has asserted itself globally as the singular hegemonic political and military power. Simultaneously, it is locked into fierce competition with the European Union and rising economic powers in Asia and Latin America for dominance of world markets. Even though Democratic and Republican administrations have pursued divergent foreign policy responses to this highly competitive global environment, both political parties remain committed to the maintenance of U.S. global hegemony. In fact, even President Obama's call for the development of green energy, health-care reform, and increased spending on education were all framed as initiatives needed to maintain U.S. economic dominance.

Despite its seemingly amorphous nature, globalization leaves its mark more prominently on certain key urban centers around the world. These urban regions constitute the nodal points of globalization where capital and information are created and then exchanged through elaborate, international fiber-optic networks linked to other cities around the world. The sociologist Saskia Sassen refers to these cities as the "command and control centers" of the global economy where cutting-edge producer services are created and marketed for use by transnational corporations that invest and produce around the globe. Cutting-edge producers within this global information and service economy prefer to work in cities, which are seen as conducive for the kinds of creative synergies that lead to innovation and new product development. Consequently, certain key cities now bring together a global workforce—a small number of which are highly educated and skilled managers along with thousands of *others* who work, often in the informal labor market, servicing the living standards of the highly paid managers.

As a result of their incorporation into empire, certain cities have become highly contested spaces as central-city locations are now regarded as the coveted work and residential locations for the global networked economy. Prior to the 2008/9 recession, land prices had been skyrocketing, creating very lucrative real estate markets in the inner urban core. This led to a dramatic reconfiguring of urban space with the wealthy moving into downtown locations while the poor were rapidly being squeezed out. This transformation has been startling in cities such as New York, Chicago, San Francisco, and. to a lesser extent, Los Angeles. For example, since the early 1990s, Chicago's downtown office space doubled, while a ring of new constructed upscale housing arose on three sides of the downtown area. Housing projects were torn down, their residents scattered into poor outlying neighborhoods, to make room for fashionable townhouses for the global managers. City and state officials were vying with one another to lure new global corporate headquarters and production facilities, yet had little interest in investing in infrastructure for neighborhoods in which new immigrants, poor African Americans and others live. Community-based activism has expanded in reaction to these dramatic transformations as congregations and other community-based institutions resist the resultant marginalization of poor African American and immigrant communities.

The Politics of U.S. Empire

In a 2005 book titled *Inequality and American Democracy,* a group of prominent political scientists led by Lawrence R. Jacobs and Theda Skocpol linked the growth of income inequality in the United States to a decline in the federal government's support of policies that "promote equal opportunity and security and enhance citizen dignity and participation, reinforcing the suspicion of many in the American public that government officials 'don't care' about the needs and values of ordinary citizens."[12] Even though globalization has exacerbated disparities in wealth within the world's richest nations, some responded by using government policies to protect the living standards of their most vulnerable citizens. However, the same study found that not to be true of the United States. The researchers concluded that "government policies and actions in the United States have been especially responsive to the values and interests of the most privileged Americans and therefore have often not undertaken active and effective steps to mute or offset market inequalities."[13] In the United States, globalization has been accompanied by the political decline of those institutions, including unions, civil rights organizations, and activist elements within religious denominations that in earlier times had played key roles in empowering marginalized groups in American society. As a consequence of this decline, independent religious justice organizations are assuming an increasingly critical role as a principal moral voice within local, state, and national political arenas.

In an earlier work, the political scientist Theda Skocpol demonstrated that in the past the voices of ordinary citizens were frequently mobilized through an extensive web of voluntary organizations, which reached across class boundaries by organizing chapters at the local, state, and national levels. These organizations successfully mobilized and trained people of modest backgrounds in the art of politics while simultaneously encouraging people of higher status to interact with their fellow citizens on a wide range of issues. At their height, organizations such as the Masons, the Elks, the Fraternal Order of Eagles, the Women's Christian Temperance Union, the General Federation of Women's Clubs, the Knights of Columbus, and various veterans groups "often rivaled political parties in affording organized leverage in civic and legislative affairs to large numbers of Americans."[14] In the early twentieth century, African Americans founded their own broad-based civic organizations aimed at the promotion of social and economic uplift, including the National Association for the Advancement of Colored People (NAACP), the National Urban League, and Marcus Garvey's more populist Negro Improvement Association. By the mid-twentieth century, these popularly based membership federations rivaled business and professional organizations for influence over national policy making. Organized labor, represented by the recently merged AFL-CIO, stood at the forefront of struggles over economic and social policies. Still others worked on agricultural, educational, and family related issues.

By the early 1970s, however, many of these older organizations found themselves increasingly sidelined. In part, they were displaced by the political upheavals of the 1960s that had brought new social movements to the forefront of American politics. New grassroots activist civil rights organizations, movements against the war in Vietnam, and an emerging women's movement increasingly supplanted the traditional organizations. African Americans finally gained full citizenship rights, which were accompanied by new legal protections of their voting rights along with a revamped immigration law that for the first time granted legal admission into the United States to people from all countries in the world. Taken together, the 1960s social movements led to a reordering of racial- and gender-based power relationships while striking a blow to U.S. ambitions of global hegemony.

The political coalitions that brought about these expansions of democratic rights proved to be quite fragile. Following the assassination of Martin Luther King Jr., moderate civil rights organizations were displaced by new militant Black nationalist organizations, which quickly alienated many Jewish and mainline Protestant supporters of civil rights. The political momentum gradually tilted toward conservatives as reaction to the expansion of rights set in, not only in the Bible Belt but in the Democratic Party's urban strongholds and within organized labor. A politico-religious realignment, coupled with the emergence of global capitalism and a reaction to the growing hybridity of the nation's racial and ethnic makeup triggered by globalization and the new immigration law, transformed the political landscape. With the election of Ronald Reagan as president in 1980, national administrative agencies responsible for the implementation of labor and civil rights fell into conservative hands. Reagan's appointees to the two agencies responsible for overseeing the implementation of labor and civil rights began to dismantle their enforcement mechanisms. The Reagan National Labor Relations Board (NLRB) displayed a pronounced hostility to unions and collective bargaining, while the Equal Employment Opportunities Commission (EEOC) labeled affirmative actions programs set up to compensate for decades of structural discrimination in the workplace and the academy as reverse discrimination.

The historic Protestant denominations that had stood at the center of American religious life for generations were not immune to this national shift toward conservatism. Roman Catholicism, having arrived early in the Americas with the Spanish conquistadors, had taken root in the United States among newly arrived working-class immigrants. In contrast, Protestants' center of gravity lay among whites living in the rural towns of the South and the Midwest. Protestant denominations were well connected to political power, preferring quiet private meetings with politicians over any public forms of protest. Their views on political matters reflected their elevated social and economic status. As we will see, the oldest religious peace organization in the United States was formed in direct response to the denominations' open endorsement of the U.S.' entry into World War I.

In the 1950s, the predominantly white Protestant denominations remained silent even as early local manifestations of the gathering civil rights movement arose throughout the South. The success of the Montgomery bus boycott, which highlighted the pivotal role of the black church in the emerging activism, made "the inaction and moral hesitancy of the major white denominations" even more glaring.[15] It was the 1963 March on Washington, the movement's penultimate national event that finally catalyzed the moderate denominations into active engagement. The white Protestant churches mobilized belatedly, bringing forty thousand people to the Washington Mall.[16] A growing number of clergy became directly involved in civil rights activism. One study of Protestant clergy in California found that in 1968 one quarter of them had taken part in some kind of civil rights demonstration.[17] Final passage of the landmark 1964 Civil Rights Act is credited in part to the grassroots efforts of local religious activists that swung midwestern Republican members of Congress into support for the legislation. This monumental effort was the fruit of a broader ecumenical movement that flourished in the early 1960s, which included the convening of Vatican II, Pope John XXIII's conciliatory overtures toward non-Catholics, and the welcoming of Catholic and Jewish representatives into the National Council of Churches as regular participants.[18]

The intervening decades have witnessed nothing less than a seismic shift in the landscape of American religion. Today, the United States is a post-denominational society, in which many people select local congregations, based not on their denominational affiliation but on whether the pastor and the church feel right to them. Fifty years ago, religion was treated as an ascribed aspect of a person's identity. A Gallup poll taken in 1955 found that only 4 percent of Americans no longer adhered to the religion of their childhood. Yet by the mid-1980s there had been a dramatic shift, with another Gallup poll discovering that one in three Americans had left the denominational faith of their childhood. Religion had increasingly become "achieved," a chosen identity that is not always or even often the same as that of one's parents or upbringing.[19] Today religion is often one more consumer-driven choice, made less on doctrine and more on the psychological or emotional fit of a local church to an individual. Simply hanging a denominational identifying sign outside a church's front door no longer draws people in, just as the old brand names of Ford and Chevrolet are insufficient. Both white and African American Protestant and Catholic churches have been slow to comprehend the implications of this sea change, often continuing to assume that their members would remain loyal from baptism until burial. The result has been a steady numerical decline in membership among the old denominations.

Within the historic Protestant denominations, conservatives reacted to these declines by arguing that they are in part the result of their progressive activism. They argued that the churches' bureaucracies continued support for progressive causes was out of step with members in the local congregations. Today, conservative caucuses exist within the United Methodist Church, the Presbyterian Church USA, and the Episcopal Church. They are committed to rooting out all forms of what they perceive as unorthodox expressions of support for various liberal justice issues, including support for the rights of gays and lesbians to marry or to become ordained clergy. They have particularly targeted what they consider to be theologically progressive clergy and seminary professors who are seen as questioning the basic tenets of the Christian faith. Their decades-long campaign to silence progressive religious lobbying has led to a decline in funding and a resultant quieting in the activism of the denominations' Washington lobbying offices. The United Methodist Church's shifting budgetary priorities have also led to declines in resources allocated to clergy training, while funding for a wide variety of resources used by local churches and regional denominational bodies has increased from a mere 3 percent in 1969 to 15 percent in 2008.[20]

The dramatic weakening of unions, civil rights organizations, and prophetic voices within denominations has left these historic advocates of expanded substantive rights unable to mount strong responses to the consequences of globalization on the rights of American workers or the urban unemployed. Working-class whites and African Americans for whom manufacturing jobs had served as a route into the middle class have seen their economic status decline. As manufacturing jobs were exported, millions of new low-wage service jobs were being created for which many employers preferred to hire undocumented immigrants who could claim no rights due to their lack of legal status. In recent years, unions have mounted aggressive new organizing campaigns among service workers, yet unions and employees are often too weak to win against the formidable array of union-busting tactics that employers throw at them. It is in the midst of these increasingly contentious battles that independent religious justice organizations now play critical roles. Not only do they provide a much-needed moral voice in support of the rights of vulnerable workers and communities, they increase support for these struggles among a broad range of American citizens. Moreover, local religious activists have opened up new spaces for dialogue between African American and Latino clergy whose communities have been deeply divided by globalization's impact on the domestic U.S. economy.

In the aftermath of the collapse of the Soviet Union, the United States also asserted its global military dominance, including claiming the right to militarily intervene in countries that it perceives as threats. Here too, religious opposition has consistently raised the critical moral questions surrounding the U.S.' foreign policies. It has been peacemaking organizations, some of which identify as religious while others have large numbers of religious members, that have consistently challenged the U.S.' support for paramilitaries in multiple Latin American nations, its invasion of Iraq and Afghanistan, its endorsement of conservative Israeli governments' support for expanded settlements in the West Bank and East Jerusalem, as well as its support of torture. Religious activists are also largely responsible for triggering what is now a remarkably broad commitment on the part of the United States and other wealthy countries to invest significant financial resources in the elimination of disease and hunger in the world's poorest nations, especially in Africa. Much has happened since religious activists embraced the call for Jubilee in the years leading up to the new millennium. It is in this arena that they have made significant progress in achieving a religious commitment to establishing right relationships among nations.

Prophetic Activism as Resistance to Empire

Resistance to these new forms of domination takes many forms, as people seek to increase their capacity to live fruitfully in the context of empire. In the United States, major advances in both formal and substantive citizenship rights tend to occur as a result of initial pressure from below, gradually finding expression in the centers of political power. Yet, certain critical foreign policy issues, which are often shrouded in secrecy, emerge directly on to the national political agenda. Much of present-day religiously inspired activism works alongside groups of people, both domestically and internationally, who resist becoming victims of the new global order. In certain international contexts, activists hold the United States directly culpable, while in others, it is seen as capable of exerting pressure on other regimes that are oppressing their citizens. We will see how, depending on the activists' social location, they are assisting the disenfranchised to be empowered to act on their own behalf or they are creatively seeking indirect means of making other people's voices heard within the halls of power. As a whole, these new types of religious activism constitute an element of a broader multidimensional global resistance to modern empire. Their efforts are constituent of what Hardt and Negri call the "multitude;" a collection of singularities that have been brought into existence by the new global order or imperial sovereignty. The forms of prophetic activism featured in this book frequently share common goals and commitments with secular forms of resistance to empire, even though they may not share common strategies or methodologies of creating change.

While much of the U.S. activism featured in this book is rooted within the Christian tradition, many current activists are increasingly working within broader interreligious and secular contexts. This is true even of a few evangelical justice organizations, which are collaborating with other Christian, Islamic, and Jewish activists. This willingness to embrace inclusive engagement places them in opposition to triumphalist forms of Christianity that demand exclusivity for the Christian message, making them hostile to interreligious collaboration. The growing multireligious nature of prophetic activism is itself a challenge to American empire since Western imperial regimes have frequently used some form of Christian triumphalism to undergird their power. Triumphalist Christianity has served to justify European empire since the time of Constantine, the first imperial ruler to embrace the faith. In fact, the very formation of a European identity of self rested on the creation of the notion of triumphal Christendom standing in opposition to Islam.[21] Following Christopher Columbus's arrival in the Americas, the idea of Christian superiority became critical to European justifications of colonial domination over the globe's non-Christian dark-skinned peoples. All forms of religious triumphalism are undergirded by the belief that adherents alone possess the knowledge of God's truth: anyone who disagrees is not only wrong but is guilty of apostasy. Contemporary Christian versions of triumphalism frequently claim to take the Bible, which is viewed as inerrant, seriously, yet in reality they rest on the use of selective proof-texting, which carefully picks out only those passages that appear to give credence to their vision of the world. They habitually personalize the readings of Scripture, reading often substandard English translations as though they were written for a singular rather than a plural "you."

Prophetic activists, who are also grounded in the texts of their religious traditions, have consistently taken an alternative approach. All religions contain some forms of "other-regarding" beliefs that can be used as powerful motivators for engagement in justice activism. Within Christian, Jewish, Muslim, Hindu, and Buddhist religious traditions, activists are mining their foundational religious texts for fresh interpretations that not only affirm the sacredness of all living beings but their interconnectedness as well. They do so either by reworking traditional literalist readings, by referring to the newest scholarly translations, or by identifying portions of the texts that are commonly bypassed by those who construct hegemonic interpretations. The reinterpretations are aimed at strengthening the scaffolding upon which religiously grounded collective justice activism occurs. In some cases, this requires shifting interpretations away from an emphasis on spiritual practices aimed primarily at strengthening individual communion with the divine toward those aimed at engaging with other people as a means of communing with the divine. For example, Jewish Reform rabbis who are engaging in congregational-based community organizing draw on new readings of the book of Exodus, claiming it not just as a narrative of redemption but as the bringing into being of a community at Sinai, culminating with the building of the tabernacle where the people would dwell in covenant with Yahweh.[22]

Christian prophetic activists also emphasize God's commitment to justice as a foundation for their religious engagement on behalf of justice for *others*. While they certainly quote specific passages of Scripture in their literature, at rallies, and in public testimony, their worldviews are shaped by the reading of whole texts as the stories of God's interactions with Moses, the Israelite prophets, and of Jesus, who lived within the borderlands of the ancient empires of the Near East. This relational approach allows them to recognize the complexities of the biblical narratives, beginning with Genesis and the covenant with Israel, through the prophetic warnings of the impeding destruction of Israel to Jesus' boundary crossing vision of radical inclusivity in the face of Roman imperial oppression. Taken as a whole, the gospels become stories of Jesus' efforts to spearhead a movement "of renewal of the people" in which he repeatedly pronounced God's judgment on their Romans rulers and their local Palestinian underlings.[23] After the destruction of the Second Temple, the apostle Paul, who possessed a cosmopolitan identity as a Jew with Roman citizenship, corresponded with newly formed multiethnic and multinational Christian communities located in various cities across Asia Minor. His letters instructed them on how to live out a new countercultural reality in the context of Roman domination. For example, contrary to the rigid social hierarchies of the first century CE, Paul instructed the church in Galatia that "There is no longer Jew or Greek, there is no longer slave or free, there is no longer male and female; for all of you are one in Christ Jesus" (Gal. 3:28).

Such alternate readings interpret sacred texts in ways that provide the scaffolding needed for a prophetic call to build shalom (peace), and care and speak for the marginalized. These activist organizations draw on their religious understandings and imagery to call a new more inclusive global vision into being. Interestingly, in the final pages of *Multitude*, the authors Hardt and Negri themselves call for the recuperation of a "public and political conception of love common to premodern traditions," going on to say, "Christianity and Judaism, for example, *both conceive of love as a political act that constructs the multitude*"(italics added).[24] Religious activists are successfully reframing demands for community, workplace, immigrant rights, peace-making, and global poverty eradication as religiously grounded moral issues. The work of these activists has grown significantly in scale and visibility in recent years. Between 1999 and 2000 there was considerable international attention focused on the campaign for global debt relief started by churches in the Two-Thirds World in alliance with churches in the United Kingdom and the United States. The movement gained visibility through the eloquent support it received from Pope John Paul II, yet media attention was also directed to the remarkable presence of the rock star Bono in the movement. In the United States, the movement's success was largely due to work done at the grassroots by countless religious people who lobbied their congressional representatives to vote in favor of the supporting national legislation. Another prominent alternative voice is that of *Sojourners*, a magazine and organization based in Washington DC, headed by Jim Wallis. Through the magazine, Web site, blogs, and Wallis's extensive speaking tours, a younger generation of evangelicals is abandoning the narrow political agenda of their parents and becoming engaged in these new campaigns for social justice. A small number are intentionally relocating into poor inner-city neighborhoods where they are establishing semimonastic communities that work among the poor.

Perhaps less visible are the hundreds of organizations engaged in organizing poor communities, low-wage workers, and immigrants, and in working for peace in Iraq, Afghanistan, Colombia, Darfur, and Uganda, for nuclear disarmament, for a resolution to the conflict between the state of Israel and the Palestinians, for just trade, for complete debt relief, for the elimination of hunger, and for improved foreign aid to the world's poorest nations. Becoming more sophisticated and networked, these organizations are gradually gaining the power to influence state and national policymakers.

The Centrality of Social Location

Scholars of Christian public engagement generally point to the existence of significant theological or doctrinal differences to explain variations in the public activities (or the lack thereof) of denominations or broader religious collectivities.[25] While it is helpful to position the various established Christian traditions along a doctrinal or theological spectrum, it is insufficient in explaining variations in the public activities present among individual congregations within the same tradition or even the same denomination. Certainly not all Southern Baptists congregations are alike, as witnessed by the remarkable range of social issues taken up by the Saddleback Church in Southern California, including its massive campaign on behalf of AIDS victims in Africa. Similarly, many suburban United Methodist churches can be as politically conservative as their neighboring evangelical churches, while urban black United Methodist churches work in conjunction with their local Democratic politicians on a myriad of issues of concern to their community. Importantly, with regard to religious institutions, social location matters to such an extent that in some cases it will outweigh doctrinal predispositions.

Religious activism does not just spring up randomly across the national landscape—it emerges in particular social locations among people with certain types of identities. Indeed, religion can never be divorced from its social location. One of the clearest examples comes from the era of slavery in the American South, where slave-owners used Scripture to justify their enslavement of Africans, while the secret congregations formed by African slaves read the same Scripture as a message of liberation from "Pharaoh."[26] Such examples force us to recognize the contingent nature of scriptural texts, which can be mined for their liberative message, while acknowledging "that this same Bible contains elements of bondage and disenfranchisement."[27] The text has stories of victims and victors, exploitation and benevolence, and enslavement and emancipation.[28]

As a religion that emerged at the interstices of the Roman Empire, Christianity has been particularly well suited to continuous reinterpretations as varying groups of people around the globe have appropriated aspects of its core tenets, reshaping them for their particularistic context. In many parts of the world, Christianity has blended with existing indigenous religious traditions and practices. This is the case within regions of Latin America where ancient Meso-American religions have become intermingled with the Catholicism brought by the conquistadores. It has also occurred in Korea where the missionaries' orthodox Christianity has been fused together with the country's much older Confucian traditions to create a uniquely Korean religion. Today Christianity is in decline in most Western societies, which had been its primary social location for a millennium, while it is experiencing remarkable growth and vitality in the global South where it is once again undergoing multiple reinterpretations.[29] In explaining the distinctiveness of South Asian Christianity, the postcolonial theologian, R. S. Sugirtharajah writes, "Religion and religious symbols have been used successfully both in the colonial and postcolonial Christendom."[30] This is true elsewhere in the global South where Christianity can be a mixture of orthodox, charismatic, and liberative. In such locations, literalist readings of biblical texts can provide not only justifications for political activism but also a command to engage. "*Deliverance* in the charismatic sense easily becomes linked to political and social *liberation*" in the global South where its message is often embraced "by exactly those groups ordinarily portrayed as the victims of reactionary religion, particularly women."[31]

In examining religiously constructed activism in this book, we seek to be attentive to the impact of varied social locations upon the work. We explore how social location impacts the overall character of varying forms of religious activism, and whether the construction of religious narratives vary from one social location to another. Are different methods of organizing apparent within distinct social locations? How does religious activism bridge between distinct social locations? Finally, does cross-fertilization occur between various social locations so that over time, praxis in one location influences religious praxis in other locations? We consider five major case studies situated within two large, distinct, yet overlapping social locations, which characterize much of current religious activism in the United States. For heuristic purposes, we identify these as the "borderlands" and "cosmopolitans." These two categories are not conceived of as being parallel or necessarily comprehensive in scope. The borderlands category describes both a geographic location and a set of identities, such as immigrant, low-wage service worker, ex-felon, lesbian or gay couple. which are most commonly present within the borderlands space. The cosmopolitan category describes certain types of people who come from positions of privilege and yet have come to identify themselves with the *other*, with people on the margins. In some cases, these categories overlap so that it is possible to be a borderlands cosmopolitan. There are also many cosmopolitans working within borderlands organizations. We will use these categories to draw out the significance of these two distinct arenas and to distinguish between various types of justice work that occurs within them.

The Borderlands as a Social Location

The "borderlands," or "*los intersticios*" as Gloria Anzaldúa calls them, are spaces being created by the extensive cross-border movement of people in the era of globalization.[32] Large scale migration is concomitant with today's form of empire. Borderlands exist not only directly alongside international borders, but in certain large urban regions in the United States and other wealthy nations that have become the destinations of a vast stream of global migrants. Researchers at the Brookings Institution have identified twenty-seven "melting-pot metros" in the United States that are the major gateways for new immigrants, making them distinct from the rest of the country by their far greater ethnic and racial diversity. The list includes the major city-regions of New York, Los Angeles, Chicago, Washington DC, Houston, and Miami that are central to the functioning of empire.[33]

The origins of borderlands in the United States can be traced back to an earlier form of global capital accumulation that led to the transportation of millions of African slaves to the Americas and the annexation of vast stretches of Mexico. The more recent large-scale immigration of people from Latin America, Asia, the Caribbean, and Africa has created regions in the United States, especially along the East and West Coasts and in Texas and Illinois, which are characterized by very heterogeneous populations. Those who are immigrants possess multiple identities—those of their home countries and those acquired in the United States. There is a duality to their existence as people in a prolonged stage of transition. Borderlands are places of displacement and marginality; home to many people with multilingual, multicultural identities. They are in-between spaces, intertwined with the mainstream, dominant society, yet separated from it. Borderlands are also dynamic spaces where new hybrid identities are formed, new ideas and commitments take root, making them places of great ferment.

As people from the global South migrate to the United States, they carry along their own contextualized ways of living out their home-country religious traditions. Religious practices continue to bind extended immigrant families and communities together by spiritually linking those who are now in the States to those who have stayed behind. The rituals and worship of the immigrants' faith affirm their inherent dignity and worth, giving meaning to the hardships of their day-to-day lives. Yet, the experience of immigrating to a new place also gradually transforms the religious traditions they bring with them, so that the new understandings of Christianity, Hinduism, Buddhism, and Islam emerging on American soil represent a hybridization of home-country religion and new forms created in response to this country's context.[34] Given the growing religious diversity in the United States resulting from the arrival of new immigrants, religious activists are increasingly seeking to contextualize their justice issues—not only in more familiar Christian religious traditions but also within Judaism, Islam, Buddhism, and Hinduism. We will see that within all three of our borderlands case studies, there are examples of emerging interreligious activism. This activism is still in its early stages as non-Christian traditions carry out the interpretative work necessary for the construction of a religious justice tradition.

Several earlier scholars who have written on borderlands (or on *Mestizaje,* which is the embodiment of hybridity within Latino/a American communities) have primarily conceptualized it as a cultural or religious phenomenon.[35] I add to that understanding by also conceiving of borderlands as spaces characterized by the presence of people who possess limited citizenship rights. Some are immigrants who currently lack access to formal citizenship within the country in which they are long-term residents. Others have experienced various forms of political disenfranchisement even though they were born U.S. citizens. For example, there are an estimated 5.3 million Americans who have lost their right to vote because of prior felony convictions. It is estimated that 13 percent of all African American men have been stripped of their right to vote due to the prevalence of racial disparities in the criminal justice system.[36] Another type of citizenship right—the right to have one's marriage recognized by the state—is still denied to gay and lesbian couples in the majority of states. As of 2010 eight states and the District of Columbia allowed gay and lesbian couples to marry, while a number of others had some form of domestic partner provisions.[37] The dominant culture has defined the poor, nonwhites, immigrants, gays and lesbians, and ex-offenders as threats to society whose lives therefore require regulation by the state.

In a world made up of nation-states, to be a noncitizen is effectively a form of being a nonperson since even universal human rights are ultimately enforced by nation-states. As new religiously inspired forms of resistance emerge in response to these circumstances, they assert the moral authority needed to engage in a politics of insurgent citizenship. Our case studies of congregational-based community organizing and worker rights highlight religious organizing in the U.S. borderlands communities where the meaning of citizenship rights is multilayered. It includes those formal rights gained through membership in a nation-state, alongside other basic human rights such as the right to work, to access education, health care, and affordable safe housing. Some immigrants now also possess certain transnational citizenship rights by virtue of rights granted to migrants by their countries of origin. Given our historical development as a federated nation in which the fifty states retain substantial powers, formal citizenship in the U.S. nation-state brings access to relatively fewer substantive rights than is the case in nation-states with highly developed national systems of social provision. Access to substantive rights has become further attenuated since the early 1980s by the progressive dismantling of national social benefits, including income support, health care, subsidized housing, childcare, and job training.

As access to national substantive rights became more restricted, the arena of contention over the provision of substantive rights shifted to local and state governments. It has been at these lower levels of government that border-lands activists have been most successful in securing new rights, even for those immigrant residents who do not possess formal U.S. citizenship.

The case studies will show how religious justice activists are using various liberative pedagogies to assist in overcoming the social and ethnic divisions inherent in borderlands spaces, thereby creating possibilities for building new alliances across a broad spectrum of cultural, ethnic, and class divides that normally disrupt the social cohesion of the globalized city. Through building various broad institutional collaborations, they are gradually creating the organized power necessary to reclaim diminished citizenships rights. Thus, they create forms of insurgent citizenship.[38] Taken together, their efforts challenge the inequalities created by globalization with its growing disparities between wealth and poverty.

The cultural anthropologist James Holston, who coined the phrase "insurgent citizenship," applied it to new movements of the urban poor for "rights to the city" and of women, gays, and ethnic and racial minorities for "rights of difference." I am using that phrase to describe struggles to empower people in the borderlands who are pushing back against the denial of their basic human rights. Movements for an expansion of substantive citizenship rights force the state to respond to the deteriorating social conditions of the working poor—which are only one of the consequences of empire on citizenship. Such movements are unprecedented because "they create new kinds of rights, based on the exigencies of lived experience, outside of the normative and institutional definitions of the state and its legal codes."[39] To interpret a wide variety of struggles for increased economic security, improvements in the quality of community life, and even the basic right to family unity in the borderlands as forms of "insurgent citizenship" acknowledges that at present, socioeconomic justice cannot be separated from access to basic democratic freedoms and ethnic and racial self-determination. The opposite is true as well; socioeconomic equality is a necessary precondition for the effective exercise of democratic citizenship rights.[40]

Within the context of empire "insurgent citizenship" is not a form of revolutionary upheaval. Rather, its assertion of the right to have rights should be understood as a expansion of basic freedoms as they are conceived by the India-born, Nobel Prize–winning economist Amartya Sen. For Sen, freedom is defined as "the capability to live really long and to have a good life while alive" in contrast to a life of misery and unfreedom.[41] Sen emphasizes the quality of people's lives and the strengthening of their own abilities to enhance that quality through their own capabilities. For Sen, the most elemental form of unfreedom is the inability to survive due to famine, inadequate health care, or a lack of sanitation, functional education, gainful employment, or economic and social security. Unfreedom also results from gross inequalities between men and women and from the lack of political rights and freedoms. We will also consider the right to migrate as both a right and a form of freedom, while current efforts to limit that right are seen as increasing "unfreedom." Sen advocates for prioritizing the creation of opportunities that enable people to achieve what they themselves would like to achieve, including the ability to participate in democratic decision making that holds their political leaders accountable. For those people lacking formal citizenship within a nation-state, expanding their freedom to have a good life is a form of "insurgent citizenship" achieved from the bottom up.

Thus, campaigns waged by congregational-based community organizations and worker-justice activists are to a certain extent able to expand the rights sphere within certain local arenas so as to increase people's capacity to live well. However, in the case of the roughly 12 million people now in the United States with no access to formal citizenship, their rights can be fully achieved only through national legislation. Yet, within a democracy, expanding citizenship to new categories of "foreigners" requires that a majority of the nation's citizens agree to such an expansion. Citizens are being asked to expand the right to U.S. citizenship at a difficult moment when they are under siege due to the severe crisis in global financial markets. In his book on the politics of immigration control, the political scientist Paul Tichenor reminds us that a majority of American citizens have never supported expansions of citizenship to new groups of immigrants. Instead, extensions of citizenship have come as a result of political support from coalitions of business and farm interests, organized labor, immigrant associations, and pro-immigrant advocacy groups.[42] Religious constituencies have historically been divided and continue to be so at present. As "illegal" immigrants have been increasingly vilified and marginalized, religious activists have stepped up efforts to provide urgently needed humanitarian aid, while also documenting the dehumanization occurring along the border and within the interior borderlands. Yet, unless religious activists as part of a larger "multitude" successfully secure equitable national immigration legislation, immigrants will continue to be cast as the *other* who is deemed unworthy of access to American citizenship. Without access to citizenship, other forms of insurgent citizenship that have been won through tough struggles are in jeopardy of being lost.

The Cosmopolitan Social Location

The second social location in which religious justice activism occurs is among cosmopolitans. We look at two case studies that highlight work primarily being done by individuals and religious communities who are predominantly middle class, occupying positions of greater power and privilege. Many cosmopolitan activists are Euro-Americans, although there are also prosperous, well-educated native-born African Americans, Latinos, and Asians as well as immigrants and their second-generation descendants. In his book on cosmopolitanism, Kwame Anthony Appiah explains it as a twin set of ideas. "One is the idea that we have obligations to others that stretch beyond those to whom we are related by the ties of kith and kind, or even the formal ties of shared citizenship. The other is that we take seriously the value not just of human life, but of particular human lives, which means taking an interest in the practices and beliefs that lend them significance"[43] Cosmopolitans recognize that differences abound within the human family, all of which are worth exploring and seeking to understand. "They neither expect nor desire that every person or every society should converge on a single mode of life."[44] Cosmopolitans have no interest in remaking the world in their image or returning to some earlier "more pure" era when Western notions of what constituted civilization dominated the world. For them there are no "good old days" before American society became multinational. They have abandoned hegemonic notions of the moral superiority of the West, making them willing to enter into true partnerships with people around the globe.

Religious cosmopolitans work in all five arenas of activism featured in this book, but they dominate among peacemaking and global justice activists. When asked, they can consistently point to certain transformational experiences in their lives, which have enabled them to see the world from the point of view of the *other*. This book contains the stories of several cosmopolitan activists who were transformed through having spent extended periods of time living somewhere in the global South, most often in Latin America. These experiences frequently occurred either while they were students or while they were serving as missionaries. Interestingly, direct missionary experiences or reports sent back to the United States from missionaries in the field have been catalytic in several religious activist movements. This is especially true of Roman Catholic missionaries who worked in Latin America beginning in the late 1960s. Since most missionaries were sent to work among ordinary people, rarely interacting with the upper classes, they were exposed to the people's hardships, their strong commitments to community, and their popular religious practices. Young religious Americans who spent extended periods of time in Latin America in the late 1960s were frequently exposed to the intellectual and social ferment surrounding the emergence of liberation theology and concomitant pedagogies, which sought to foster critical consciousness among the masses of Latin American people.

For still others, early experiences in U.S.-based movements including pacifist, civil rights, antiwar, farmworkers, Nuclear Freeze campaign, and others proved to be so transformative that they embarked on a lifetime of justice activism. In a few cases, people even referenced the impact of their parents' activism. Still others grew up in poor or immigrant families where they have personally experienced being treated as the *other*. Through access to education, including seminary degrees, they have since gained middle-class status, yet their childhood experiences give them a strong affinity to those who remain on the margins. It is important to emphasize that these varied experiences are processed and interpreted through the lenses of each person's deeply held religious and ethical percepts. Their life experiences are indeed transformative as they connect with their understandings of the sacredness of all life and one's responsibility to show compassion for the *other*. Such beliefs can be found in some form in every religion. As a result of these varied transformative experiences, cosmopolitans learn to embrace an "other regarding" worldview, leaving them open to engaging social issues that are in the interests of people who have little power, but are not necessarily in their own direct personal self-interest. They frequently come to see themselves as world citizens rather than being deeply attached to any one nation or racial/ethnic identity. At the same time, their expanded sense of belonging compels them to make use of their privileged identity as American citizens to advocate on behalf of those who do not possess that status. Thus, they acknowledge their own privilege and chose to use it in ways that places them in solidarity with those who are suffering at the hands of the very nation-state through which American cosmopolitans hold their privileged citizenship.

In order for religious belief to provide the grounds for justice activism, it must have the capacity to move a person from empathy for those who are suffering to anger against the societal practices that cause that suffering. Yet, given the broad commitment to nonviolence among most religious activists, anger at injustice cannot be allowed to turn into acts of violence against the perpetrators. We trace the emergence of active nonviolent resistance back to its origins in Gandhi's concept of *satyagraha,* which recast elements of the Hindu tradition to ground a commitment to nonviolence as a form of *no-*

harm. We note that these ideas were carried into the U.S. Christian context through several activist streams and have now been broadly embraced by religious activists.

Both Christian and Jewish justice activists find religious frameworks for their work within the books of the Hebrew Scriptures. Each religion also draws on still other texts central to their tradition: the New Testament for Christians and the Talmud for Jews. Christian cosmopolitans frequently see themselves as the inheritors of earlier generations of religious social activists whose justice work also grew out of their faith commitments. Depending on their religious orientation and the issues in which they are primarily engaged, they may claim the historic legacy of the nineteenth-century abolitionists, the proponents of the social gospel, the Catholic Worker movement, or the more recent civil rights, farmworkers, antiwar, or sanctuary activists. Activists in other religious traditions are building their own frameworks for justice activism and finding inspiration for social activism from earlier activists within their religious traditions. For example, Jewish activists make frequent reference to the image of Rabbi Abraham Joshua Heschel marching arm-in-arm with Martin Luther King Jr. in Selma, Alabama.

Religious justice organizations often act as a bridge between borderlands and cosmopolitan social locations. This is most evident in cases where organizations were established to intentionally bring cosmopolitans into solidarity with people on the margins, such as much of the work of the religious worker-justice organizations including Clergy and Laity United for Economic Justice (CLUE) and Interfaith Worker Justice (IWJ). In both cases, a great deal of their work is accomplished in close collaboration with unions that are organizing directly among low-wage workers. CLUE and IWJ function to bring religious cosmopolitans into solidarity with what are often hard-fought unionization campaigns. The same is true of organizations such as Witness for Peace (WFP) and Christian Peacemaker Teams (CPT), both of which send American volunteers overseas to give witness to and provide accompaniment for rural villagers living in the midst of violent conflict zones. These volunteers in turn send back very graphic reports of the suffering people are enduring to their networks of mostly cosmopolitan supporters in the United States.

While religious activists working in borderlands social locations make extensive use of liberative pedagogies to instill people with an awareness of the root causes of their oppression, cosmopolitans generally possess a far greater sense of their own political efficacy. There certainly are immigrant activists who arrive in the United States with significant prior political or organizing experience in their home countries, enabling them to readily become active here, yet cosmopolitans who were born and educated in the United States generally have a greater familiarity with the workings of American institutions and politics. Those who have gone through multiple tiers of the American educational system have been exposed to the basic mechanics of the political process in this country and have been taught to believe that they have a voice in policy decisions. They are also more likely to have social networks that can connect them to various funding sources, especially those that exist within religious institutions. As a result, organizations whose primary constituency is among cosmopolitans employ very different mobilizing methodologies. They rely heavily on email and increasingly on YouTube, Facebook, MySpace, and Twitter to educate and mobilize their constituencies. We will encounter one organization that actually sends its supporters instructions on how to organize mass actions in their local communities via YouTube. There are a few organizations whose primary objective is to generate letters to members of Congress in support of whatever issue they are currently working on. Others combine such email letter-writing campaigns with mass actions, including acts of civil disobedience. However, as the head of one religious peace organization pointed out, being able to participate in acts of civil disobedience is itself a form of privilege. Only those who are U.S. citizens with jobs that allow them to possibly miss a few days of work can risk arrest resulting from an act of civil disobedience.

To the extent that cosmopolitan organizations are largely composed of middle-class whites, they are always challenged in their ability to connect to broader multiethnic constituencies. Some have wrestled with this dilemma and yet were largely unsuccessful in moving beyond their historic base of supporters. During the 1980s, as WFP was sending delegations to Nicaragua, despite their efforts they attracted very few nonwhites to join their delegations. Yet, as Clare Weber, a former WFP staffer points out, "it is whiteness to the degree that it intersects with middle- or upper-class standing in U.S. society that is privileged in the body politic."[45] Thus, in large part the very whiteness of WFP activists gave the organization its political clout. More recently, Bread for the World is finding greater success in finally building networks of supporters for its anti-hunger advocacy among African American and Latino congregations. Perhaps the distinction is that Bread has consciously maintained a dual focus on global hunger as well as hunger in the United States. Thus, they are able to access borderlands constituencies in a way that solidarity with Nicaragua could not do in the 1980s.

Methodological Approach

The content of this book is based on qualitative research. I sought to portray the broad sweep of American religious justice organizing, although there are certainly other important issues, such as environmental justice or LGBTQ-rights organizing, which are not included. There are undoubtedly organizations I missed that should have been incorporated, for which I apologize. I quite intentionally made heavy use of a narrative style of research that mirrors these organizations' widespread emphasis on storytelling.

I made extensive use of my own personal connections to the religious activists involved in this work, especially those in Chicago and Los Angeles. In January 2008, I spent a week in southern Arizona visiting the various humanitarian activists who are active in saving immigrants' lives in the desert. In writing the peacemaking chapter, focused on a movement with which I was less familiar, I began by consulting a number of scholars who are active peacemakers, asking them to provide me with assessments of who were the most important organizations active in the field.

I conducted dozens of individual, open-ended interviews with staff from each of the organizations referenced in the chapters that follow. I want their voices to come across the pages of this book. Since every activist organization now has a Web site, I also made use of online materials as well as material from newsletters and regular email postings. In the case of a number of older organizations, I was able to draw on some excellent secondary literature, which is generally not yet available for those organizations that have come into existence in more recent years. I have been careful to include only those organizations with which I was able to conduct a phone interview with a staff member, since there are clearly inactive organizations that still have a presence online.

The Plan of the Book

Chapter 2 presents a fuller explanation of what the prophetic traditions within both the Hebrew Scriptures and the New Testament have to say about various justice issues. It also includes a more extensive discussion of the trajectory of various methodologies prevalent throughout religious activism. The first is a broad based commitment to active nonviolent resistance. The chapter also traces another important thread that shapes much of American justice organizing, namely, the influence of Latin American liberation theology and pedagogies, which have also been contextualized in the United States.

The next three chapters focus on borderlands activism. Chapter 3 begins by discussing the distinctive legacy of Catholic social action and the entrance of Latin American liberative models of praxis into community organizing in the late 1970s. It then introduces the major national organizing networks and recounts the personal stories of a number of professional organizers to demonstrate their understanding of the prophetic nature of their own involvement. The chapter then addresses the use of popular education models in various aspects of community organizing's day-to-day praxis. Finally, it examines a variety of concrete forms of insurgent citizenship that have been created by these organizations' work. Chapter 4 begins by examining the decline of the American labor movement and the barriers to successful organizing created by the dismantling of the federal labor regulations. It then focuses on the work of two major religious worker-justice organizations, Interfaith Worker Justice (IWJ) and Clergy and Laity Concerned for Economic Justice (CLUE), both of which were constituted as interreligious organizations. Both have established their own identities in the midst of significant on-going turmoil within the ranks of organized labor. They both act as moral voices in the midst of an increasingly difficult union organizing climate and also function as bridges between borderlands and cosmopolitan social locations. In recent years, IWJ has birthed a number of worker-justice centers, which embody the institutional hybridity common among borderlands organizations. As a result, IWJ has also become more active in national advocacy, recognizing that only stronger enforcement and legislative reform can protect the most vulnerable workers. CLUE has recently initiated a series of dialogues between African American and Latino clergy and is successfully recruiting evangelical clergy to support worker justice.

Chapter 5 begins by tracing the contested history of immigrant rights in the United States. It then looks at the religious humanitarian work along the Arizona border with Mexico, some of which has roots in the 1980s sanctuary movement that also originated in that region. These organizations are also engaged in documenting human rights abuses and advocating for a more humane set of immigration laws. The chapter then looks at the work of the new sanctuary movement and the religious responses to the massive 2008 federal raid of a meatpacking plant in Postville, Iowa. Finally, it analyzes the broad based multiethnic interreligious coalition that is lobbying for national comprehensive immigration reform.

Chapter 6 marks the shift toward cosmopolitan religious activism by looking at various forms of religious peacemaking, including traditional pacifist support for conscientious objectors, solidarity work, and human rights work. While there is a long-standing pacifist tradition within Christianity, the dominant position among Christians has been just war theory, versions of which have undergirded justifications of empire throughout the centuries, including the 2003 U.S. invasion of Iraq. The Fellowship of Reconciliation (FOR), which is the oldest U.S. religious pacifist organization, has over the decades been joined by a diverse array of other religious peace-making groups. A commitment to peacemaking is now central to the identities of a wide range of religious adherents. More than any other arena this work includes distinctively Catholic, Jewish, Buddhist, and Muslim peace organizations, as well as a younger generation of evangelicals who are important new voices within a religious community marked by strong triumphalist tendencies. Less concerned with empowering individuals to act, peace-making activism focuses on the intricacies of the issues, making heavy use of email to reach its supporters. Most organizations also engage in various types of mass actions, including civil disobedience, yet there are a few whose outreach is entirely done online.

Chapter 7 looks at a range of global justice organizations, includes ones that are engaged in advocacy work on debt relief, hunger, and global poverty. Beginning with the Jubilee 2000 campaign, much of this work has been focused on Africa. Its deepening poverty has directly contributed to growing violence throughout many parts of the continent. As a result, global justice has become closely aligned with efforts to reverse Africa's growing humanitarian crisis through massive infusions of public and private funding into the poorest regions of the continent. This chapter also features several anti-genocide organizations that have formed in response to ongoing conflict in various parts of Africa. Although not necessarily religious in their identities, they organize among religious communities. They are also using innovative, creative organizing strategies that attract large numbers of young adults to work on their issues. These new methodologies clearly suggest new emerging forms of future organizing.

Finally, chapter 8 concludes the book with an assessment of the overall significance of this work in bringing renewal to communities, creating new citizenship rights, and ultimately confronting American empire. While activism occurring in both borderlands and cosmopolitan social locations seeks to lessen the impact of the most negative consequences of globalization and empire, the case studies also reveal clear distinctions in the actual character of the work in the two settings. Indeed, it is apparent that religious activism frequently serves as a bridge between the two.

All quotes from the Hebrew Bible and the New Testament use the New Revised Standard Version (NRSV) or in some cases, an individual translation.

2

Identifying the Qualities
of Prophetic Activism

In everyday parlance, "prophetic" is often defined as "telling the future," which in some translations of the Hebrew Bible takes on the meaning of a fortune-teller.[1] Within the Abrahamic religious traditions, prophets were messengers from God. There is no commonly agreed-upon meaning of "prophetic" among contemporary religious activists, although when asked many will define it as "speaking truth to power." In the context of this book, which focuses specifically on progressive prophetic activism, that is a somewhat inadequate understanding. Conservative Christian religious activists are as likely to use the same phrase to describe their work. Thus, in this chapter we will set out to identify certain qualities of the prophetic commonly found among progressive activists, which distinguish their work from that done by conservatives. We begin by examining the approach and use of prophetic texts within the Christian tradition since that is the starting point of the majority of organizations featured in this book. Even some of the organizations now engaged in interreligious work are still led by Christian activists and thus bear a degree of Christian DNA in the basic theological understandings of their work.

Both conservative and progressive Christians draw on the multiplicity of narratives present in Scripture to lend authority to their work. Conservative Christians generally construct their theological scaffolding on the foundation of the exclusivity of God's claim upon the people of Israel. After rescuing them from slavery in Egypt, God declares, "I am the LORD your God, who brought you out of the land of Egypt, out of the house of slavery, you shall have no other gods before me" (Exod. 20:2). As long as the people obeyed God's covenant, God pledged to protect them and defeat their adversaries. However, that very claim of exclusivity later sanctioned the slaughter of the Canaanites, rendering God as both liberator of the Israelites and conqueror of the Canaanites. The text describes the Canaanites as sexually deviant, thus giving tacit justification to their slaughter. Such acts of labeling and violence on behalf of God's chosen people continue to be employed by conquering nations, including the United States, to justify their own acts of aggression against other peoples.

In his book on Jewish renewal, Rabbi Michael Lerner seeks to come to terms with such passages by claiming that they are not actually God's voice but a human distortion that resulted from "a legacy of pain that is passed on from generation to generation, creating a tendency toward malevolence."[2] The texts of the Hebrew Bible certainly contain many passages that portray God as a caring and compassionate parent who is reluctant to use force. For example, in Genesis 18:22–33, Abraham is able to convince God not to destroy the cities of Sodom and Gomorrah as long as ten righteous people can be found living in them. After Israel becomes a monarchy, God's stance toward its leaders becomes increasingly critical. In much of the subsequent prophetic tradition, God warns the Israelites of their impending destruction at the hands of their enemies, not just if they fail to abandon their worship of other gods but, even more importantly, because of their continued acts of injustice.

The framing of the prophetic has historically been used in the United States to either enhance or restrict the space necessary for a democratic politics in which "meaningful and intelligible innovation can occur."[3] Acknowledging its use by both conservative and progressive social movements requires that one explore the constructed social locations from which both have employed prophetic rhetoric. For example, in his book on prophetic politics, David Gutterman contrasts the rhetoric of two pairs of prophetic voices—Billy Sunday versus Martin Luther King Jr., and Promise Keepers, an evangelical organization that urged men to reclaim their place as the head of the family versus Call to Renewal, a Christian anti-poverty coalition founded by Jim Wallis, the founder and president of Sojourners. Call to Renewal and Sojourners merged in 2006. It becomes apparent that both Billy Sunday and Promise Keepers construct a triumphalist narrative of national chosen-ness, while Martin Luther King Jr. and Call to Renewal position themselves as conscious pariahs located in a state of exile. According to Gutterman, Sunday's use of prophetic rhetoric emphasizes uniformity, with only decent Christians possessing the right to claim membership within God's chosen nation of America.

In contrast, King challenged the very notion of American chosen-ness, emphasizing instead the universality and inclusivity of chosen-ness, applying it equally to the newly independent nations of Africa from whom the

United States could learn. King positioned African Americans as sojourners in the wilderness who are awaiting entrance into the Promised Land at some point in the future. Rather than being dictated by God, the future is open to human creativity, an attitude that "demands active human engagement in the making and remaking of history."[4] As Gutterman makes clear, one's social location shapes the very character of one's use of the prophetic rhetoric. It can be employed to advance a hegemonic, exclusive political agenda or it can be employed to open up the possibilities of multiple visions of the future that are broadly inclusive.

The texts most commonly used by justice activists are not necessarily the dominant narratives found within the scriptures of the world's religions. Since there is a multiplicity of voices present in both the Hebrew Bible and New Testament, quotes from both continue to be used to justify hegemony, militarism, racial, ethnic, and gender exclusion. Returning to the earlier example, God's willingness to slaughter the Canaanites is still used to justify savagery and genocide against present-day so-called enemies. Prophetic texts have also been appropriated as tools for the maintenance of dominance. Reflecting on the Algerian colonial experience, Franz Fanon described how the symbol of "Jesus" was used by the colonialists to maintain order; "The colonialist bourgeoisie is helped in its work of calming down the natives by the inevitable religion. All those saints who have turned the other cheek, who have forgiven trespasses against them and who have been spat on and insulted without shrinking are studied and held up as examples."[5] In this case, French colonialists made use of the same passages from the Sermon on the Mount to argue for Algerian passivity that religious activists use to support their commitments to nonviolent resistance.

As was the case with the Hebraic prophets and with Jesus, contemporary prophetic activism emerges in response to the myriad forms of injustice found among people living in the slums of the world, who are hungry or excluded from full citizenship, exploited in off-shore manufacturing plants, are AIDS orphans, child soldiers, or widows who watched as their husbands and children were slaughtered. Confronted with pain and exploitation, contemporary prophetic activists ask God to speak in the midst of human suffering. This is theology done from the bottom up, which is less concerned with doctrine and more concerned with hearing God's voice in the midst of suffering. This may mean recognizing that the Virgin of Guadalupe, who is revered by the mestizo people of Mexico, brings healing and comfort to those whose land has been occupied and those forced to leave their homes and go into exile in El Norte. It could also mean enabling a young gangbanger in south Los Angeles to recognize himself in the thief who hung on the cross next to Jesus, or making it possible for a young single mother forced into prostitution to feed her family in Zimbabwe or in Harlem to envision herself in the Canaanite woman. It also sees the possibility that a gay couple might experience Jesus turning water into wine at their wedding. These are just a few of the contemporary contexts at the margins that cry out for a prophetic presence.

In response to the multiple forms of injustice and violence unleashed by empire, prophetic activists in various religious traditions construct meaning and vision by weaving together the stories of people who are now suffering from injustice with stories taken from their textual traditions. This weaving together of multiple stories results in the creation of new, context-specific ethical and theological scaffoldings that draw on ancient religious texts, the legacies left by earlier justice activists, and stories of pain and suffering told by those living on the margins. In many cases, present-day activism entails both words and actions that are purposefully constructed to link the realities of human misery and oppression to situations, which the founders of various religious traditions also condemned as immoral or against the will of God. These activists use the prophetic as a framework for shaping the character of their work, articulating their goals to others, and giving reality in the present to a vision of a new future among the people with whom they work. The use of such prophetic images to create ethical frameworks for their work distinguishes them from secular justice activists. One of this book's key premises is that the shared commitments to act within these prophetic traditions creates the possibilities of engaging in other-regarding activism, which runs counter to standard assumptions of political behavior as largely self-centered.

In addition to the widespread use of prophetic texts, religious justice activists consistently employ certain common methodologies in their work. There is a current understanding of activism as nonviolent resistance. Borderlands organizations consistently use various popular education models, often based on the use of personal narratives, to empower people with a critical consciousness. There are also a number of both borderlands and cosmopolitan organizations that conceive of their work as forms of accompaniment. This may entail activists' use of their privileged status as American citizens to protect others from harm. These methodologies are particularly prevalent among those who understand their work as empowering or standing in solidarity with the *other*. A number of peacemaking organizations include the use of civil disobedience within their tactical repertoires. Cosmopolitan organizations, whose primary form of activism is legislative advocacy, generally do not use these methodologies. Instead, the most effective advocacy organizations use well-established American strategies in which they build extensive grassroots networks that are invested in the establishment of long-term relationships with key national legislators. A cohort of younger organizations, established since 9/11, is developing new types of activist methodologies that are more appropriate for organizing in the age of Google. Like everything else about progressive activism, these organizations' methodologies must be understood within their social contexts.

Although the concept of civil disobedience is homegrown, many of the other methodological paradigms now embedded within American religious activism originated outside of the United States. Much of the praxis that is distinctive to contemporary religious activism was adapted for use in the United States by activists who first encountered its use in the contexts of colonial and postcolonial struggles for justice. These global influences have further strengthened American religious activists' increasingly cosmopolitan and interreligious outlooks. They are aware of having learned from activists working in the global South and within multiple religious traditions. Since quite a few American religious activists have also spent extended periods of time in non-Western parts of the world, they gained firsthand knowledge of various ideas and praxis that have emerged in those places. These experiences often led them to abandon any lingering notions of the moral superiority of the West, making them willing partners with activists around the globe.

Most religious activists have also been profoundly shaped by the legacies of earlier exemplars of prophetic activism. The most commonly mentioned is the legacy left by Dr. Martin Luther King Jr. and the American civil rights movement. It is almost astounding how often the legacy of Dr. King is evoked by contemporary activists, including a Muslim woman activist who emigrated to the United States from Pakistan. The civil rights movement remains the premiere example of the capacity of nonviolent resistance to transform a nation. Over the decades it has inspired activists around the world in such disparate places as East Germany, South Africa, and China. Jewish activists frequently allude to the image of Rabbi Abraham Joshua Heschel walking alongside Dr. King during the 1965 march in Selma, Alabama, as the symbol of their own activism.[6] A great number of people also reference Mahatma Gandhi, whose experiments with nonviolence eventually forced the British to depart from India. This is indicative of the extent to which nonviolent methods of social change are now widely embraced by religious activists. Other people and movements whom contemporary activists frequently mention as their models are Dorothy Day, the founder the Catholic Worker movement; Archbishop Oscar Romero of El Salvador, a proponent of liberation theology who was assassinated in 1980; and César Chávez, the founder of the United Farm Workers Union (UFW). What these people have in common is that while their work was shaped by the lived realities of marginalized people, communities, and nations, they were able to speak to wider audiences, including those who are in positions of power and authority.

The Prophetic Tradition within the Hebrew Bible

Prophets existed among many of the peoples who inhabited the ancient Near East, including Egypt, Canaan, Aram (ancient Syria), Mesopotamia, Israel, and Judah. The Hebrew Scriptures abound with prophets, including Abraham, Aaron, Samuel, Elijah, Elisha, Amos, Hosea, Jeremiah, Ezekiel, Nathan, Isaiah, Habakkuk, Haggai, and Zechariah, as well as a number of women: Deborah, Miriam, Noadiah, Huldah, and the wife of Isaiah.[7] Christians then add John the Baptist and Jesus, who are both referred to as prophets, while Muslims add Muhammad, whom they regard as the final prophet.

Scholars are by no means in agreement as to the historicity of either the biblical narratives or the prophetic writings, since much of the literature makes extensive use of poetry and allegory. However, there are historical markers within certain texts enabling one to locate individual prophets in a broad relationship to historical events. A number of the books can be largely located within the late monarchic period in the Northern Kingdom of Israel and in the Southern Kingdom of Judah. Certain passages in the book of Ezekiel situate him in Babylon after the Israelites' forced exile from Jerusalem, while others were written in the postexilic period of Persian domination. Overall, the books of the twelve minor prophets make little mention of specific historical contexts. In these accounts, one finds "Israel" construed "as a transtemporal entity whose manifestations included the Israel of the Exodus, Sinai, the monarchic politics, exilic Israel and of course the community centered around Jerusalem in the Persian period." This allows each of the texts to focus on conveying certain essential lessons concerning "Yahweh, Israel, and the relationship between the two in the past and in the future" to later readers who were no longer connected to the immediate events.[8] It is this very quality that allows contemporary activists to appropriate these texts for use in radically different social and historical contexts.

Many of the prophets are identified as members of the priesthood, although they speak and act from varied social locations; those speaking from exile can be read as occupying "borderlands" locations, while others speak from the centers of power such as Nathan, who was a member of David's royal court, and First Isaiah, who is presented as an advisor to the kings in Jerusalem during the latter half of the eighth century BCE. Isaiah's oracles and actions are consistently rooted in the royal theology of the house of David.[9] Jeremiah was a Levitical priest whose oracles were informed by his role as a Deuteronomistically oriented teacher of the Mosaic Torah, while Ezekiel was a Zadokite priest whose oracles were shaped by a keen sense of the Jerusalem temple as the holy center of all creation.[10] Amos identifies himself as a shepherd, placing him among the marginalized. In the New Testament, John the Baptist and Jesus both occupied positions of marginality. The same can be said of the prophet Muhammad, who was orphaned as young child, having experienced "poverty, oppression, and cruelty as well as power and dominion."[11]

The Scriptures are not only replete with examples of the prophetic as spoken words, but they contain powerful examples of the prophetic embodied in actions that bear witness to the presence of God in a particular time and space. Both Jesus and Muhammad organized their followers into active engagement in the process of societal transformation. These two became the founders of new religions and social structures, with Muhammad doing so after militarily defeating his adversaries. While other prophets may not have had large followings, were at times spurned and even threatened by their listeners, they too engaged in prophetic action as visible signs of God's presence, power, and the future realities of which they prophesied. Isaiah walked naked and barefoot for three years as God's visible sign that the Assyrian king would lead the Egyptians, from whom the Judean monarchy had sought protection, away as captives (see Isa. 20:3). Jeremiah wore a yoke around his neck to symbolize his warning that God would place the yoke of a foreign power onto the necks of the people of Jerusalem.

Taken as a whole, the prophetic books are a form of theodicy that seek to explain tragic events in the history of Israel as God's punishment for Israel's sins. The literature embodies an overarching metanarrative composed of multiple subcomponents: (1) Israel has committed grievous sins in violation of its covenant with God; (2) its punishment was announced to it at the time of its sinning by the prophets who at times unsuccessfully called it to repentance; (3) from the perspective of later readers of these books, though not necessarily those who populated the world of the book, Israel's punishment was fulfilled; and (4) a utopian future already decided by God was explicitly announced by godly speakers (the deity or the prophets) and was announced to Israel at precisely the time of and despite its seemingly incurable sin.[12]

Of the four components of this metanarrative, the first and the fourth are most relevant to contemporary justice activists. The prophetic texts speak of a multiplicity of "sins" including the worship of other gods, which has defiled God's temples, the greed and selfishness of the dominant economic and political powers, which has led to the oppression and exploitation of the weak and powerless, the failure to care for "the widow, orphan, and stranger" who are emblematic of all who could not protect themselves, the corruption of both religious and governmental leaders, including temple priests, kings, and judges, and the inappropriate pursuit of foreign alliances by Israel's leaders.

The prophets insisted that the human condition could be understood only in conjunction with the divine presence. They rejected the belief that humans are the masters of their own destiny. According to Heschel, prophetic reflection begins "with the abuse and consequent failure of freedom, with the irrationality of human conduct, and it points to God who stands above history."[13] Human history is not history's only dimension. While it is generally assumed that war, politics, and economics are the substance and subject of history, the prophets regarded God's judgment of human conduct as the main issue. God was not perceived as a silent immutable God but as an active presence within the flow of history who remained engaged with humans. Humans are seen as having choices, but not sovereignty. Rabbi Jonathan Sacks interprets God's call to Abraham in Genesis 17:1, "Walk ahead of Me and be perfect" to mean that God "empowers us to make mistakes and get it wrong. That is what it is to be human, and God does not ask us to be superhuman."[14] There were times when God hid his face from Israel, seemingly indifferent to Israel's plight; leaving the prophets pleading with God for a response.

God's justice and righteousness was a priori of biblical faith, self evident, not an added attribute to God's essence.[15] This conceptualization of God as just stands in sharp contrast to the dominant Western philosophical paradigms that have been derived from Greek philosophy. Greek religions did not stress the connection between religion and morality, offering no precepts for the regulation of human conduct.[16] For Israel's prophets, learning to act righteously was one of the principal means by which humans served God. The value of all forms of worship, including sacrifice and prayer, was contingent upon moral living. The prophets believed that humans principally served God through the practice of love, justice, and righteousness. Anything else was regarded as hypocrisy. In one of his complaints to God, Jeremiah asks "Why does the way of the guilty prosper? . . . You are near in their mouths, yet far from their hearts" (Jer. 12:1b, 2b). Heschel explains

God's perspective in this way: "How supremely certain ancient man was that sacrifice was what the gods most desired may be deduced from the fact that fathers did not hesitate to slaughter their own children on the altar. . . . To add paradox to sacrilege: all this grandeur and solemnity are declared to be second rate, of minor importance, if not hateful to God, while deeds of kindness, worrying about the material needs of widows and orphans, commonplace things, platitudinous affairs, are exactly what the Lord of heaven and earth demands![17] Heschel explains that justice was so important to God because "righteousness is not just a value; it is God's part of human life. *God's stake in human history.* Perhaps it is because the suffering of man is a blot upon God's conscience; because it is in relations between man and man that God is at stake. . . . People act as they please, doing what is vile, abusing the weak, not realizing that they are fighting God, affronting the divine, or that the oppression of man is a humiliation of God."[18] The book of Proverbs states this point very succinctly, "Those who oppress the poor insult their Maker" (Prov. 14:31).

Emmanuel Levinas, a twentieth-century French Jewish philosopher, embraced this biblical centrality of justice, recasting it in contemporary terms as a commitment to just systems of human rights that are grounded in a human responsibility to the *other*. As a European Jew and survivor of the Holocaust, whose own parents were put to death by the Nazis, Levinas constructed his philosophy based on humans' one-on-one encounters with the face of the *other*. Levinas regarded the traditional philosophical foundations of the West's commitments to human rights as weak and unstable because they rest on a self-interested, egocentric model of society, grounded in the totalizing will to freedom of the autonomous ego. In this model, the ego can relate to the *other* only in a totalizing manner that is unable to see her as a particular person in the here and now, but instead, immediately places her into a category so as to dominate over her. At its most extreme, this denial of *otherness* is the foundation of all forms of racism, which "consists in accepting only what is the 'same' and excluding what is different or "foreign."[19]

In contrast to this self-centered worldview Levinas, following the covenantal tradition, placed priority on human responsibility to the *other*, even to the point of sacrificing one's own life so that the *other* may live. This responsibility begins through an encounter with the face of a singular *other* but is then extended to all others. For Levinas, the encounter with the *other*'s face is also the point at which God breaks into the worldly situation. The call to responsibility becomes a commitment to peace with the *other* through the creation of bonds of solidarity. For Levinas, the most fundamental dimension of responsibility that is accepted and realized is "justice" in the broad sense of the term.[20] Justice therefore does not originate with an empowered ego, but rather from the disenfranchised *other*: "the one whose rights we must defend is primarily the other person and not myself."[21] Levinas's *other* becomes analogous to the biblical depiction of the other in the form of the "widow, orphan, and stranger." In other words, God's glorious transcendence consists in descending from His majesty and aligning Himself with the suffering of the helpless and needy.[22]

Activists' Use of Hebrew Bible Texts

Contemporary Christian activists frequently draw on the prophetic literature in the Hebrew Bible and New Testament, while Jewish activists draw from the prophetic literature as well the Torah and later rabbinical writings found within Talmudic literature. Similar to Levinas's recasting of the prophetic message as a philosophical justification of a responsibility for the *other*, they contextualize it to address specific forms of contemporary injustice and exclusion. The prophetic tradition lives through its use in holding politicians and corporate leaders accountable to ethical standards beyond those offered by contemporary corporate capitalism and democratic rule. The texts upon which they draw address economic exploitation by the rich and powerful, the rights of the alien, how to live as exiles in empire, and peacemaking. The religiously constructed worldviews that animate prophetic activists generally make use of one or more of these four themes, using them to connect their work to the sacred, to erect an ethical scaffolding for their vision of a new future, and to shape the character of their actions. These are by no means comprehensive since activists engage these texts on a continuous basis as new situations and issues arise in their work.

Ancient Israel was a patrilineal tribal society in which inheritance of the land, which constituted the basic means of production, was passed down through the male members of extended family or kinship networks. Protecting a family's land through the generations is critical to the survival of the clan in any subsistence agricultural economy. A person who lacks direct familial blood ties has no standing within a tribal community. To protect and regulate inheritance, traditional tribal cultures throughout the world have evolved complex sets of rules to ensure that land remains within the extended family. Since land is inherited through the male, widows, orphans, and foreigners are at risk of being excluded from the ownership of land, which would deny them access to the principal means of securing a livelihood.

Given the dynamics of this inheritance system and the critical link between land ownership and status within the clan and community, the Mosaic Law sought to protect all those who were most at risk of losing access to the land. To do so, it erected an elaborate set of laws protecting inheritance rights. To the extent to which these laws were followed, it ensured the continuation of a relatively egalitarian social structure. This is expressed in the following passage in Deuteronomy, which states, "There will . . . be no one in need among you, because the LORD is sure to bless you in the land that the LORD your God is giving you as a possession to occupy" (Deut. 15:4). But, ignoring the Mosaic Laws would inevitably lead to an increasingly unequal society as some lost access to their hereditary land rights, while others became land wealthy.

The covenantal laws sought to quickly restore the property rights of the poor. If someone who had fallen into economic difficulty had been forced to sell a piece of his property, another member of the extended family was required to buy it back. If a member of one's family became so poor that he were forced to sell himself to another member of the family, that member could not make him a slave. Furthermore, all debts were to be forgiven and each person restored to his inherited land in the year of Jubilee (see Lev. 25). Even at that point, the poor person was not to be sent out empty-handed; instead, the landowner was instructed to "provide liberally out of your flock, your threshing floor, and your wine press, thus giving him some of the bounty with which the LORD your God has blessed you" (Deut. 15:14).

Generosity, not profit, was regarded as a central economic principle. Israelites were instructed not to withhold wages from their laborers, who were to be paid by the end of each day, and not to charge interest when lending money to those in need. Since the poor were not just economically poor but also lacking in social status, the law sought to protect them from abuse by the courts, prohibiting judges from perverting "the justice due to the poor in their lawsuits" (Exod. 23:6). Nonetheless, these protections for the poor did not extend to all marginalized others. To the extent that women had status, it was only in the context of marriage. Widows and orphans, who had became disconnected from the patrilineal family, were granted the same rights as foreigners, while slaves were left entirely outside the boundaries of the Israelites' prescribed rights.

These relatively egalitarian practices remained intact until the emergence of a monarchy in Israel. The new hierarchical social structures provided the wealthy with increased leverage over the poor. The monarchy, which paid tribute to the Assyrians, imposed taxes on its citizens; those who could least afford to pay were at the mercy of the wealthy. Credit was available, but borrowers were now required to pay high interest rates. With a lack of regulation and a corrupted judicial system, creditors could demand payment of a debt at any time, leading to the creation of a permanent class of very poor people.[23] The prophets condemned such exploitation as manifestations of the breakdown in the covenantal relationship between God and God's people. The psalmist spoke of God's displeasure, saying, "Because the poor are despoiled, because the needy groan, I will now rise up, says the LORD; I will place them in the safety for which they long" (Ps. 12:5).

Isaiah offers one of the most poignant condemnations of land grabbing by the wealthy. Metaphorically, Isaiah compares Israel to a vineyard planted by God, which was expected to yield grapes, but had produced only wild grapes. God will now trample the vineyard down, for the LORD of hosts had expected justice, but saw only bloodshed. Then, Isaiah makes the target of God's anger clear by saying, "Ah, you who join house to house, who add field to field, until there is room for no one but you, and you are left to live alone in the midst of the land" (Isa. 5:3–8). Isaiah condemns the accumulation of land that once supported numerous households into the hands of a single household. Elsewhere, using the same image of the vineyard, Isaiah points his criticism directly at the powerful leaders, saying, "The LORD enters into judgment with the elders and princes of his people: It is you who have devoured the vineyard; the spoil of the poor is in your houses. What do you mean by crushing my people by grinding the face of poor says the LORD God of hosts" (Isa. 3:14–15).

Other prophets were equally harsh in their condemnation of the abuse suffered by the poor at the hands of the rich. Jeremiah also employs the image of building a house, exclaiming, "Woe to him who builds his house by unrighteousness and his upper room by injustice; who makes his neighbors work for nothing, and does not give them their wages" (Jer. 22:13–17). Similar statements criticizing the wealthy who mistreated and oppressed the poor are found in Ezekiel 16:49; 18:2–4, 22:29; in Amos 4:1 and 6, 5:11–12 (which contains another image of a finely built house to represent unjustly gained wealth), 8:4 and 6; and in Zechariah 7:9–10. Each of these passages points to quite specific violations of the Mosaic Laws that sought to protect the rights of the poor and thereby maintain relative equality among the people of Israel.

These are among the passages most frequently used by borderlands activists who engage in community, worker rights, and immigrant rights organizing. The prophets are condemning the abandonment of God's covenantal laws that were intended to avoid forms of exploitation very similar to those occurring today. Immigrant workers are frequently not paid fair wages or not paid at all, new laws are being enacted to exclude the modern "alien," and some communities are experiencing disinvestment while others undergo gentrification, displacing the poor to make room for new luxury housing. In the midst of contemporary inequalities, these prophetic texts are powerful reminders of the gap between God's expectations and present-day realities. Later we will see how the Levitical requirement of Jubilee became the ethical foundation of a global campaign for granting debt relief to the world's most highly indebted nations.

As the issues surrounding immigrant rights have become increasingly contested, certain conservative Christians have opposed justice for undocumented immigrants because they are "breaking the law." They justify the primacy of upholding the law on the basis of a particular passage in the New Testament that reads, "Let every person be subject to the governing authorities; for there is no authority except from God, and those authorities that exist have been instituted by God" (Rom. 13:1). Rejecting this approach as incompatible with their commitments to policy reform, immigrant rights activists, the congregations that join them, and many denominations have developed alternate biblical foundations for their positions. This is a clear example of different texts being used by conservatives and progressives to support polar opposite views on a contentious issue.

Progressive Christians have relied heavily on passages that speak of the provision of "hospitality" to the stranger, which is perhaps articulated in its clearest form in Matthew's narrative of the final judgment in which God will bless those nations which welcomed the stranger. The Hebrew Bible also contains a number of very significant stories of hospitality to strangers, each of which contain elements of mystery and surprise For the Israelites, acts of hospitality revealed the underlying good or evil of a community and are seen as demonstrations of covenantal loyalty to the God of Israel since the Jews themselves had lived as aliens in a foreign land. After Abraham welcomed three strangers into his tent who, unbeknown to him, were actually angels, he was told of his elderly wife's miraculous pregnancy as well as the impending destruction of Sodom and Gomorrah. In another story, when an elderly widow shared her last meal with the prophet Elijah, her food supply was miraculously replenished in the midst of a widespread famine.

Within the prophetic tradition, resident aliens were not only to be welcomed, they possessed certain rights. This actually moves the framework for religious immigration work beyond one grounded in notions of hospitality, which are normally granted to visitors, to one grounded in rights.[24] These are not just citizenship rights within individual nation-states, but international human rights. Here Levinas's grounding of human rights in humans' encounter with the *other* becomes extremely relevant. In early Israel blood ties connected each person to one of the twelve tribes, which in turn determined that person's right to inherit the lands God had given to each tribe. This right of inheritance marked an individual as an Israelite. Those who did not possess such blood ties were considered to be aliens, even though, given the ethnic hybridity of the region, they may have been long-term residents of the land given to Israel. This situation demanded that the Mosaic Law pay considerable attention to the rights of immigrants or resident aliens. In Exodus God instructed Moses as follows; "You shall not wrong or oppress a resident alien, for you were aliens in the land of Egypt. . . . If you do abuse them, when they cry out to me, I will surely heed their cry; my wrath will burn, and I will kill you with the sword" (Exod. 22:21–22). This admonition is reframed positively in Leviticus where it states, "The alien who resides with you shall be to you as the citizen among you; you shall love the alien as yourself" (Lev. 19: 34). Repeatedly, the rights of aliens are grounded in the remembrance that Israel had been given refuge in a foreign land.

The book of Numbers instructs the Israelites that "you and the alien shall be alike for the LORD. You and the alien who resides with you shall have the same law and the same ordinance" (Num. 15:15b). Like all Israelites, aliens were to be given rest on the Sabbath and were allowed to gather the gleanings from a harvested field, as well as leftover olives and grapes. Judges were to give aliens a fair hearing and judge them as they would any citizen, and they were even to be granted refuge if they had killed someone unintentionally. Every third year the tithes of produce were to be given to the aliens, orphans, and widows. Since within a theocratic state, full citizenship is defined in religious terms, the distinctions between citizens and aliens were more sharply drawn on access to the elements of religious worship. Aliens were not permitted to eat of the ram of ordination, holy anointing oil was not to be placed on an alien, they could not eat the holy donations, they were prohibited from approaching the tabernacle or the altar, and they could not become priests. Only foreigners who had been circumcised could partake in Passover.

The pain and anguish brought on by Israelites' experience of exile echoes in the lives of all people who have been displaced, forced to leave their homes as refugees from violence and persecution, or as labor migrants. They find themselves far from home, having often lost family members, living in refugee camps or on the margins of societies, which they do not understand. Exiles face the challenges of reconstructing their lives and communities in similar ways to those experienced by the Israelites. In these contexts, the encouraging letter sent by the prophet Jeremiah to the exiles in Babylon addresses the challenges of building peace within the context of empire. The letter begins with "Thus says the LORD of hosts" making it clear that God is speaking through Jeremiah. "Build houses and live in them; plant gardens and eat what they produce. Take wives and have sons and daughters; take wives for your sons, and give your daughters in marriage, that they may bear sons and daughters; multiply here and do not decrease. But seek the welfare of the city where I have sent you into exile, and pray to the LORD on its behalf, for in its welfare you will find your welfare" (Jer. 29:5–7).

Jeremiah's understanding of Babylon as God's agent in his punishment of the people of Israel is problematic, since it requires an acceptance of empire. Yet, it also contains a vision of exiles creating the capacities to live well, which can inform justice activism under many of the present conditions created by globalization. Jeremiah encouraged the exiles to establish themselves and their families in their new land and flourish through the generations, and then to actively work and pray for the well-being (welfare) of all who reside in this alien city because their well-being (welfare) is directly tied to the well-being (welfare) of the entire city. True peace will come to the exiles only when peace has come to their enemy's capital city. Here is a vision of how peace and reconciliation with one's enemy leads to one's own ability to heal and flourish once again. God is telling the Israelites that there is no separate "peace'" for exiles, no private deals with God, no permitted withdrawal from the affairs of the empire. This small vulnerable community is being invited to engage with the larger public processes of the empire rather than being allowed to withdraw into a safe sectarian existence.[25]

To become a refugee or immigrant leads to a profound sense of loss that can also open up spaces for self-examination and reflection, which eventually lead to a redefinition of a people's identity and purpose. Certainly, the Babylonian exile was an intellectually fruitful time for the Jews. Hebrew Scriptures contain a number of stories that provide glimpses of how the exiles navigated the dangerous waters of exile and dislocation as foreigners within their enemies' countries. There are stories of Jews who had attained positions of high status within the courts of foreign rulers and used those positions to protect other Jews from harm. Such stories of survival are not only forms of encouragement but also contain wisdom on the importance of ingenuity under circumstances where one is a small minority in the midst of a domineering empire. The theologian Daniel Smith-Christopher argues that these stories point to the use of wisdom rather than brute force as the survival strategy of the Diaspora. "It is the clever and wise insight of the Diaspora community that their life as the people of God is far more important than the success or failure of the empire" whose existence is only temporary. Indeed one may serve the emperor only as long as such service does not conflict with the *real* world.[26]

Although peacemaking is not a dominant theme within the Hebrew Bible, it is nonetheless present. The creation story found in Genesis 1 portrays God alone and in peace creating the universe. Yet, chapters two through four portray a series of revolts against God's original peaceful creation, culminating in Cain's murder of his brother Abel. This is followed by further stories of violence. In what reads like the histories of certain contemporary anti-colonial struggles, once freed from slavery in Egypt, the Israelites turn around and commit genocide against the Canaanites. The narratives of Israel's monarchical period are also filled with stories of battles won and enemies slain. Psalm 72 offers an image of a powerful, triumphant king of Israel who has dominion from sea to sea, whose foes bow down before him, whose enemies lick the dust, while all other kings fall down before him and the nations give him service (Ps. 72:8–11).

These stories of warfare are presented as historical narratives of the Israelites' relations with neighboring peoples. Despite humanity's propensity to engage in war, Rabbi Jonathan Sacks argues that "the prophets were the first people in history to conceive of peace as an ideal."[27] They did so most clearly in the famous words of the prophet Isaiah, which read, "they shall beat their swords into plowshares, and their spears into pruning hooks, nation shall not lift up sword against nation, neither shall they learn war any more" (Isa. 2:4b). According to Sacks, though, the prophets envisaged peace "*not* within historical time but at 'the end of days,'" and even more importantly saw it as the work of God, not humankind. Moreover, the later rabbinic tradition distinguished the peace that was possible in the not-yet-fully-redeemed world as one that required living with *difference,* including "with those who have another faith and texts. . . . The prophets articulated a utopian peace; the sages, a *non*-utopian programme for peace in the here and now."[28]

Another glimpse of the prophetic nature of peace is found in Second Isaiah (Isa. 40–55), where after announcing that God will soon return Israel from exile in Babylon, Isaiah tells the exiles that rather than seeking revenge for their suffering, they (Israel) will be given "as a light to the nations, that my salvation may reach to the end of the earth" so that "Kings shall see and stand up, princes, and they shall prostrate themselves, because of the LORD, who is faithful, the Holy One of Israel, has chosen you." (Isa. 49:6b, 7b). After the pain and suffering of exile, here is an image of Israel as the peace and salvation of the nations. This is counterintuitive since "humans are typically capable only of revenge, or even more typically thinking that their own violence is pure and innocent while the enemies' violence is bad and evil."[29] And yet, Second Isaiah (Isa. 40–55) proposes that we be "a light to the nations," not just a source of recovery for ourselves.

Jesus Expands the Prophetic Tradition

Jesus worked within the context of the Hebraic tradition, stating that he had come not to abolish the law or the prophets but to fulfill them (Matt. 5:17). In preaching from Isaiah in his hometown synagogue, Jesus evoked the Deuteronomic vision of an egalitarian society, while appealing to the subversive tradition of the great prophetic social critics of Israel.[30] Yet, he went well beyond the old law by challenging creditors not only to forgo interest but to not ask for any repayment (Luke 6:34b). In contrast to the ethno-centrism of the Mosaic Law, justice now defined all human relationships, not just those among friends or people of the same nationality, ethnicity, gender, or religious identity. As was the case with the earlier prophets, Jesus understood justice to define the actions not just of individuals but of whole cities, which were the centers of administrative power and wealth under Roman rule in the ancient Near East.[31] The same was true of nations since the extended passage found in Matthew 25 concerns the judgment of nations based on whether they have fed the hungry, given the thirsty something to drink, welcomed the stranger, clothed the naked, visited the sick and those in prison. For, "just as you did it to one of the least of these who are members of my family, you did it to me" (Matt. 25:40) The expectation that nations would direct their resources toward the least of these is a radically anti-imperial understanding of the role and responsibilities of nation-states.

In his own actions Jesus broke down the hierarchical boundaries that had defined Israel's social structure for generations. He included women as members of his community of followers, some of whom were single and unattached to a male head of household, which was the only circumstance under which Mosaic Law accorded status to women. He set aside the old assumptions of religious purity by healing those who were ostracized as being unclean—including the blind, the lame, and even lepers, who were akin to people with HIV/AIDS of today. In his words and actions he conveyed a vision of who would be included in the reign of God, which defied the religious establishment that functioned as the boundary preservers within postexilic Jewish society. For Jesus, the act of healing was more important than maintaining the Sabbath.

His vision of the reign of God was no longer ethnically exclusive. His acts of healing broke through the restrictive boundaries of nationality to include people who were non-Jews, including some who were the historic enemies of the Israelites. When a Roman centurion appealed to Jesus to heal his servant, he did so. Amazed by the soldier's faith, he announced to the crowd that was following him, "I tell you, many will come from the east and west and will eat with Abraham and Isaac and Jacob in the kingdom of heaven, while the heirs of the kingdom will be thrown into the outer darkness" (Matt. 8:11). This pointed to the inclusion of people from other ethnic and religious traditions within God's reign, while certain descendants of Israel would be left out. In another border crossing encounter, a Canaanite woman approached Jesus asking for healing for her daughter. His first response is ethnically exclusive, "I was sent only to the lost sheep of the house of Israel" (Matt. 15:24) But, then, recognizing her faith, he healed the daughter. There was a new universalizing dynamic at work.

Jesus made repeated use of the metaphor of a banquet to represent his vision of new forms of radical hospitality, in which the economic and social outcasts would be elevated above those with wealth and social status. This is further articulated in his Sermon on the Mount in which he teaches his disciples: "Blessed are you who are poor, for yours is the kingdom of God. Blessed are you who are hungry now, for you will be filled. . . . But woe to you who are rich, for you have received your consolation. Woe to you who are full now, for you will be hungry" (Luke 6:20–21a, 24–25). Jesus was telling his followers that it was the poor, along with the meek and brokenhearted who would inherit God's coming reign on earth. In parable after parable Jesus spoke of the reign of God using images drawn from farming and women's work, not warfare or mighty palaces. His images stand in sharp contrast those found in certain postexilic prophetic literature that proclaimed God's triumphal reestablishment in Jerusalem.

Jesus' emphasis on peacemaking is particularly striking given the extreme violence of the Roman occupiers. In his clear rejection of the military option as the way to oppose the Romans, he was breaking with all those who sought the reestablishment of the Davidic kingdom by force. The ethic of nonviolence is present in the Sermon on the Mount: "Blessed are the peacemakers, for they will be called children of God" (Matt. 5:10), which is coupled by his teaching his followers to love their enemies and pray for those who persecute you (Matt. 5:44). Jesus practiced nonviolence and expected it of his followers to the point of even scolding the disciple who, in attempting to protect him at the moment of his arrest, cut off the ear of the high priest's slave (Matt. 26:51). According to the theologian Walter Wink, the Last Supper celebrates Jesus' nonviolent breaking of the spiral of violence by absorbing its momentum with his own body. And in his crucifixion Jesus refused to turn to violence as a "last resort" but instead trusts God with the outcome. "Through the history of his people's violent and nonviolent struggle for survival, Jesus discovered a way of opposing evil without becoming evil in the process."[32] Jesus presents the full-blown alternative to what Wink calls "redemptive violence," which enshrines the belief that violence saves, that war brings peace, and that might makes right.

Activism as Nonviolent Resistance

Today there is widespread unanimity among American religious activists on a commitment to work within the parameters of nonviolent resistance. There are some groups, especially among those engaged in peace activism, who engage in civil disobedience as a form of protest. The term "civil disobedience" was coined by Henry David Thoreau, who published a small pamphlet in 1849 explicating his refusal to pay taxes in protest against the U.S. government's unwillingness to end slavery and its pursuit of war against Mexico.[33] He argued that if injustice "is of such a nature that it requires you to be the agent to another, then, I say, break the law. Let your life be a counter friction to stop the machine."[34] Thoreau's challenge is said to have influenced Mahatma Gandhi, and it certainly continues to resonate among some contemporary activists.

Many activists link their understanding of nonviolence to its best-known American manifestation, the civil rights movement, without fully realizing that in modern times its use can be traced back to Mahatma Gandhi. Gandhi's methodologies, which were grounded in innovative reinterpretations of Hindu texts, were subsumed into a Christian context through concurrent interactions between Gandhi and his followers and key American pacifists and African American leaders. As a result, Gandhi's ideas were incorporated into the self-understanding of the civil rights movement and from there have entered the mainstream of progressive religious activism.

Gandhi developed the central principles of his concept of active nonviolent struggle during his successful campaigns against the South African regime and later against British colonial rule. His methodology, known as *satyagraha,* is a fusion of traditional Jain and Hindu concepts with ideas Gandhi found in the writings of Leo Tolstoy and in Jesus' Sermon on the Mount. Often translated as "soul force," *satyagraha* is a complex idea that includes the use of civil disobedience as well as the commitment to nonviolence, the belief in the power of truth and self-suffering, and the desire to win over one's opponent, thereby transforming the conflict situation.[35] In India, *satyagraha* involved the progressive use of a multiplicity of nonviolent actions, including strikes, picketing, sit-down strikes, economic boycotts, the non-payment of taxes, noncooperation, ostracism of community members who refused to join in, and finally, civil disobedience. All of these actions embodied some form of coercion since the *satyagrahis* were attacking the status quo. Yet, even when they were met with violence, they refused to engage in any form of retaliation. According to an account written by one of Gandhi's followers, the refusal to retaliate had the effect of destabilizing the attackers. "'The non-violence and good-will of the victim act like the lack of physical opposition by the user of the physical *jiu-jitsu*, to cause the attacker to lose his moral balance. He suddenly and unexpectedly loses the moral support which the usual violent resistance of most victims would render him.' The non-violent spirit of the *satyagrahis* bothers the opponent's conscience and makes a tangle of his habitual behavior patterns."[36]

Reinhold Niebuhr, one of the twentieth century's most influential Christian ethicists, recognized the inherent advantages of Gandhi's methodology of nonviolent resistance. In *Moral Man and Immoral Society,* first published in 1930, Niebuhr wrote that as a method of expressing moral goodwill "it protects the agent against the resentments which violent conflict always creates in both parties to the conflict," and "it proves this freedom of resentment and ill-will to the contending party in the dispute by enduring more suffering than it causes. If non-violent resistance causes pain and suffering to the opposition, it mitigates the resentment, which such suffering usually creates, by enduring more pain than it inflicts."[37] Niebuhr displayed remarkable prescience in noting that "the emancipation of the Negro race in America probably waits upon the adequate development of this kind of social and political strategy."[38]

Gandhi's ideas of nonviolent praxis were adapted for use in the United States context by two distinct, yet intertwined, streams of American activists, which then took practical form within the African American struggle for freedom. The first pathway consisted of a series of encounters between the Indian independence movement and key African American leaders.[39] Already in the 1930s, African American leaders were extremely interested in Gandhi and the movement for Indian independence. Comparing Gandhi to the Buddha, Mohammed, and Jesus Christ, African American writers, leaders, and spokesmen continuously encouraged their people to learn from India.[40] Writing in the *Norfolk Journal Guide* in mid-March 1931, Gordon Hancock, a celebrated educator, clergyman, and journalist, pled for the emergence of an African American Gandhi. For Hancock, not only had Gandhi moved India closer to freedom, "but even more important was the fact that the Indian leaders, by opting for 'the more excellent way' of nonviolence, 'have set the world an example of soul greatness that must bear fruit through many ages.'"[41] Over the next decades, such news coverage continued, as the African American press avidly followed Gandhi and his leadership of the Indian independence movement.

Beginning in the mid-1930s there were also a series of meetings with Gandhi in India by delegations of prominent African American intellectuals, including Howard Thurman, Mrs. Sue Bailey Thurman, Benjamin E. Mays, and Channing Tobias. After his return from India, Mays wrote a series of articles on his trip, one of which was titled "Gandhi and Nonviolence." Here, Mays emphasized the active nature of nonviolence and traced Gandhi's doctrine of nonviolence back to Jesus, Tolstoy, and the Hindu scriptures.

The second pathway was through contacts made by key members of the Fellowship of Reconciliation (FOR), an American pacifist organization. Howard Thurman is the connector between these two pathways, having been one of the very first African Americans to join this organization. Its commitment to pacifism naturally led its members to pay close attention to Mahatma Gandhi's *satyagraha* movement in India. Two of the organization's leaders visited Gandhi in his ashram in 1929, while another met him in London two years later.[42] Beginning in 1926, still another FOR member, Richard Bartlett Gregg, spent four years living in India. His stay included several months in Gandhi's ashram and well as at the school run by the great Bengali poet and philosopher Rabindranath Tagore. As a result of his time in India, Gregg published three books on nonviolent resistance, the most influential of which is *The Power of Nonviolence,* published in 1934; this book has been called FOR's Bible.[43]

Recognized as the first American theorist of nonviolent action, Gregg effectively "translated" Gandhi's theories of nonviolence into a psychological framework that could more readily be understood by Westerners. According to Gregg, the power of nonviolence lay in its ability to evoke sympathy. The practice of nonviolent resistance requires that those seeking change voluntarily undergo suffering for their beliefs while refusing to strike back against their adversaries, believing that their voluntary suffering will move both the assailant and the beholders to change their hearts and feel a kinship with the sufferer. Believing that Gandhian methods had applicability to U.S. labor disputes and the struggle for racial equality, Gregg maintained an ongoing correspondence with W. E. B. Du Bois, the famed editor of the National Association for the Advancement of Colored People's *Crisis* magazine. Dubois, in turn, republished Gregg's letters describing *Gandhiji's Satyagraha* in the magazine, thereby further contributing to the popularization of Gandhi's methods among African Americans.

Remarkably, a number of key civil rights leaders had been active in the FOR prior to joining the civil rights movement. According to the historian Joseph Kosek, "a disproportionate number of black civil rights leaders, including Bayard Rustin, James Farmer, James Lawson, and Martin Luther King, were members of FOR at key points in their careers."[44] Rustin had been FOR's youth secretary for twelve years. During World War II he protested Japanese internment and refused military service, for which he was imprisoned for two years. Rustin would later become one of Dr. King's closest advisors.[45] By the 1940s, an interracial group, including a number of FOR members, launched a series of nonviolent direct actions against restaurant segregation in Chicago. Three of the group's leaders, James Farmer, Bernice Fisher, and George Houser, would later form the Congress of Racial Equality (CORE), which Farmer described as "a coordinated movement of mass noncooperation as with Gandhi."[46] The CORE "Statement of Purpose" and "Action Discipline" specifically committed it to Gandhian principles, vowing to confront racial segregation "without fear, without compromise, and without hate." Its literature "expressed the belief that direct action should always be accompanied by a spirit of good will toward the discriminator, a frame of mind calculated to change not only his actions, but his attitudes as well."[47] This organization later became the lead organization behind the Freedom Rides, which contributed to ending all forms of segregation in interstate public transportation. Farmer served as its national director during the Freedom Rides.

Even after Gandhi's death, connections continued to be cultivated between Gandhi's followers and individuals who would come to play key roles in the civil rights movement. Martin Luther King is said to have undertaken a serious study of Gandhi and his nonviolent methods after being profoundly moved by a lecture given by Dr. Mordecai Johnson, the president of Howard University, who had gone to India in 1949. While there, Johnson had long talks with Gandhi's followers in which he gained a deeper understanding of the spiritual dimension of nonviolence.[48] However, Rev. James Lawson is the person who most directly brought his experiences of Gandhian praxis into the civil rights movement. Lawson, who had become a pacifist as a child, spent three years working for the Methodist Church in India, where he had extensive interactions with Gandhi's followers. When Lawson returned to the United States in 1956, he quickly went to work with Dr. King, bringing a wealth of practical experience with him.[49]

King and his followers successfully contextualized these Gandhian concepts into the African American religious worldview in part because it had a preexisting tradition of subversive reading of the Scriptures. Sudarshan Kapur, a peace studies expert who has thoroughly documented the links between African Americans and Gandhi's followers, stated, "African Americans were drawn to Gandhi because they too had been taught not to make distinctions between the personal and the public, the political and the religious, the sacred and the profane; all of life was viewed as a piece of the whole, inextricably connected." In addition to these shared religious values, Jesus' teaching in the Sermon on the Mount was another important meeting ground. Although Gandhi was a committed Hindu, he never tired of drawing parallels between his movement and the one headed by Jesus. Manifesting their inclusive understanding of Christian faith, African American leaders spoke of "the great power (Gandhi) has won through sincerity and love," and emphasized the need to take him seriously because "he has Christ in him."[50] These various intertwining streams of Gandhian influences upon American activists would eventually result in the recontextualization of Gandhi's ideas within an African American religious and cultural setting. The successful use of nonviolence to finally end racial segregation in the American South would in turn establish nonviolent resistance as the model for most subsequent religious activism in the United States. Having entered the Christian context through the work of the civil rights movement, Gandhian concepts are now emblematic of all contemporary American religious justice activism.

Contemporary religious activists continue to build on the legacies left by Gandhi and King. John Dear, a Jesuit priest who served as FOR's director for three years, has written extensively about the American peace movement. In *Put Down Your Swords*, in which he shares global examples of nonviolent resistance, Dear writes, "We stand up publicly and resist injustice with creative love, trusting in the God of peace. Nonviolence begins in our hearts, as we renounce the violence inside ourselves, and then practice active nonviolence toward our families, communities, churches, cities, nation, and the world. We practice it personally in the face of violence and join the international grassroots movement of nonviolence for justice and peace."[51] Dear shares stories of activists, including himself, who have willingly served prison sentences as a result of their acts of civil disobedience. The readiness to violate what are regarded as unjust laws or to defy police orders continues to be a characteristic of some of the activist groups featured later in this book. This is especially true of a number of peacemaking groups. No More Deaths (NMD), a religious, immigrant rights organization providing aid to migrants crossing the Sonoran Desert to gain ingress to the United States, practices "civil initiative." This concept is a legacy of the 1980s sanctuary movement that also started in southern Arizona. Civil initiative is a willingness to break laws that are seen as being legitimate, yet harmful in a particular situation. For example, NMD activists have continued to place plastic water jugs in a wildlife refuge, recognizing that they are violating antilittering laws, which they admit are important for protecting the environment. Yet, they remain willing to break these laws and accept the accompanying punishments in their attempts to save migrants from dying of thirst in the desert.

Learning from Latin American Liberative Praxis

The emergence of liberation theology in Latin America was set in motion by Vatican II, held from 1962 until 1965. Taken as a whole, this Vatican council was an event and process "that redefined the Roman Catholic church's self-identity and its relationship with contemporary societies, moving what had remained an inward focused, isolationist institution into active engagement.[52] While Vatican II issued a total of sixteen documents, all but one dealt with internal matters, such as changes in the traditional Latin liturgy. Only at the very end did the council address the church's relationship to society, resulting in the issuance of a brief document titled *Gaudium et Spes* (Joy and Hope). Unlike all previous encyclicals, which were grounded in church doctrine and natural law, *Gaudium et Spes* rested on an examination of contemporary social, cultural, and political realities in light of the gospels and human experience, and affirmed the basic dignity of every human being. Consequently, every form of discrimination, whether based on race, color, sex, social condition, language, or religion came to be seen as contrary to God's intent and therefore should be eliminated. In seeking to walk with humanity and placing human liberation at the center of the church's work, this document opened the door to the development of theologies from below, done from the perspective of the oppressed. *Gaudium et Spes* set the foundation for a series of further papal encyclicals that outlined specific strategies of building solidarity with the poor in developing nations, rectifying the inequalities between nations, and the need for universal charity that includes welcoming migrant workers and treating those who have crossed borders as equals. These teachings transformed the basic posture of what had earlier been a conservative, backward-looking church hierarchy into one of active engagement on issues of global peace and justice.

The debate that occurred between liberal and conservative forces within the church at Vatican II took place within a largely Western framework, with those participating arguing over issues that were of primary concern to theologians from Northern Europe and North America. On the whole, the bishops from the global South, while present in large numbers, were not very involved or significant in the debate over the content of *Gaudium et Spes*. Yet as Vatican II progressed, there was a growing realization that the church was no longer just Western and Eastern, but also Asian, Latin American, and African, and therefore council documents would have to take those regional contexts far more seriously. However, Donal Dorr, an Irish missionary priest writes, "a fully elaborated Third World theology did not emerge at the Council to challenge both the liberal and conservative approaches, both of which were quite Western in their concerns."[53] A coherent theology emerging out of the global South was still missing, and in the absence of a body of theologians who could articulate such a theology, the problems of that part of the world were still predominantly looked at from a Western perspective.

Ultimately, the movement for change within the Roman Catholic Church unleashed by Vatican II was sufficiently widespread that it began to be articulated in various localized gatherings of church leaders. These new pronouncements proved to be most transformative in the Latin American context, where church hierarchies had long been intertwined with the ruling oligarchies. A 1968 gathering of Latin American bishops in Medellin, Colombia, issued a series of documents which would constitute a turning point in the life of the Latin American church and of committed Christians around the world. What has come to be known as "liberation theology" emerged as a contextualization of *Gaudium et Spes* in the conditions of poverty and oppression in Latin America. The Medellin conference placed the church in solidarity with the misery and exploitation of Latin America, which the bishops identified as a "situation of injustice that can be called institutionalized violence."[54]

In response to the economic dependency of Latin America, an insistence emerged on the need for the oppressed peoples of the continent to control their own destiny. Therefore, Medellin called for "liberating education" or *concientización*, which was understood as a means of awakening the masses to the injustice of their situation. One of the most important themes running through the Medellin statements is that liberation requires the active participation of the people themselves. The assessment of institutional injustice and the need for liberation in turn required a revision of the church's own presence in Latin America. Claiming the prophetic tradition in both the Hebrew Bible and the New Testament, the bishops acknowledged that "the God whom we know in the Bible is a liberating God, . . . who intervenes in history in order to break down the structures of injustice and who raises up prophets in order to point out the way of justice and mercy. He is the God who liberates slaves (Exodus), who causes empires to fall and raises up the oppressed."[55] The gospels then came to be read in light of Jesus' proclamation, when he read the Torah text from Isaiah, that he had come to bring good news or liberation to the oppressed. And this, in turn, was interpreted as Jesus having a preferential option for the poor, which needed to be manifested in the church's work and one's own lifestyle.

Liberation theology's call to become the church of the poor resonated deeply with many priests and laypeople who reoriented their praxis toward transformative work among the poor, many of whom were landless, rural peasants in the late 1960s. Christian activists, including priests, quickly found themselves under threat from not only the right-wing military regimes in power in many Latin American countries but also the conservative ecclesial leaders who maintained that the Church should remain apolitical. One of the most significant forms of community that emerged out of liberation theology were the Christian base communities that sought to intentionally live out their interpretations of Jesus' call to renewal in the context of engagement with the poor. Certainly, the message of liberation emanating from Medellin had many critics who accused the bishops of fomenting socialist revolution, yet its reverberations were quickly felt not only within Latin America but in the United States and beyond as well.

There are at least three distinct avenues by which the concepts and praxis connected to liberation theology became integrated into U.S.-based religious activism. Virgilio Elizondo, the first executive director of a newly formed Mexican American Cultural Center (MACC) in San Antonio, Texas, spearheaded liberation theology's contextualization within the emerging Chicano rights movement. Returning missionaries, especially those sent to Latin America through various Catholic orders, also implemented the ideas and praxis of liberation theology within U.S.-based justice organizations with which they become affiliated upon their return. The same is true of Protestant seminarians who returned to the States after seeing liberation theology put into practice while in Latin America. The third route was through the Central America peace movement, which arose in reaction to the Reagan administration's support for the contras in Nicaragua. However, in that case, the need to translate Spanish texts into English for American audiences suggests that it probably impacted the broader U.S. activist community after its arrival through the work of MACC. The Maryknoll mission movement's publishing house, Orbis Books, was the first to translate and distribute many important works of liberation theology for English language audiences in the United States.[56] As was true of Gandhian concepts of nonviolence, American theologians also began incorporating elements of liberation theology into their own writing. As a result, thousands of American religious activists would come to adapt elements of liberation theology for use in their particular contexts.

The embrace of elements of liberation theology was accompanied by the incorporation of certain liberative methodologies, which emerged alongside the new theological perspectives as people sought to concretely apply them to their day-to-day praxis. These liberative methodologies are particularly common within borderlands contexts where activism aims to empower people with limited citizenship rights. But they also appear among cosmopolitan organizations, especially those founded during the 1980s, that conceive of their work as forms of solidarity with people in the global South.

The most frequently used methodologies consist of varying models of popular education. The goal of popular education, or what are also called liberative pedagogies, is to develop critical consciousness—*concientización*. Fundamental to all forms of popular education is the idea that the task of changing society primarily rests on the shoulders of the oppressed. According to Paulo Freire, a Brazilian educator and one of the foremost theorists of popular education, "to surmount the situation of oppression, people must first critically recognize its causes, so that through transforming action they can create a new situation, one which makes possible the pursuit of a fuller humanity."[57] Freire understood that without a process of *concientización*, the oppressed would not be able to objectively understand the role of the oppressor. As a result, their only model of what it meant to achieve full humanity would be to become like the oppressors. Furthermore, "the oppressed who have adapted to the structure of domination in which they are immersed, and have become resigned to it, are inhibited from waging struggle for freedom so long as they feel incapable of running the risks it requires."[58] Popular education was designed to enable the oppressed to see their situation not as a closed world from which there was no escape, but as a limiting situation that they could transform.

Although various adaptations of Freire's model of popular education are most commonly used among justice activists, the sociologist Aldon Morris has documented the equally critical role of the Highlander Folk School in training key civil rights leaders during the 1940s and 1950s. A number of future civil rights leaders met there for the first time. Rosa Parks attended the school just four months before she choose to sit down on the bus, thereby kicking off the Montgomery bus boycott.[59] The school was founded by Myles Horton, who had been encouraged by the theologian Reinhold Niebuhr to create a school in the mountains of Tennessee for mountain people. Highlander's basic philosophy was that "oppressed people know the answers to their own problems and the 'teacher's job is to get them talking about those problems, to raise and sharpen questions, and to trust people to come up with the answers.'"[60]

Popular education is also used as a means of enabling the oppressors or those who possess privilege in a society to enter into solidarity with the oppressed. For those with privilege, this requires that they abandon any lingering notions of the inferiority of the oppressed, which would lead them to engage in various forms of paternalistic charity toward them. Freire explains that, "true solidarity with the oppressed means fighting at their side to transform the objective reality which has made them these 'beings for another.' The oppressor is solidly with the oppressed only when he stops regarding the oppressed as an abstract category and sees them as persons who have been unjustly dealt with, *deprived of their voice,* cheated in the sale of their labor, when he stops making pious, sentimental, and individualistic gestures and risks an act of love."[61] The emphasis on giving marginalized people opportunities to tell their stories, to give voice to their suffering, or in cases of global solidarity, to speak on their behalf, is a recurring theme throughout the case studies that follow. This praxis stands at the center of congregational community organizing, efforts to build solidarity between more privileged religious cosmopolitans and low-wage workers, the work of the workers' centers, and global solidarity work. It is striking that even certain elite institutions, such as the Bill and Melinda Gates Foundation, which spend millions of dollars underwriting advocacy on behalf of increased foreign aid for poverty alleviation, also rely heavily on the use of personal narratives, although not in the context of liberative pedagogies. Given the accessibility of video and the Internet, stories of suffering and redemption gathered from around the world can easily be employed in U.S.-based justice organizing and advocacy work. Clearly, following Levinas, the face and the voice of the *other* can indeed become powerful motivators of justice action.

Some organizations use popular education to enable people from privileged backgrounds to become self-reflective about their own sense of entitlement as well as any negative views they may have of people living in poverty. If left unaddressed, such elitist views could easily lead to practices that dominate over rather than work alongside with people who are poor, those without proper visa documents or who are living in slum housing in the global South. At the same time, solidarity organizations also consciously make use of middle-class Americans' privilege by organizing them to become advocates in the halls of power for those whose marginalization does not enable them to access those same centers of power. The WFP staff person Clare Weber highlights the complexity of this use of privilege in the case of that organization's 1980s advocacy against the contra war in Nicaragua, "Interestingly, it is the privilege of whiteness that was used against the U.S. government, whose hegemonic strategies usually served to maintain the very privileges that the majority of White, middle-class WFP activists were working to undermine."[62] Such a use of privilege becomes especially important in international solidarity work, where the citizens of a war-torn country in the global South often cannot gain permission to enter the United States. Americans who visit those countries with the intention of returning with eyewitness accounts play critical roles as truth-tellers about conflicts, which the United States may be attempting to conceal. In addition, those few refugees who are fortunate enough to gain permission to resettle in the United States also become important spokespersons. By telling their own experiences of suffering, they give voice to their compatriots who remain in their home country.

The use of privilege is also at the heart of accompaniment, another methodology used by a number of organizations. Accompaniment is used by activists within the United States as well as in overseas solidarity work. It can involve the physical presence of volunteers who seek to protect people in danger of being harmed or deported. In some contexts outside of the United States, it involves the presence of foreign volunteers who provide protection for civilian activists or organizations against violent, politically motivated attacks while encouraging them to continue their democratic activities. Human rights accompaniment was used by the U.S. solidarity movements active in support of Central American activists during the 1980s. In such situations, it is hoped that the presence of a volunteer who is an American citizen will serve as a deterrent against any attempts to physically harm local activists. Clearly, this has to be regarded as a form of nonviolent resistance in which U.S. citizenship is used as a protective shield. Accompaniment can also be combined with various forms of advocacy in which the volunteers either enable local activists to more safely tell their own stories or, in some situations, act as the storytellers for others who are under too great a threat to do so on their own. This use of privileged citizenship was a tactic used during the civil rights movement where northern, white volunteers at times purposely accompanied southern African American activists into dangerous areas to serve as a visible deterrence against violence. This methodology undergirded the Freedom Rides, in which integrated buses were sent to the Deep South, knowing that they would encounter violence from segregationists.

The Advocacy Organizations

None of the organizations that primarily do advocacy work make use of the various liberative methodologies described in the previous section. Instead, the most effective advocacy organizations are those that have successfully built national networks of grassroots activists that effectively reach into every congressional district in the country. They have been able to motivate, educate, and organize their volunteers to successfully conduct in-district meetings with their congressional representatives. By building a stable base of volunteers, many rooted in local congregations that also identify with the issues, these advocacy organizations have been able to establish long-term relationships with key members of Congress. Over time, they come to rely on the volunteer advocates' expertise. They also recognize that these volunteers represent a larger mobilized constituency within their districts.

The strongest of these advocacy organizations have built the capacity to function much like many of the older broad-based constituency organizations described in the previous chapter. Today, this requires sizeable financial and staff resources. Organizations with small staff and limited budgets cannot achieve this capacity and thus end up resorting to relying on email networks, which can mobilize letters to members of Congress but do not build up long-term personal relationships with those members as is done by those with grassroots networks of volunteers.

There are also several cosmopolitan organizations founded during the last decade in response to genocides in Africa, which do not use the various liberative methodologies or confine themselves strictly to legislative advocacy. Both the Save Darfur Coalition and Invisible Children organization have been successful in attracting large numbers of youth and young adults to their events, something that many of the older cosmopolitan organizations are struggling to do. Neither organization is overtly religious, although the Save Darfur Coalition has a large number of religious organizations as members of its coalition, while individual staff and participants of Invisible Children are involved out of their religious convictions. Both organizations make extensive use of new media to encourage creative local initiatives and independent support actions among their youthful supporters. They are producing films and YouTube videos not only to convey their stories of African genocide, but also to send out instructions for local activities to supporters who are linked to the organization's staff and each other through Facebook, MySpace, and Twitter. The use of these social networking tools allows them to connect vertically to the organizations' staff as well as horizontally to each other, undoubtedly strengthening the relational bonds that can germinate further activism. As a result, these organizations are unleashing a great deal of local energy and creativity among their young supporters that bears close watching into the future.

All religious activists are engaged in the development of fresh interpretations of their religious texts. Although this chapter emphasized texts that are commonly used by Christian as well as Jewish activists, we will encounter similar textual work taking place among Muslims and Buddhists, as justice activists emerge within those traditions. Regardless of religious tradition, at its core, justice activism is characterized by its conscious engagement with the face and voice of the *other* as the embodiment of the sacred, however that is understood within each religious tradition. We will also see how frequently the various organizing methodologies are being used by activists within very diverse settings, ranging across borderlands and cosmopolitan contexts.

3

Organizing in
Borderlands Communities

Today congregation-based community organizing is one of the most powerful forms of prophetic "insurgent citizenship" within borderlands communities. It is estimated that congregation-based organizing now exists in at least 180 cities in the United States and involves more than four thousand congregations.[1] Taken as a whole, it is the most compelling grassroots response to the negative consequences of urban restructuring and the withdrawal of resources from marginalized communities. It has effectively given power to thousands of marginalized, voiceless people, some of whom are not yet American citizens. They have been transformed into skilled leaders with the ability to organize their congregations into powerful networks that can both confront and collaborate with local, regional, state, and in some cases, even national political leaders and government officials. The success of these efforts rests on their responsiveness to the multiplicity of present-day urban contexts by intentionally building networks of institutions representing multiple ethnic, class, and religious backgrounds. The use of the prophetic becomes a means of holding together a common vision in the midst of what can easily become tense diversity.

The roots of present day congregational based community organizing reach back into the deep soil of early twentieth-century efforts to organize industrial workers in the United States. Later, as the communities in which they were working increasingly became borderlands spaces, they adopted theologies and praxis more suitable to these new cultural contexts. By the 1970s, organizers were constructing new paradigms drawing both on the civil rights movement's legacy and on Catholic social justice traditions, especially the emergence of Latin American liberation theology. Both of these contextualizations draw analogies between the contemporary exploitation of society's most vulnerable people and that which existed in the ancient Near East against which the biblical prophets once raged. Congregational-based organizing is now grounded in the use of popular education models, which are particularly appropriate to the cultural predispositions of borderlands people. Many professional organizers and clergy have been drawn into this work out of cosmopolitan perspectives that lead to them to make conscious decisions to work in solidarity with marginalized people. For them, the work offers rich opportunities to live out of their religiously grounded commitments to social justice. Yet, they too must learn to use popular education as a praxis suitable to the borderlands. Indeed, staff organizers, pastors, and local leaders generally anchor their decisions to engage in activism within prophetic frameworks shaped by various pieces of these contemporary traditions, which ultimately rest on interpretations of the biblical texts on justice. Thus the work is transformative for the cosmopolitan organizers and clergy, and the people rooted in the border-lands. For people living in marginalized communities who become leaders in congregational organizing, the use of popular education leads them to an awareness of the root causes of the ills besetting their communities, of God's commitment to justice, and of their own capacity to transform their collective well-being.

The Emergence of Community Organizing

Urban congregations made up of recent migrants, whether they were African Americans migrating from the southern regions of the United States or earlier European immigrants, have long provided both spiritual and material sustenance to new arrivals and their families. They re-created familiar forms of worship, often reassembling migrants who came from the same towns or regions, while providing informal job and housing referrals for the new arrivals. Over time, increasingly well-established African American churches and immigrant Catholic parishes became active participants in urban politics. Politicians saw the churches as a solid source of votes, while individual pastors positioned themselves as community brokers, able to secure certain resources to benefit not only their own congregation but the larger community in which they were situated. These relationships were defined by the wider systems of patronage politics in which they were embedded, leaving the pastors in a clientage position, basically dependent on the largess of party politicians who retained the dominant power over municipal resources.

The economic collapse of the 1930s gave rise to new political ferment, including widespread industrial union organizing and more militant forms of neighborhood based organizing such as the "Don't Shop Where You Can't

Work" campaigns. These coalitions, led by a combination of Garveyites, church leaders, and businesspeople in northern African American communities, targeted local storeowners who refused to hire black clerks.[2] In the midst of this ferment, Saul Alinsky, who is widely recognized as the originator of contemporary forms of community organizing, began to build an organization in the Back-of-the-Yards neighborhood on the near Southside of Chicago. Back-of-the-Yards, an impoverished immigrant neighborhood built around Chicago's enormous stockyards, had been immortalized in Upton Sinclair's *The Jungle,* which described the heavy toll that this raw form of industrial capitalism exacted on human lives. Alinsky launched the Back-of-the-Yards Neighborhood Council to support the Congress of Industrial Organizations' (CIO) union organizing drive among the immigrant and African American packinghouse workers and to serve as a vehicle for neighborhood empowerment. At that time, the community consisted of various first-, second-, and third-generation Irish, Italian, and Bohemian immigrants, of whom 90 percent were Roman Catholics. Alinsky, who had been trained by John Lewis, the renowned president of the United Mineworkers Union (UMW), built an organization consisting of union leaders, neighborhood merchants, and local church leaders. The new organization employed militant union organizing tactics such as sit-downs and boycotts, all of which he drew from the CIO's repertoire.[3]

Significantly, the Roman Catholic bishop of Chicago, Bernard J. Sheil, played a pivotal role in the creation of the Back-of-the-Yards Neighborhood Council by helping to convince local pastors to support the CIO unions and the new neighborhood organization. The significance of Bishop Sheil's willingness to fund the Alinsky-led community organization should be understood in the context of the larger Catholic social tradition that not only supported the rights of workers to organize and but also sought to build an alternative to atheistic socialism within the working class. When Alinsky wanted to extend his work to other parts of the country, it was the support of Sheil and the Chicago philanthropist Marshall Field III that enabled him to raise the funds needed to found the Industrial Areas Foundation (IAF) as the vehicle through which he would work elsewhere.

The Catholic Church, both its U.S. hierarchy and local parishes, is still an important presence in the flourishing field of congregation-based community organizing. In 2001, Catholic parishes comprised one-third of all congregations engaged in this work.[4] Yet that alone does not adequately capture the Catholic presence in the work: Catholic parishes are generally far larger than Protestant ones and have also often been among the first congregations to sign onto a newly forming organizing committee. Equally significant, the Catholic Campaign for Human Development, the social justice arm of the United States Catholic Conference of Bishops (USCCB), awards roughly $10 million annually to a wide variety of community-based justice organizations, consistently making it the single largest source of support to congregational-based community organizing. As John Carr, then the director of the USCCB's national lobbying office, explained in a 2001 interview, "One reason there are lots of Catholics in faith-based community organizing is that we pay for it."[5]

The Catholic Church's Divergent Trajectory

The Catholic Church's engagement in community organizing in the United States is a testament to the distinctive trajectory of its social justice involvement. It established a commitment to poor people in the 1960s, which has remained important ever since. This can be attributed to two distinctive factors: its long history as a pariah religion in the United States, and the presence of a coherent Roman Catholic social tradition. While today it is by far the single largest denomination in the United States (23.9 percent of the U.S. population is Catholic), historically it stood on the margins of American society.[6] Indeed, throughout the latter half of the nineteenth and early twentieth century, virulent anti-Catholicism animated much of northern Protestantism. Mobilized through the Whig Party and its successors, native-born Protestants sought to contain or weaken the perceived Roman Catholic threat by calling for laws prohibiting the sale of alcohol on Sundays and public funding for parochial schools. "To Yankees, the Irish were English 'blacks' who were now infesting Protestant America."[7] The surge in Catholic immigrants in the 1840s and 1850s led directly to the nation's first anti-immigrant backlash. In the mid 1850s the Know-Nothing movement sought unsuccessfully to enact new restrictive federal immigration and naturalization laws aimed at limiting continued Catholic migration and attainment of citizenship.[8] As late as 1960, John Kennedy's Catholicism was viewed as an obstacle to his ability to win the presidential election as opponents raised the specter of papal control over the White House.[9]

In sharp contrast to the major historic Protestant denominations, which were primarily centered in mid- to small-sized midwestern and southern towns, Catholic immigrants had settled in central cities. As is the case with contemporary immigrants, they lived in co-ethnic neighborhoods centered on a parish church and grade school through which they sought to preserve their homeland language and culture. These immigrants joined the emerging industrial working class and became active in ethnically based urban Democratic Party politics, using access to government as a means of upward mobility. Only after the Second World War did Catholics join the great exodus of whites out to the suburbs, leaving behind their older parishes to African Americans and more recently to new arrivals from Latin America, Vietnam, and the Philippines. This lived immigrant experience led to far more active Catholic engagement in union and community organizing long before Protestant denominations gravitated to activism in the heady decade of the 1960s. Furthermore, earlier generations of the church's ordained priests and nuns often shared the same urban working-class origins as the majority of their parishioners. As they rose to positions of prominence within the hierarchy, they were able to institutionalize ongoing support for grassroots justice work within the life of the Church as a whole.[10]

Catholics are also grounded in a justice tradition whose roots lie deep within the medieval church and which was further elaborated both theoretically and in praxis over the course of the past 120 years of the Church's history. The Catholic social tradition emerges out of the blending of an accumulated body of official doctrine and the praxis of Catholic-led and inspired grassroots justice movements. The Church's first comprehensive statement in support of social justice was an encyclical written in 1891 by Pope Leo XIII, titled *Rerum Novarum* (Of New Things), which called for the promotion of human dignity through a just distribution of wealth and affirmed workers' basic human rights including to right to a living wage and the right to organize. Written as an explicitly Roman Catholic alternative to the growth of socialist ideologies among Europe's working classes, it called for collaboration between owners and workers rather than class struggle, taking a more critical stance against socialism than against capitalism.[11] The encyclical gave raise to a movement of worker-priests in France and Belgium who left their monasteries to live among and work on behalf of the working classes.

In 1931, on the fortieth anniversary of *Rerum Novarum*, another encyclical explicitly supported the organization of trade unions, while encouraging Christians to enter into politics because economic affairs could not be left solely in the hands of business. It also gave encouragement to more active lay involvement in social movements, of which the Catholic Worker became one of the most significant. Co-founded by Dorothy Day and Peter Maurin in 1933 in the midst of the Great Depression as both a newspaper and a movement, it sought to catalyze a radical renewal of Catholicism and the larger society. As an organization working among the poor, the Catholic Worker sought to embody the prophetic nature of Jesus' life. It was one of the first American religious organizations to premise its work on the incarnation of Jesus' words in Matthew 25:40 where he says "just as you did it to one of the least of these . . . you did it to me" along with the early church's traditions of radical hospitality, and the holy lives of the saints. "Dorothy spent her life putting flesh on the bones of Mathew 25. If there ever was a mission statement of the Catholic Worker Movement, this was it. Through the great mystery of the incarnation, persons in every generation are able to respond to Christ himself in the poor. As Dorothy put it, 'He made heaven hinge on the way we act toward Him in His disguise of commonplace, frail, ordinary humanity.'"[12]

Intellectuals and ordinary working people alike responded to this Catholic vision of social and personal transformation, offering an alternative at a time when many thought that only communists cared about the masses.[13] Dorothy's understanding of the gospels and the early monastics also led her to oppose all war, beginning with the Spanish Civil War and extending through the Vietnam War. She was among the small group of people who started what would become Pax Christi. Dorothy's activism, which continued until her death in 1980, serves as a contemporary prophetic role model for many younger Catholic and Protestant activists, including those born since her death. Today there are 185 Catholic Worker communities in the United States, Mexico, New Zealand, and several European countries, all of which continue to practice simple living while serving as places of hospitality among the poor.[14]

Throughout much of the civil rights activism of the 1950s and early 1960s Catholic activists were preoccupied with the rights of workers, remaining largely blind to issues of racial injustice in American society.[15] Protestants, especially African American Protestants, dominated the leadership of the civil rights movement, while Catholic clergy, both black and white, made few significant contributions. Apparently even black priests shared the dominant opinion within the Catholic Church that it was unseemly for either clergy or religious to engage in "public spectacles like demonstrations."[16] Dorothy Day's *Catholic Worker* newspaper was the exception, carrying articles about racism, the exploitation of black labor, and justice for people of color.[17] It was not until 1965 when Monsignor Jack Egan, the head of the Chicago archdiocesan Office of Urban Affairs, marched alongside Martin Luther King in the Selma march for voting rights that this resistance began to break down and other priests joined.[18]

Catholic Commitments to Organizing

In response to the new orientations brought about by Vatican II, many Roman Catholic clergy and religious expanded their ministries beyond the traditional foci on education and charity into the empowerment of the poor. John Bauman, a Jesuit priest and founder of the Pacific Institute for Community Organizing (now known as the PICO [People Improving Communities through Organizing] National Network), recalls a 1966 letter coming from his superior in which the order was for the first time encouraged to do work in urban settings.[19] The emergence of farmworker organizing was another response. Catholic involvement in congregation-based community organizing in the United States is certainly an outgrowth of Vatican II as well as the emergence of Latin American liberation theology, contextualized in the turbulent circumstances of American cities in the late 1960s and 1970s.

In 1969 the U.S. Conference of Catholic Bishops established the Catholic Campaign for Human Development (CCHD) to serve as a vehicle for furthering the church's national anti-poverty strategy. The CCHD's mission was to raise funds to support "organized groups of white and minority poor to develop economic strength and political power" and to "educate the people of God to a new knowledge of today's problems . . . that can lead to some new approaches that promote a great sense of solidarity."[20] According to Bill Purcell, who worked at CCHD in the 1990s, "Creating the Catholic Campaign for Human Development was a prophetic act because it laid out a national program that would challenge present structures with gospel values that are thousands of years old."[21]

In its forty-year history, the CCHD has been one of the nation's largest funders of all types of community organizations working among marginalized people. Its funds originate from a single Sunday's offering taken up in Catholic parishes nationwide. That offering has fairly consistently raised $15 million, of which 75 percent is distributed through the CCHD's national office, with the remainder dispersed through its local diocesan counterparts. By 1999, the CCHD had awarded more than $250 million in grants and loans to over 3,500 organizations that were working to empower people living in poverty.[22] Eleven years later, it had awarded a total of 7,800 grants to self-help projects in local communities.[23] The CCHD gives preference to organizations that are run by the poor, requiring that at least 50 percent of any organization's board of directors be composed of low-income people. It prioritizes organizations that seek to empower the poor to change unjust social structures, which has made it a major financial underwriter of all forms of community organizing. In 1999 alone it made eighty-nine separate grants to various congregational-based organizations and another fifty-three grants to other organizing networks including the Association of Community Organizations for Reform Now (ACORN), the Center for Third-World Organizing, the Southern Empowerment Project, and the Center for Community Change.[24] By 2001, CCHD was also funding increasing numbers of both national and local immigrant-rights organizations, including the National Coalition for Dignity and Amnesty and the Illinois Coalition for Immigrant and Refugee Rights.[25]

The CCHD enjoyed widespread support within the Catholic Church during much of its first twenty-five years. In part this was the result of a conscious strategy of integration where the Catholic social tradition with its priority on the needs of the poor and oppressed was woven into the Church's prayer and worship life. According to John Carr, who currently heads the national Church's Department of Justice, Peace, and Human Development, while there was opposition, the CCHD and the Church's lobbying office drew less flak than their mainline equivalents because they took "less 'prophetic,' less predictable stances, using fewer pious platitudes."[26] Essentially, conservatives within the Roman Catholic Church were satisfied as long as justice for the poor was balanced with conservative stances on abortion and gay rights.

Things began to shift in the mid 1990s as the CCHD came under increasing attacks from conservative forces within the Catholic Church. As is the case among mainline Protestants, these attacks have in part been launched by well-funded outside organizations that are committed to ending what they characterize as a leftist bias within the CCHD's funding priorities. The Heritage Foundation and the Capital Research Council, a conservative think tank funded by William Simon, former secretary of the treasury under Presidents Nixon and Ford, charged that the CCHD had funded organizations that promoted "gays, communists, and abortions."[27] Remarkably, despite these attacks, parish giving to CCHD continued to climb. However, these attacks have reverberated throughout the field of community organizing because the CCHD's national office began scrutinizing whether the local organizations they fund were working in coalitions with gay rights or pro-abortion groups. Some networks were threatened with a loss of funding if they did not disassociate from organizations that supported gay rights or abortion rights. As a result, there is a growing perception that the "Catholics are in turmoil and no longer provide a solid source of funding for community organizing."[28] Even Bill Purcell admits that the CCHD's funding and visibility has declined in recent years, which he attributes more to the financial constraints brought on by the enormous settlements that many archdioceses have paid out to the victims of sexual abuse. These settlements have forced staff and program cuts within the church's national offices.²⁹ Nonetheless, religious leaders active in community organizing recognize that the decline in the Catholic presence is a blow to the vitality of the field.³⁰ Fortunately, other Christian denominations such as the Evangelical Lutheran Church of America (ELCA) have increased their institutional support for organizing by creating a national staff position to support it. The Unitarian Universalists are also stepping up their presence in this work.³¹

The decline of a Catholic presence is also offset by a significant increase in the presence of Jewish synagogues affiliated with the Union of Reform Judaism, which has made community organizing one of its strategic areas of work. While there had been a minimal Jewish presence in local organizing networks the past, as of 2010, there are now at least one hundred synagogues that are becoming leaders in local affiliates connected to all four of the national umbrella organizations: the Industrial Areas Foundation (IAF), the PICO National Network, the Gamaliel Foundation, and the Direct Action Resource Center (DART). The Union of Reform Judaism sponsors Just Congregations, which is supported by a grant from the Jewish Fund for Justice, to act as a catalyst among Reform synagogues to engage in organizing. Its founding director, Rabbi Jonah Pesner, tells the story of his own conversion to community organizing. Having grown up in New York City, he had regularly ridden the subway through the South Bronx. He says, "I was afraid of those neighborhoods." Then in 2000, the veteran organizer Rev. John Heinemeier invited Jonah to visit IAF's Nehemiah Homes that had transformed portions of the South Bronx. Pesner remembers, "I went and I couldn't believe it. I asked Heinemeier, how did you do this?" Heinemeier responded, "We did it!" Since then organizing has become one of Jonah's highest priorities.³²

As Jewish congregations fully enter into congregational community organizing, their leaders are engaged in constructing a distinctively Jewish understanding of the work. They are drawing a distinction between traditional Jewish service work, such as volunteering in soup kitchens, and the work of redemptive social justice. The authors of several articles found on the Just Congregations' Web site draw on Isaiah 58:6: "Is not this the fast that I choose: to loose the bonds of injustice, to undo the thongs of the yoke, to let the oppressed go free, and to break every yoke?"³³ Pesner understands, redemptive social justice as being a "'repairer of the breach,' which means being dissatisfied by feeding hungry people. It means acting with power to reshape this world, to be an agent of systemic change. *Real* repair is the sacred transformation of this world into the world as we know it should be: 'like a watered garden' overflowing with justice."[34] Pesner is also reclaiming the book of Exodus not just as a narrative of redemption but as a story of how the Israelites were brought into being through their creation as a mixed community at Mount Sinai. The narrative begins with the Israelites groaning under their bondage in Egypt, which Jonah interprets as the beginning of their redemption and then climaxes with God's giving of the Torah.[35]

The Emergence of a Focus on Congregational-Based Organizing

Following his success with the Back-of-the-Yards Neighborhood Council, Saul Alinsky extended his community-organizing models into several other cities during the late 1940s and 1950s. He began to hire and train a staff of organizers capable of leading projects in various cities, many of which involved responses to the growing presence of African and Mexican Americans in northern cities and on the West Coast. In California, Alinsky worked with Fred Ross, the founder of the Community Service Organization, to organize Mexican Americans. Ross later hired César Chávez, founder of the United Farmworkers, as one of his organizers. Alinsky was asked to work in several Chicago neighborhoods fractured by racial transitions. In 1959 Catholic pastors invited Alinsky to set up the Organization for the Southwest Council in an all-white neighborhood on Chicago's southwest side. The neighborhood had been wracked by racial violence and rioting in reaction to an attempt by an African American World War II veteran to move his wife and children into the community. The next year Alinsky was asked by a local coalition of Protestant ministers to set up a community organization in Woodlawn, a neighborhood just south of the University of Chicago that had undergone an almost complete transition from white to black during the 1950s. The Woodlawn Organization (TWO) became the first of the Alinsky organizations to draw its inspiration from the contemporaneous civil rights movement. TWO engaged in picketing, boycotting, and voter-registration drives to force neighborhood merchants, landlords, as well as Mayor Richard J. Daley's city government, into improving public and private services in the community.[36] This represented one of the African American community's first direct challenges to racially biased provision of city services by the vaunted Chicago political machine, in which Irish Catholics occupied the key positions of power.

Alinsky's basic approach was to establish organizations that mobilized the leaders of existing community organizations including churches, block clubs, and small businesses to build what were neighborhood-based coalitions that together possessed the power to win concessions from public and private institutions. His IAF staff organizers were taught ways to enter into a community, and to identify and organize its existing leaders around a common vision and strategy. Those leaders were in turn responsible for mobilizing their constituencies when needed. As the local organization gained experience and won small victories, its power increased, so that over time its capacity to win ever larger concessions would expand. Alinsky believed that poor people could achieve political empowerment by forming alliances among existing neighborhood organizations. He also believed that "the end justifies the means," and his preferred strategy for forcing elites to share power was to expose his targets in dramatically staged confrontations and subject them to ridicule.[37] Alinsky conceived of his organizing staff as an elite, all-male group largely without personal commitments, who would be willing to move from city to city as needed. Organizers were expected to train local leaders so that they were capable of carrying on the work in the absence of an ongoing presence of an IAF staff person.

Alinsky laid out his theories of organizing in *Reveille for Radicals* (1945) and *Rules for Radicals* (1971), and was frequently asked to lecture on the subject, thus influencing generations of subsequent activists. Yet, in reality not a single one of the organizations he started maintained their original vision, and the vast majority are no longer in existence. By the 1960s, the original Back-of-the-Yards Neighborhood Council had become an outspoken proponent of housing segregation. TWO was transformed into a community development corporation, becoming the recipient of substantial government grants to construct and manage large subsidized housing complexes in the Woodlawn neighborhood. Alinsky's approach to community organizing, which rested on organizing the existing leaders and placing staff organizers into communities for short periods of time, proved unable to construct sustainable organizations.

The viability of this early phase of neighborhood-based community organizing peaked during the volatile 1960s. The civil rights movement, although focused on racial exclusion in the South, had also brought unprecedented attention to black poverty and exclusion in the urban North and West. In response, a host of new forms of community organizing emerged during the decade—some of them were spinoffs of Saul Alinsky's model, and others were intentionally constructed as alternate models. Young, radicalized

African Americans, Chicanos, and Asians took up community organizing as a means of transforming poor ethnic communities that had remained untouched by the broad legislative pronouncements contained in the Civil Rights and Voting Rights Acts of 1964 and 1965. Students for a Democratic Society (SDS) established "bottoms-up" community organizations in thirteen predominantly black, white, and racially diverse urban neighborhoods. While these organizations never involved large numbers of people, they borrowed from the civil rights movement in their commitment to directly involve poor people in decision making and leadership development.[38]

As the processes of neighborhood demographic transition accelerated in the 1970s, many community organizations, which had relied on what was considered a stable membership base, began to find it increasingly difficult to turnout the large numbers required to carry out actions against local business or political leaders. Don Elmer, a United Methodist pastor who has been active in organizing for almost forty years, recalls, "In the early 1960s, pastors at Northwest Community Organization (in the West Town neighborhood of Chicago) could make an announcement on Sunday morning and five hundred people would show up at just one ethnic church. By 1970, that same pastor could make the same announcement and five people would show up. Relationships within the parish had vanished."[39] The decline in the neighborhood-based approaches required a reassessment of organizing strategies, eventually resulting in the emergence of congregational-based community organizing as the new dominant model of community organizing.

By 1977 Ernesto Cortes, who had been trained by the IAF, succeeded in creating the first community organization in the country to be primarily grounded within congregations. He did this in collaboration with a highly engaged group of Mexican American Roman Catholic clergy and lay leaders in the borderlands city of San Antonio, Texas. Within three years, Communities Organized for Public Service (COPS) was strong enough to break the city's Anglo elite's historic monopoly on political power.

San Antonio had long been a borderlands location. Having originally been in Mexican territory, it was ceded to the United States in the Treaty of Guadalupe-Hidalgo, which also offered American citizenship to Texas's Mexican population. Yet, in the 1850s the anti-immigrant Know-Nothing Party had run active campaigns against San Antonio's Mexican population, vilifying their Catholicism and continued use of Spanish in the public schools, and actually winning the mayoralty in 1854.[40] Little had changed by the 1970s—even though Latinos were now the majority population, they held a single seat on the City Council.

The redevelopment of COPS as an organization represents a form of hybridity, fusing together traditional Alinsky-style organizing with liberative models of empowerment emerging out of Latin America. By the late 1960s San Antonio had become a hub of the incipient movement among Latino Catholics that sought to empower Chicanos by integrating Latin American forms of popular religion into the Catholic Church and by promoting civic engagement to deal with discrimination and social justice.[41] In 1969, fifty priests had met in San Antonio to form PADRES (Padres Asociados para Derechos Religiosos, Educativos y Sociales).[42] This group was created to serve as a national organization of priests who modeled themselves on French worker priests and who believed that it was imperative that they become actively engaged in Chicano communities. Father Virgilio Elizondo, a founding member of PADRES and one of the foremost Chicano theologians in the United States, was based in San Antonio in the 1970s. Having attended the 1968 Medellin conference at which liberation theology was first presented, Elizondo was deeply affected by its description of Latin America's glaring social and class inequalities as a "social sin" and its call on the church to take the side of the poor instead of its historic allegiance to wealth and power.[43] He was also the first Mexican American theologian to name the historical and cultural location of the *mestizo/a* people—who were engendered by the mixing of the conquistadors' Spanish blood with that of the indigenous people—as the experience from which theological reflection needed to emerge. For him, this meant that a Mexican American theology needed to arise out of collective faith experiences, identity, and wisdom of the *mestizo/as*.[44] In an effort to give concrete form to these ideas, in 1971 Elizondo founded the Mexican American Cultural Center (MACC) in San Antonio "to promote the unique culture, religious beliefs, and theological articulation of the Mexican-American people.[45]

MACC was committed to the furtherance of the Chicano inculturation of the Roman Catholic Church and to the empowerment of Chicanos in both sacred and secular matters. As an institution, it adopted a Freireian approach to leadership formation by beginning with what people already knew and could relate to.[46] In practice, MACC stressed the importance of priests serving as community organizers. Working together with PADRES and Patricio Flores, the archbishop of San Antonio and a strong supporter of Chicano empowerment, MACC collaborated with Ernesto Cortes and the IAF in the ongoing development of COPS. According to Cortes, "There was a lot of cross-fertilization and some priests from MACC got involved in COPS."[47] Both PADRES and MACC came to conceive of congregational-based community organizing as a contextualization of the Latin American concept of base communities (*communidas de base*) in its establishment of more permanent and extensive organizations, which were rooted in the parishes. While not strictly speaking a base community, COPS did reflect the communidas' stress on linking reflection with action, borrowing the "see, judge, act" model that draws upon Freireian concepts, as a means of developing critical consciousness.[48] Cortes himself was more influenced by the writings of certain American Catholic theologians, although over time he taught more elements of liberation theology as they proved helpful in sustaining the organizations he had helped to create.[49]

Much of the initial funding for COPS came from the Catholic hierarchy. Of the $40,000 used to start the organization $4,000 came from the San Antonio archdiocese, $3,000 from the Jesuits, and $15,000 from the Campaign for Human Development. The remainder came from a variety of denominations, including the Unitarians and the United Methodists.[50] Priests who were leaders in PADRES later worked closely with Ernesto Cortes in starting UNO (United Neighborhoods Organization), a counterpart to COPS in East Los Angeles, by bringing together eighteen parishes in LA's largest Mexican community.[51]

Ed Chambers, who had taken over as the executive director of the IAF after Alinsky's death in 1972, embraced the new congregation-based organizing model. While Alinsky had little interest in the religion or culture of the churches he had recruited, Chambers, a former seminarian, could see "religious leaders as more than instruments for mobilizing resources. He thought their ideas and traditions might provide important values to sustain participatory politics."[52] Under Chambers's leadership, the IAF institutionalized the model developed in San Antonio as its core strategy. In a public document titled *Organizing for Family and Congregation,* the IAF framed the crisis in the United States not just in economic and political terms but as a crisis of values. While Alinsky had regarded self-interest as the critical motivator for individuals' engagement in organizing, the IAF now began to argue that people's basic concerns were not simply focused on themselves but on their families' and communities' well-being and dignity.[53] These basic assumptions resonated deeply with religiously committed people, especially those whose lives were being battered by the increasingly free-market orientation of American national and local policy. Furthermore, placing religious identity at the center of the work enabled people from a multiplicity of ethnic backgrounds and social locations to form bonds of commonality grounded in their religious beliefs and identity as "children of God." This in turn allowed them to recognize the mutuality of their concerns so that the organizations no longer rested on individual self-interest, but rather on a collective sense of self-interest. Once congregations became the locus of community organizing, activists and organizers alike began to draw on the ancient prophetic traditions, thereby grounding their concrete demands for change in an ancient set of ethical values. In linking their demands to the prophetic tradition, people who had long been marginalized were now convinced of the sacred righteousness of their complaints against public and private authorities.

The shift away from the old Alinsky model to a congregational-based model was further hastened by the massive federal budget cuts that occurred following Ronald Reagan's election as president in 1980. Reagan successfully eliminated several federal programs that had been utilized to funnel funding through city administrations to local community organizations, which in turn used that money to hire organizing staff. According to Don Elmer, organizations that had six to twelve organizers suddenly found themselves left with only one or two. As a result, organizers needed a model that could succeed with fewer staff and less money.[54] By the early 1980s, the PICO National Network also made the shift to a congregationally based model. By centering this work in congregations and weaving together a shared religious identity and set of values, these organizations have been able to construct large effective regional and even statewide networks composed of people from diverse ethnic and class backgrounds. Nonetheless, centering the work in congregations has also had a moderating effect by forcing certain issues on which a broad cross-section of religious institutions would disagree off the agenda. Certainly, gay marriage as a citizenship right is marginalized and silenced within these networks.

Employing elements of Paulo Freire's pedagogy has become a common practice within all forms of congregational community organizing. Organizations use the methodology to determine the key issues on which they will focus by holding upward of several thousand individual conversations known as "one-on-ones." Local network leaders conduct these short, listening meetings with congregational and community members to hear the most common heartfelt pains present within their midst. Those issues surfaced through the one-on-ones are then gathered together and used to shape the organization's issues agenda. By gathering input from a broad array of people, the use of "one-on-ones" shifts the power of shaping the organizing agenda downward. Popular education models also inform the extensive and ongoing leadership training that occurs within these organizing networks. While most clergy and lay leaders are initially invited to attend a ten-day training in which they are exposed to the basic philosophy and approaches to community organizing, the training of leaders takes place in the course of praxis. Leaders are continuously trained through the process of identifying issues, doing research, mobilizing, and preparing for actions at which the issues are presented to policymakers, and then evaluating the effectiveness of the work. Thus, popular education models are at the center of the rhythm of the continuous cycle of planning, action, and reflection.

Today each of the four organizing networks have affiliated local groups in many states. The affiliated groups are essentially local or regional networks of varying sizes, consisting primarily of congregations and, in some cases, other types of organizations as well. The oldest national network, the IAF, which is based in Chicago, reportedly has fifty-seven local affiliates in twenty-one states, Canada, the United Kingdom, and Germany.[55] The PICO National Network has "50 affiliated federations working in 150 cities and towns and 17 states. More than one million families and one thousand congregations from 50 different denominations and faiths participate in PICO." PICO, headquartered in Oakland, California, tends to be strongest in the West, Southwest, and South[56] The Gamaliel Foundation, set up as an organizing institute in 1986, states that it now has sixty affiliates in twenty-one states across the United States and five provinces of South Africa, representing more than a million multifaith, multiracial, churchgoing people who work on social justice campaigns.[57] Finally, the smallest of the national networks, DART, was founded in 1982 and is based in Miami, Florida. It has more than twenty local affiliated organizations, of which half are in Florida and in five other states, including Virginia, Indiana, Kentucky, Ohio, and Michigan.[58] There are also several smaller regional or local congregational organizing networks, including the more recently formed InterValley Project that works in mid-sized cities in several New England states, and the Regional Congregations and Neighborhood Organizations Training Center (RCNO), which brings together small African American congregations in California, Pennsylvania, Illinois, Alabama, and Georgia.[59] The RCNO organizes congregations on the issues of substantive citizenship rights that are particularly relevant within African American communities.

In their 2001 assessment, which remains the most comprehensive assessment of the field of congregational organizing, the sociologists Mark Warren and Richard Wood estimated that between 1 percent and 1.5 percent of all congregations in the United States were affiliated with one of these networks. Taken as a whole, that figure represented a significant form of grass-roots popular political activism.[60] In addition to the one-third that are Catholic parishes, another third consisted of mainline Protestant congregations and the final third was composed of varying African American Protestants (including black evangelicals), Jewish synagogues and Islamic mosques.[61] Recent declines in Catholic participation are being replaced by a growth in Jewish, Unitarian Universalist, and immigrant institutional involvement.[62] Given their greater commitment to theological exclusivity and their relative political conservatism, few white evangelical congregations are present in this work.

The 2001 report confirmed that this work is indeed concentrated in the borderlands. The five states with the highest concentrations of congregational-based community organizations were all in borderlands regions, with California ranked as number one, followed by Texas, New York, Florida, and Illinois.[63] In 2001, 36 percent of all member institutions surveyed were predominantly white, 35 percent were African American, and 21 percent were Latino with another 6.5 percent consisting of racially mixed institutions. Eleven percent of the participating institutions were predominantly composed of immigrants. However, in the intervening years, the immigrant presence in this work has mushroomed. Kathy Partridge, who directs Interfaith Funders, an umbrella organization to which all the major national networks belong, reports that since 2001 there has been "a very significant increase (by far) in the percentage of immigrant institutions involved, and indeed immigrant issues have emerged as a key sector for action by the organizations. This has resulted from both a shift within existing member congregations (especially Catholic), as well as the addition of immigrant-defined member congregations and institutions such as sports clubs."[64] There is now some Asian immigrant presence, which had been noticeably lacking in the past. The heightened presence of immigrant member institutions has in turn led to more of the local networks becoming racially, ethnically, and socio-economically diverse. Given the often conflictual nature of the racial, ethnic, and class transitions occurring within borderlands regions, community organizing is emerging as a critical location in which those tensions can be bridged as people from very divergent backgrounds work on policy issues that are of shared interest. More importantly, it potentially creates a formal space within which relationships of mutuality can be built.

Linking to the Prophetic Tradition

Many of the professional organizers who serve as staff in these networks have been drawn to this work out of their sense of religious calling. Corey Timson, who is a PICO organizer in Southern California, is emblematic of many other staff organizers. Timson attended the University of Notre Dame with the intention of going to medical school. Through his exposure to Catholic social teaching while at Notre Dame, he decided instead to go to Chile as a Holy Cross associate. During his two-and-a-half years in Chile he worked with Construyendo Juntos, a Chilean organization similar to Habitat for Humanity. Using Paulo Freire's pedagogical methods, he also taught adult women how to read and write. On his return to the United States, he began working for PICO.[65] Jared Rivera, who works as an organizer for another PICO affiliate, has a similar biographical story. His father is a first-generation Mexican immigrant. Jared attended the University of California at Berkeley, where he was exposed to activism. While at Berkeley he began studying liberation theology, finding inspiration in César Chávez's life, which led to Jared's interest in organizing. He went to work for PICO shortly after graduating from college. His organizing work for PICO has stimulated a further exploration of his Catholic faith because he sees what he is doing as the embodiment of being Catholic.[66] Paula Cripps, a former organizer for CLUE, grew up in a Sioux City, Iowa neighborhood of Vietnamese, Laotian, and Mexican immigrants. In college she studied to become a teacher, doing her practicum in low-income schools where she observed teachers treating refugee children from Somalia with disdain. She was in Spain at the time of 9/11 and was embarrassed by the American media's vilification of Muslims in its aftermath. These rich cross-cultural experiences continued after coming to seminary in Southern California, where she first interned and then took a job as an organizer for CLUE. She has come to view the Bible as a story of migrants, sojourners, and people of God who are oppressed.[67] These are very typical biographies of the college-educated young adults whose faith and life experiences among the marginalized have led to their embrace of a cosmopolitan worldview, which in turn sparked a conversion of sorts to the work of social justice. They constitute much of the professional organizing staff in these religiously inspired justice organizations.

Each of these organizers also articulates clear connections between their work and the biblical prophetic tradition. Because religious understandings of the prophetic permeate this work, even those organizers who do not bring a personal religious commitment into the work must, over time, become conversant with the various religious traditions present within their network. Those who are rooted in a religious self-identity often interpret the distinctive components of organizing as forms of prophetic engagement. A veteran such as Ernesto Cortes, who remains one of the leading architects of IAF's national work, is remarkably well read, not only in the Catholic social tradition but in other theological traditions as well. As increasing numbers of synagogues have joined IAF's affiliated networks in recent years, Cortes has invested considerable time in deepening a distinctively Jewish understanding of organizing, which has undoubtedly contributed to its growth among Reform synagogues. Cortes sees community organizing as the nexus between the Jewish and Christian prophetic tradition and Alexis de Tocqueville's notions of citizens' democracy.[68]

Younger organizers also understand organizing as an embodiment of the prophetic. Routinely, they connect the prophetic to an embrace of the *other*. Corey Timpson sees PICO as the epitome of the Hebrew Bible's understanding of the prophetic where a right relationship with God required a right relationship with one's neighbor. For Timson, PICO's efforts assisting in the repair of various relationships between community residents and their elected officials are a form of prophetic work. Regina Martinez, a former PICO organizer in Orange County, California, understands her work as prophetic because it "helps people actually speak their own truth, giving them the tools to speak this truth in a public arena to the powers that be, in the company of large numbers of other like-minded people."[69] Timpson also sees his work as prophetic because it enables people to speak truth to power, which is a familiar refrain in organizing circles.[70] Pat Kennedy, a PICO organizer in Long Beach, California, views the "one-on-ones" as prophetic acts because they are designed to break down the barriers that separate people from each other, thereby enabling them to form a real community of shared interests. In Long Beach, a community that has in recent years experienced violent interethnic confrontations, intentionally breaking down ethnic barriers is critical. Like many other borderlands spaces, the city is now populated by a number of different ethnic and immigrant groups whose relationships to the American state are quite different. For instance, the granting of refugee status to Cambodians has created seeds of resentment among other immigrants who were not offered that privilege and are therefore living in the United States illegally. Similarly, African Africans who are U.S. citizens believe they are being targeted by largely immigrant or second-generation Latino gangs. In such highly fractured contexts, the existence of established relationships can, potentially, enable people with disparate interests to identify *their* common issues.[71]

Pastors and church leaders of activist congregations reflect the same commitments to the prophetic. When asked about their sources of inspiration for engaging in organizing, the majority either cited specific passages from the Hebrew prophets, the teachings of Jesus, and the early church fathers, or they named people they view as contemporary prophetic activist "heroes." Pastoral leaders of congregations engaged in organizing uniformly embrace liberative interpretations of Scripture. For them, the stories of the prophets and Jesus are alive with calls to liberation in the present. Especially for Roman Catholic priests rooted in their social tradition, there is no dichotomy between the work of justice and the task of evangelism. Indeed, they see organizing as a means of connecting and responding to the needs of the broader community to which their parish belongs. In interviews, pastors will frequently quote well-known "justice" passages from the Hebrew prophets such as Isaiah, Ezra, Jeremiah, and Micah. One person recited Jeremiah's call on the exiles in Babylon to care for the well-being of the enemy's city. Even more frequently they recite from Jesus' stories and sayings such as those in the Sermon on the Mount (Matt. 5:3–11), his reading of Isaiah in his hometown synagogue calling for good news to the poor and release of the captives (Luke 4:18–19, and the passages where Jesus warns the nations that they will be judged by what they did to "the least of these" (Matt. 25:31–40).[72] Religious leaders also draw inspiration from certain contemporary theologians including Abraham Joshua Heschel, Martin Buber, Rosemary Radford Reuther, Gustavo Gutierrez and other liberation theologians, along with exemplars of prophetic activism such as Dorothy Day, Martin Luther King Jr., Oscar Romero, and Desmond Tutu. Taken as a whole, they contribute to the creation of the theological scaffolding necessary for the public articulation of the ethical nature of the organizations' demands and the maintenance of activists' continued engagement in this work, despite its substantial time commitments.

Rooted in Narratives

The use of narrative infuses the praxis of congregational-based community organizing. The work intertwines biblical narratives with the stories of ordinary people who have become active in the organizing to construct a prophetic understanding of whatever issues the network of congregations has taken on. Since congregations generally constitute the basic building blocks of this form of organizing, the use of scriptural narratives are especially prominent in their public events. However, the hundreds of one-on-ones, which bring forth people's stories of pain, form the backbone of the popular-education method of strategy formation. Storytelling is used within the networks as a means of building relational power, and used publicly as a means of confronting recalcitrant officials and corporate executives. The centrality of narrative is especially well suited for the borderlands context in which so much of this work is now situated. African Americans and many immigrants from Latin America, the Caribbean, and Asia have deep cultural roots within oral, storytelling traditions. Furthermore, their ethnic identities have been fundamentally shaped through the repeated hearing of certain symbolically powerful religious narratives, such as the story of the Exodus among African Americans or that of the apparition of the Virgin of Guadalupe among Mexican Catholics.

When the biblical prophets condemned Israel's departure from God's justice they were referring to certain very tangible transgressions. The same is true of the congregational activists who choose to become engaged in community organizing. They too arrive at the decision to become active, to join one these existing networks through the merging of their understandings of the calls for justice within their particular faith tradition and the all-too-concrete realities of injustice within their own or their neighbors' communities. Thus, the employment of narratives and storytelling lies at the very heart of this work.

Indeed, engaging in organizing emerges out of personal stories of collective pain and grievance. Interviews with the leaders of twelve congregations active in local community-organizing networks in Milwaukee, metropolitan Chicago, and New Orleans offer a glimpse at the range of grievances that moved church leaders to join one of these networks. Each congregation's pastor or justice coordinator was asked to reflect on those events or circumstances that had led to their decision to join. Not surprisingly, the responses varied substantially, depending on the local context. The most frequently told grievance stories among pastors serving poor, predominantly African American central-city congregations, especially those in Milwaukee and New Orleans, spoke of poor-quality public education and the persistence of racial injustice. These issues were followed by homelessness, the lack of decent, affordable housing, the prevalence of drug addiction, chronic joblessness, and violence against children. One of the most powerful stories was told by the pastor of an inner-city New Orleans parish who said his greatest pain was "the violence that our children are subjected to—every child in our parish school has either witnessed a murder or knows someone who was murdered." Immigration was mentioned by a number of clergy, including the pastor of a predominantly black congregation in Milwaukee. Several of the churches located on Chicago's rapidly gentrifying Northside, mentioned the lack of affordable housing. Three clergy of large Hispanic Catholic parishes were most grieved by the resistance they encountered among elderly white parishioners to accept the new immigrants into their community and into the life of the parish. To quote one response, "The English-speaking population sees that it's no longer the same neighborhood."[73] Interviews with leaders in other cities invariably yielded a somewhat different list of grievances. For example, in Los Angeles a pastor active in the regional IAF network named his deepest pain as the high number of deaths from gang violence; the environmental contamination of his neighborhood by Caltrans, the state's transportation authority; a lack of access to health care for the immigrants in his parish; low-paying jobs, and poor-quality schools.[74]

Moving from concentrating their work within a relatively homogeneous constituency in a few well-defined neighborhoods to building larger, diverse metropolitan networks has given the congregational organizing networks the power to take on more complex regional and statewide issues. Yet, it has also exponentially increased the complexities of issue formation. Many of the networks increasingly include some middle-class institutions with very different concerns from those voiced by central-city pastors. For example, when interviewed, few suburban pastors mentioned immediate community hardships as their primary grievances. They were most concerned about matters such as broken marriages, the shortage of clergy in the Catholic Church, developing greater spirituality among the laity, misunderstandings of homosexuality, and a lack of understanding of the destruction of this world by business people. By encompassing middle-class congregations within broader regional networks, congregational community organizing is bridging between borderlands and more privileged communities.

Through the use of popular education, communities of privilege can be empowered to understand their role in this work as a form of accompaniment or solidarity. While members of middle-class congregations may also be facing financial difficulties or an inability to secure affordable health care, these concerns are more likely to remain hidden and managed in private. Yet, pastors of middle-class congregations do report that engagement in organizing networks increases the congregation's consciousness of their own social role. It also provides them with rare opportunities to work across economic class boundaries, which often results in a greater sensitivity to the struggles facing poor families.

This increasing hybridity, encompassing multiple racial, ethnic, and class identities is a major challenge for the creation of a coherent, commonly agreed-upon strategy out of very disparate grievances. In borderlands regions characterized by high levels of *in-migration*, such hybridity has often bred mutual suspicion between communities of people who live in close proximity but do not interact. It is here that the networks' intentionality in building relational power becomes crucial to their ability to create a common voice out of diversity. Central to that process is the creation of spaces where leaders from the varied cultural contexts, which are now represented in these networks, have opportunities to listen to each other's stories. Renee Wizig-Barrios, the IAF lead organizer in Houston, explains that enabling people to share their own experiences of racial injustice "teaches people to cross the boundaries of religion and race by talking to each other."[75] In Los Angeles, for example, Salvadorian members of IAF's network who have heard of the civil rights movement but know very little about it, needed to hear the stories of those struggles. Similarly, a rift between Filipinos and Latinos was addressed by pulling together a small group of people who shared each other's stories, which enabled both of them to recognize their shared experiences of colonial rule. They realized that contrary to common beliefs there were well-off Salvadorans and poor Filipinos, and they could see the commonality of the U.S.' role in the School of the Americas and in the Philippines. Similarly, stereotypes that Armenian, Latino, and white members had of each other were dispelled by exploring their common stories of genocide.[76] This mutual storytelling breaks down the barriers of isolation that normally divide people of varied ethnic and class backgrounds from one another in a large, amorphous, urban space such as Los Angeles. The construction of a new sense of commonality is what enables otherwise isolated, marginalized communities to collectively build the power necessary to confront public authorities as well as corporate executives.

The networks' carefully planned and rehearsed public actions offer yet another venue for storytelling. What are in many cases massive events are purposefully designed to put the networks' strength on public display before an array of public or private-sector officials. These individuals will be asked to give their assent to a well-researched set of demands concerning a particular issue on which the network has chosen to focus. Tightly orchestrated, the events revolve around the use of individual narratives; these are told to clarify the all-too-human dimension of the grievances that are to be remedied. For example, a public action demanding that state politicians expand publicly funded health care for poor families, an issue that has topped the agenda of several of the national networks, will bring forth personal testimonies of families' suffering as a result of a lack of health insurance. Perhaps a single mother will tell officials how their program now covers her children but offers no insurance for her, their caregiver. While the network is prepared with a well-rehearsed policy proposal to present at the end of the event, the actions emphasize these personal narratives. Not only are they forcing the invited officials to confront real people who are suffering as a result of their policies, these actions also serve as a real-life training ground for ordinary congregants who have never before spoken in public, let alone used their public presence to demand remedial action from those with power over their lives. However, it is within these interactions that community organizing is creating exactly the kind of public space that Ernie Cortes refers to when he speaks of it bringing together the biblical tradition with the Tocquevillean democratic tradition.

Congregational Organizing as Insurgent Citizenship

Over the last thirty years, congregational organizing has significantly increased its capacity to build the necessary relational power to attain more comprehensive forms of substantive citizenship rights. While continuing to work on a wide variety of neighborhood specific issues, such as an over-concentration of liquor stores, a lack of adequate playgrounds, the presence of hazardous waste material, or open drug dealing, the networks are now capable of fighting for substantive rights affecting larger collectivities. Some researchers have disparaged community organizing's shift into congregations as a moderation of its earlier more militant forms, but it has proven to be the most viable model for building sustained civic participation among ordinary people.[77] It is undoubtedly true that community organizing does not call for a radical rearranging of political and economic power. Yet, it has succeeded in achieving very observable improvements in the quality of life of marginalized people and the communities in which they live. Many of the networks' campaigns are tangible responses to the negative impacts of complex urban transformations, including massive demographic shifts, declines in public investment, and the restructuring of work. In the midst of these organizing campaigns, participants who run the gamut from clergy to undocumented immigrants gain a new political consciousness of the workings of power in a democratic society as well as their own capacity to create change. Many ordinary people have been transformed from uninformed political outsiders to engaged citizens. In essence, it forces capitalist democracy to become more inclusive and accountable to those who singularly have little economic or political clout. Drawing on Amartya Sen's understanding of freedom in its broader sense of "possessing the capabilities to do the things one has reason to value," organizing should be understood as directly contributing to an increase in freedom. It enhances freedom by improving the quality of and accessibility to those institutional structures that generate opportunities for upward mobility such as schools, recreational space, health insurance, job training, and decent affordable housing.

Already in the 1980s, congregational community organizing demonstrated an ability to win substantial improvements in communities' basic well-being. As early as 1982, East Brooklyn Congregations (EBC), an IAF affiliate, had built sufficient power to secure a combination of local, state, and private financial backing for the Nehemiah Plan, whose goal was to remake the once devastated neighborhood of Oceanhill-Brownsville by building 2,900 new homes. Prior to the construction of the Nehemiah homes, the price of a home, even in one of the worst areas of New York City, exceeded what many well-paid workers such as letter carriers or bus drivers could afford, forcing families to flee the old neighborhoods. The EBC intentionally set out to build more new homes rather than the lesser numbers done by most community-based builders so the homes could regenerate a sense of community.[78] Thus, EBC's efforts led to the creation of a revolving loan fund with seed money from the Missouri Synod Lutherans and the local Roman Catholic archdiocese. Its organizing campaign eventually resulted in an agreement by New York State to subsidize the mortgages, thus making them affordable to many first-time homeowners. The organization also pried an agreement out of Ed Koch, the mayor of New York City at the time, that the city would condemn any remaining abandoned structures and provide tax deferrals and interest-free loans totaling $10 million, thus making the purchase price of each house affordable for middle-income families. The result was quite literally the rebirth of a community. Obviously, the choice of the project's name was an intentional signal of the project's prophetic intentions: the Hebrew Bible's book of Nehemiah tells the story of the rebuilding of Jerusalem following the Israelites' return from their exile in Babylon. As a story, Nehemiah resonated deeply among the largely African American population of Oceanhill-Brownsville who found themselves living in a form of internal exile. The IAF has since replicated the model on a smaller scale in Philadelphia and Washington DC.

The IAF affiliate in Baltimore, Baltimoreans United in Leadership Development (BUILD), is recognized as the originator of the national livable-wage campaign and a leader in creating innovative responses to the changing nature of work. Another of the older networks, BUILD was founded in 1977 by many of the same African American pastors who were active in the city's earlier civil rights movement. It had spent its first decades working to improve the dismal state of the city's public schools. By the late 1980s it reoriented its attention onto the shifting nature of work in a city that had long relied on heavy manu-facturing as the source of long-term stable jobs. New global manufacturing platforms had drained Baltimore of many of its reliable industrial jobs, replac-ing them with low-wage service-sector employment. Even the public sector had subcontracted jobs that had once paid $13.00 an hour to outside contrac-tors who were paying $4.25 an hour without any benefits.

BUILD decided to fight for the enactment of a living-wage ordinance for employees of the city's subcontractors: one-on-ones conducted with people who were using member churches' food pantries revealed that many peo-ple were working but did not earn enough to feed their families through-out the month. This discovery angered church leaders because they realized that their volunteer services were, in fact, subsidizing low-wage employers.[79] BUILD decided to pursue the enactment of a city ordinance requiring all city contractors to pay a living wage, set at $7.70 an hour at that time, after their research revealed the highly fluid nature of service employment. They recog-nized it would be difficult to successfully win wage increases from individual private contractors, since doing so would only give a competitive advantage to those firms that kept their wages at a minimum. Instead, the point of lever-age over these firms was to force the city, which was a huge purchaser of their services, to require the payment of an adequate wage. Passage of the ordi-nance helped stabilize the workforce of the city's contractors so they could in turn be organized into a union, which BUILD accomplished in conjunction with the American Federation of State, County and Municipal Employees (AFSCME). Living-wage ordinances were eventually passed in forty-nine other cities and ten counties, largely through the efforts of ACORN, the now defunct neighborhood-based organizing network. Baltimore remains the only city where the contract employees were unionized.[80] The creation of the union was possible because BUILD's strong congregational base of sup-port protected the workers as they organized. "The politically savvy black churches were able to lend these vulnerable workers their political clout."[81] Religious worker-justice organizing is providing similar protection to vul-nerable workers, who are now often undocumented immigrants.

In recent years as networks have expanded their reach beyond central-city boundaries into outlying suburbs, they have used their increased power to confront state legislatures on issues such state funding for schools and health insurance for low-income families. These efforts have also brought them into broader alliances with other types of institutions that share similar goals but do not always have organized grassroots constituencies, including unions and health-care providers. In Texas, San Antonio's COPS has joined with IAF affiliated networks in other cities to create a statewide network that waged a multilevel campaign for school reform. Recognizing that upgrading the quality of public education in poor communities required a wholesale restructuring of local schools, the Alliance Schools sought to transform schools into communities of learners. In a document outlining their emerging vision of educational reform written by a team of local IAF leaders, they called for a model that "shifts from efficiency to effectiveness: from that of students as passive learners to that of a community whose members are committed to learning the skills of problem-solving, teaching themselves and others, and collaboration."[82] Using its statewide network, the IAF affiliates successfully lobbied the Texas legislature for the additional resources, while at the same time securing funding from the Rockefeller Foundation to hire educational coordinators in local schools who used one-on-ones to engage parents and other neighborhood residents surrounding the Alliance Schools. This approach has since been adopted by other schools throughout the West and Southwest. The Greater Boston Interfaith Organization, also an IAF affiliate, was instrumental in securing the passage of Massachusetts' 2006 landmark health-care reform legislation, which, when fully implemented, will mean that hundreds of thousands of people will for the first time receive quality, affordable health care.[83]

In Wisconsin, a Gamaliel-affiliated statewide network also prioritized educational reform. By the late 1990s demographic shifts had drained Milwaukee's public schools of many of their middle-class families: 87 percent of the children in the city's public schools were from families with incomes below the poverty level. Overall, Milwaukee's schools were educating one-third of all the poor children in the state. The consequences of such high concentrations of poverty were reflected in a 60-percent high school dropout rate. After doing extensive research to identify a winnable strategy that could effectively tackle the education dilemma, the statewide network decided to focus on lowering the teacher/pupil ratio to fifteen students per teacher. In 1998, the network succeeded in its efforts to secure more state funding for classroom size-reduction in the Milwaukee schools.[84]

PICO has also worked on educational reform, seeking to bring schools more in tune with the needs of local neighborhoods through the creation of smaller schools, increased parent participation, better qualified teachers, and more avenues for youth involvement. However, it has made an expansion of access to heath care the primary focus on its state and, more recently, even its national organizing. Having focused on expanded health insurance coverage for all children in California, PICO affiliates secured greater access to health care in California, although the network fell short of its goal of winning universal state health insurance in the state. In 2007, in its first attempt at waging a national campaign, PICO networks worked with other health-care advocacy organizations to win congressional reauthorization of the State Children's Health Insurance Program (SCHIP). In enacting SCHIP in 1997, Congress had amended the Social Security Act to provide $20 billion over ten years to help states insure low-income children who were ineligible for Medicaid but whose families could not afford private insurance. Although the PICO staff had already recognized that it was critical that their type of organization do some national work, SCHIP's reauthorization brought health-care insurance to the forefront.[85] It decided to hold a national teach-in focused on health-care delivery; afterwards it asked its local affiliates whether they wanted to work on this issue in their local areas. The issue took off around the network with most PICO affiliates deciding to do one-on-ones on the issue, followed by a survey on health insurance in their member congregations. Given that the legislation was crucial to the well-being of 6.6 million children, health care emerged as an immediate issue. While PICO collaborated with Washington DC–based health-care advocates, they focused their organizing among their local members who used relational organizing to hold their state's congressional delegation accountable on this issue. In June 2007 PICO brought some of their local leaders to "Pentecost," a conference sponsored by Sojourners/Call to Renewal, a progressive evangelical organization based in DC. The two organizations collaborated in doing joint training, and then visiting congressional delegations on Capitol Hill. Although SCHIP was reauthorized at its preexisting level, the campaign to expand SCHIP failed in Congress at the end of 2007, falling fourteen votes short of the number needed to override a presidential veto. This was probably the most complex organizing effort PICO has ever engaged in. "We were told by the leadership in the House and the Senate that we had brought a whole new dimension to lobbying—we had brought sustained citizen voices to the debate" marking their return to DC after several decades' absence.[86] The work on national health care prompted PICO to create a new position for a national policy director and open an office in Washington DC. An expanded SCHIP, covering an additional 4 million children, was finally signed into law by President Obama in April 2009. Since then, PICO has continued to focus its national campaigning on healthcare, working to secure congressional approval of the 2010 health-care reform bill.

Like PICO, the Gamaliel network has moved into the national legislative arena by joining a broader campaign for comprehensive immigrant rights: this network is a member of the steering committee of the Fair Immigration Reform Movement (FIRM),a national umbrella coalition fighting for comprehensive immigration reform. Gamaliel has included two of their high-level faith leaders in national strategy sessions with FIRM so that they can take a leadership role in deciding how the Gamaliel network will implement its own immigration strategy.[87] However, they too remain primarily focused on local immigration work: following the demise of national immigration reform, states and local governments became the frontlines in the battle over immigration. Not only have various states and cities begun to enact laws requiring proof of citizenship under all sorts of circumstances, the federal agency responsible for immigration control (Immigration and Customs Enforcement [ICE]) began carrying out massive raids targeting undocumented immigrants. Viewing the massive assault on immigrant rights as a virtual state of siege where "the federal government's militaristic wing has become domestic policy," Gamaliel has done extensive educational work among its member organizations.[88] They have sought to bring their historic African American church constituency into support for the rights of the organization's emerging immigrant constituency. For example, the Detroit Gamaliel affiliate secured the passage of an anti-profiling ordinance, and the Atlanta affiliate held a prayer vigil outside the headquarters of CNN, demanding that the network provide more balanced coverage on immigration while working with the city's mayor to curtail the collaboration between local police departments and ICE. Gamaliel in Atlanta is also collaborating with other immigrant rights organizations to create a rapid response network that will have churches' leaders, including bishops, come out in opposition to raids as they occur.

While the larger national networks are investing heavily in the creation of broad-based regional networks comprising ethnically and economically diverse constituencies, the RCNO has built a smaller, though credible, network by organizing only small- to midsized African American congregations. Having originated in Philadelphia in 1987, the network is now centered in Los Angeles where it has effectively pursued a racially exclusive strategy in the midst of the region's heterogeneity. Rather than seeking commonality across racial and ethnic divides, it focuses on addressing issues critical to African Americans. RCNO has sought to build the capacity of clergy and lay leaders in those black congregations that are often overlooked by the larger national networks. Like the larger networks, RCNO's work is based on the "see, judge, act" paradigm designed to enable leaders to think critically about the issues that afflict their communities. It also receives funding from the Catholic Campaign for Human Development and the Presbyterian Church USA. One of its most significant campaigns has focused on the extraordinarily high rates of incarceration among African American men, which continues to result in their loss of formal and substantive citizenship rights. Eugene Williams, the executive director of LA Metro, the Los Angeles RCNO affiliate, regards the rise of the prison industrial complex as analogous to the loss of democratic rights experienced by African Americans at the end of Reconstruction. Drawing on liberation theology's methodology, Williams asked what God was saying to his people in the midst of these circumstances.[89] The result has been the creation of a number of church-based programs designed to stop recidivism, including obtaining funding from the state legislature to establish GED programs in African American churches. The mandate for LA Metro's ex-offenders' programs are, again, Jesus' prophetic words in Matthew 25 where he proclaims the judgment of the nations according to whether they visited the prisoners.[90]

Concluding Remarks

According to Amartya Sen, freedom entails the possession of citizenship rights that give people opportunities to influence the society in which they live. Certainly organizing accomplishes that by creating active citizens even among people who do not necessarily possess formal citizenship rights at the level of the nation-state. This is true for numerous groups of people within the borderlands, including both recent immigrants and a disproportionately large number of African Americans who have lost citizenship rights, despite having been born in the United States. Given organizing's ability to create new spaces for the exercise of substantive citizenship rights, it is a form of insurgent citizenship that is being generated from below rather than granted from above by the state. Yet, creating this type of citizen activism requires a continuous renewal of these congregational-based networks. Referring to COPS, Ernie Cortes asserts that the organization has been rebuilt at least seven times since its inception in the 1970s. "After a while we were not able to meet the challenges. We have to constantly revisit what's going on in the world. We also have to make hard, tough critiques of our own approach because the situation has changed and we can no longer do our work in the same old way."[91] This makes organizing a complex, time-consuming proposition for its many volunteer leaders. There is a continuous need to identify new leaders, which requires an ongoing process of one-on-ones and listening meetings: as issues shift, new people emerge with the passion to address the new circumstances. This commitment to continuous organizational regeneration may well contain great wisdom for other prophetic activist organizations who find themselves in the midst of generational transitions.

4

Religious Organizing for Worker Justice

Workers' basic rights are flagrantly violated on a daily basis in the United States. For example, a 2008 union campaign to organize car-wash workers in Los Angeles revealed that a group of laborers familiar to most Angelenos were working under horrible conditions. They were being paid $40 a day, well below the minimum wage, had no protection against exposure to hazardous cleaning chemicals, were denied rest breaks, and were constantly harassed on the job. "They are the most dispossessed workers in the formal economy!" declared Rev. Bridie Roberts, the program director for the CLUE affiliate in Los Angeles.[1] As with these car-wash workers, it is frequently first-generation immigrant men and women who are being exploited. Many of them have risked their lives crossing through the desert to come to the United States in order to support their families back home. They come from countries whose domestic economies simply create far too few jobs to support all of their citizens. For some of the biggest immigrant-sending countries, such as Mexico, El Salvador, and the Philippines, remittances sent home by their citizens working overseas are one of the largest sources of national income. As globalization weakened these countries' domestic sources of income, the income received from their citizens working abroad has become a critical source of economic stability. "Migration helps pacify people," says Romualdo Juan Gutiérrez Cortéz, a teacher in the Mexican state of Oaxaca, and "poverty is a ticking time bomb, but as long as there is money coming in from family in the United States, there is peace. To curb migration our country must have a better employment plan."[2]

The steady stream of income flowing from immigrants working in the United States is highly dependent on the ability of immigrants to send substantial portions of their earned income back home. Deep job losses resulting from the economic recession in 2008/09, along with increased workplace immigration raids and border enforcement, had immediate repercussions on the well-being of immigrants' families in their home countries. By early 2009, there had been an estimated 13 percent decline in remittances to Latin America. Almost all the money sent home is spent on such basic necessities as food, clothes, utility bills, education, and health care.[3] Declines in this income flow therefore not only pose hardships for individual families in Latin America, Asia, and the Pacific Islands, but they could also become a source of violence and political unrest back home, thus only increasing the number of people seeking to leave.

Immigrant workers who lack U.S. citizenship or legal visa documents, and who have limited English language skills also have limited job options outside of the low-wage sectors of the labor market where employment is often informal. Unscrupulous employers routinely violate existing labor laws by paying less than the minimum hourly wage, failing to pay overtime, and providing minimal break times, while violating all manner of workplace safety regulations. Yet, attempts at collective organizing or protest are met with swift retaliation, including cases of employers reporting the presence of undocumented workers to federal and state authorities. Prophetic worker-justice activism has emerged in reaction to globalization's exacerbation of low-wage workers' exploitation in the United States. According to Rev. James Lawson, who is regarded as one of the nation's most prominent veterans of nonviolent social change and a founder of an interfaith worker-justice organization in Los Angeles:

> What historians of the Civil Rights Movement seem not to understand is that the Memphis sanitation workers' strike was operating on ending the economic injustice that resulted from slavery. I see economic injustice as a human rights—as a civil rights issue, but that alone is too narrow of a gauge. More critically, it entails the ability of people to create healthy communities where they are able to raise their children.[4]

Here, Lawson is framing justice for low-wage workers not only as a matter of rights but, understood through a religious lens, as a matter of building shalom, of building a sustainable community in which peace will reign.

By 2009, there were forty-nine local interfaith worker-justice groups, six student groups, and twenty-one interfaith workers' centers spread across the United States. These centers represent a small portion of a still much larger number of workers' centers, some of which are affiliated with other nonreligious networks. Here, religious activism is one element of a broader movement for worker justice, much of it led by immigrant activists themselves.

The forty-nine local worker-justice committees have all formed since the mid-1990s. Today, their leadership is largely composed of multiracial, ethnic, and religious cosmopolitans who have committed themselves to stand in solidarity with low-wage workers. Again, these activists draw upon their varied religious traditions' historic texts that call for just treatment of workers and woe upon all those who abuse them. They also draw on the legacies left by earlier generations of both Christian and Jewish labor activists. Indeed, the presence of religious activists standing in solidarity with low-wage workers is not a new phenomenon. It has occurred at other significant moments in American history, including the eighteenth- and nineteenth-century's European immigration, which was also met with great hostility.

In her book on *Old Labor and New Immigrants*, the historian Gwendolyn Mink argues that in seeking new sources of lower-priced labor, employers have consistently "made ethnic choices in favor of people whose experience with capitalist institutions lags behind that of workers already in place."[5] Today that description characterizes immigrants from rural regions in Mexico, Central America, and China, whereas 150 years ago it was Catholic and Jewish immigrants from southern and eastern Europe. Between 1880 and 1920, nearly two-thirds of all new immigrants came from outside of the northern and western European Protestant ethnic groups that had immigrated to the United States during the first half of the nineteenth century. Native-born workers responded by creating union structures and membership rules that excluded the new arrivals. Their unions stood at the forefront of legislative lobbying efforts aimed first at excluding Chinese and by 1924 greatly restricting all further immigration from eastern and southern Europe.[6] While this strategy protected the wages of the skilled craft workers, it left the newly arrived Jewish and Catholic industrial laborers working under conditions similar to those experienced by present-day, low-wage immigrant workers.

Like many of today's immigrant labor activists, earlier Jewish and Catholic immigrant labor leaders often came to the United States with considerable political experience. For example, many of the eastern European Jews who found work in New York City's garment, hat, fur, and other needle trades came out of social democratic or communist political movements in their home countries. Such backgrounds gave them the experience and ideological commitment to establish new unions and quickly ascend into newly created leadership positions. Similarly, the Transport Workers Union originated in part from among the clubs and social groups made up of Irish Republican Army exiles during the first two decades of the twentieth century, who had brought their organizational savvy and a relish for political intrigue into union organizing in the United States.[7] The legacy of the early Jewish labor leaders lives on in the work of the Progressive Jewish Alliance, for whom worker rights are a core issue. Their work in California is focused on support for garment and hotel workers. "We looked at the complexity of Jewish history—Jews were the sweatshop workers as well as owners. There is also a Jewish history of rabble rousing—of forming unions and being active in the civil rights movement."[8]

The Catholic Church was an active participant in the 1930s efforts by the Congress of Industrial Organizations (CIO) to unionize industrial workers in the then burgeoning manufacturing plants. Priests and sometimes even the Church's hierarchy became directly involved in organizing campaigns. Some spoke at union organizing rallies, often for the CIO, others acted as chaplains or became full-time labor activists. The appearance of a priest or a bishop on a union platform was designed to assure Catholic workers that the Communist Party USA did not dominate their unions. Labor priests also functioned as delegates to union conventions, as educators operating labor-education schools for workers, or as arbitrators and mediators during labor disputes. The archbishop of Cincinnati established a clerical labor-education program, while Monsignor Reynold Hildebrand from Chicago arranged for labor-education classes for priests from the city's industrial parishes.[9] These programs are the precursors of today's interfaith workers' centers. While there was never an exact religious breakdown of CIO membership, nonetheless, according to John Brophy, the first executive director of the CIO, Catholics made up "the largest creedal body" in the federation's early days.[10]

The union contracts that were eventually negotiated transformed what had been low-paid, hazardous, industrial work into jobs that enabled subsequent generations of industrial workers to ascend into the American middle class. In 1997 Thomas Balanoff, the son of a steelworker, captures the unions' impact on his family, "In Gary [Indiana], the steel industry and the Steelworkers' contract allowed our family to realize the American dream: to own a home, to own a car, to put four children through college."[11] By the 1960s many third- and fourth-generation children of earlier European immigrants had entered white-collar professions. They were replaced on the production lines by African American migrants from the South who gained access to the shop floor just as American manufacturing began its long, steep decline, eventually taking the industrial unions down with it. At the pinnacle of the unions' strength in 1953, 32.5 percent of the total U.S. workforce was unionized; in the private sector it was 35.7 percent. After decades of decline, in 2003, only 12.9 percent of the nation's workforce remained unionized, with a meager 8.2 percent of all private sector workers in unions.[12]

The Weakening of Organized Labor

By the new millennium, unions were widely viewed as a relic of a bygone industrial age that held little relevance for the global workforce. Over the previous three and a half decades, organized labor had increasingly found itself caught in a vise, under pressure from all sides. Following the passage of the 1964 Civil Rights Act, black workers pressed the unions to end the vestiges of discriminatory workplace practices, which too frequently were still sanctioned by union contracts. Simultaneously, the lowering of global transportation and communications' costs led corporations to gradually shift production to overseas manufacturing platforms, leading to massive plant closings and the wholesale loss of power on the part of the larger industrial unions. With the support of a transformed National Labor Relations Board (NLRB), companies mounted aggressive campaigns to defeat new efforts to organize nonunion workplaces. A whole new industry of firms emerged that specialized in assisting corporations defeat their employees' unionization efforts. De-unionization has been accompanied by a steady weakening in the enforcement of existing federal and state fair labor laws. Employers had regained the upper hand as whole new sectors of low-wage work flourished at the bottom of the labor market. Writing on the occasion of the NLRB's fiftieth anniversary in 1985, the labor-law expert William Gould observed that "many of the characteristics of American labor-management relationships are identical to those of the 1920s and early 1930s—the eve of the New Deal and the Wagner Act (the National Labor Relations Act of 1935). . . . Today, as then—slightly more than fifty years ago—the unions are in retreat on virtually all fronts."[13]

Forty-five years ago, organized labor had been the dominant voice in favor of increased federal support for the unemployed, elderly, and the poor. Its mighty lobbying prowess was crucial in the passage of civil and voting rights. In election after election, the unions provided the bulk of the Democratic Party's get-out-the-vote foot soldiers in its urban strongholds. The AFL-CIO, the nation's umbrella labor federation, served as the largest counterweight to organized business interests, both in the workplace and in Congress. All of that changed as manufacturers began to abandon their urban factories in the late 1960s for more lucrative locations in rural America and overseas.

The gradual ascendancy of conservative politics led to a simultaneous frontal assault on the institutional apparatus that guaranteed labor rights at the national and state levels. The National Labor Relations Act, which had regulated an orderly process of union recognition since its passage in 1935, was decimated; while employer violations of those laws that survived greatly increased. "The resulting deregulatory trend was at least as detrimental for workers and their unions in service-producing industries like communications and transportation as deindustrialization was in manufacturing."[14] Emboldened by these regulatory and policy changes, employers doggedly resisted attempts by workers to unionize, effectively putting a brake on new organizing. In an article that appeared in the *New Labor Forum*, Linda Chavez-Thompson, who was elected as the executive vice president of the AFL-CIO in 1995, the first person of color to hold such a position in the federation's history, writes, "Today's labor laws are slanted so heavily in favor of employers that the right to form a union—which is recognized around the world as a basic human right—has all but disappeared from the American workplace."[15]

The unions contributed to this dismal state of affairs. By the early 1990s, the win rate of organizing campaigns in manufacturing facilities was only 31 percent. Organizing in the service sector had dramatically higher rates of 70 percent; yet unions remained focused on manufacturing.[16] Unions that had become stodgy and lethargic were slow to respond to the changed circumstances. Instead, mass-production unions often sought to accommodate employer demands for concessions in the hopes of forestalling further plant closings. In national politics, they championed protectionist policies against foreign competitors. Organizing efforts relied on top-down campaigns, using professional, paid organizers who would try to persuade workers to risk joining an organizing drive while they stood safely outside the companies' gates. Unions made only episodic efforts to build leadership among rank-and-file workers, even though research had shown that organizing strategies, which empowered workers themselves, were far more successful.[17] In their haste to expand their ranks, many unions, along with the AFL-CIO, shifted resources into organizing at the expense of funding union education departments and programs. Writing in a 2001 article in *The Nation*, the labor expert Kate Bronfenbrenner opined, "Thus, at the very time the labor movement most needs structural and cultural change, it is depleting the funds of the single most effective force for that change—membership and leadership education. Increasingly, this has meant that the frontline work of organizing is being done by a flying squadron of new and inexperienced organizing hires, not by member volunteers or rank and file leaders within the unit being organized."[18]

In many cases, unions had justifiably earned reputations as being corrupt and undemocratic. Their leadership became bureaucratic and nepotistic, often functioning more like businesses than worker advocates, all the while collecting dues and managing large pension funds for their members. Issues of shop-floor democracy, dignity and self-expression received little attention from their unions' hierarchy. Even though it had supported the new civil rights laws, the leadership of the AFL-CIO feared the 1960s era of mass mobilization. The labor federation refused to support the 1963 March on Washington, César Chávez's Delano marches, or the 1968 Poor People's Campaign. George Meany, the federation's president, was extremely hostile to the protests against the Vietnam War, ignored the emerging women's and gay rights movements, and in the 1972 elections led his AFL craft unions into endorsing Republican Richard Nixon for president. The more progressive United Auto Workers backed Lyndon Johnson and the Democratic Party's leadership in excluding the Mississippi Freedom Democratic Party from the 1964 Democratic Convention, contributing to the growing disillusionment among many younger African American civil rights activists.[19]

The long-term weakening of organized labor has resulted in a wholesale deterioration of pay and benefits for the average American worker. Since the late 1980s, even periods of economic growth have left wages stagnant. As of 2003, 45 million people living in the United States had no health insurance. Women and people of color, especially immigrants, are now disproportionately employed in the contingent labor force, with women making up as much as two-thirds of the "temporary help supply in the late 1990s."[20] The unions' decline also contributed to the decimation of the state and national regulatory agencies that were created to protect workers' rights. The U.S. Department of Labor's budget has been continuously slashed. As of 2008, there was only one wage-and-hour investigator for every 175,000 workers covered by the Fair Labor Standards Act, which guarantees that workers are paid the minimum wage, receive overtime pay, and which outlaws child labor. When FLSA was passed in 1938 the Department of Labor employed 1,500 investigators to enforce the law, which covered 14 million workers, but in 2008, there were only 750 investigators for 135 million workers.[21]

There are signs of revival within the AFL-CIO since John Sweeney, the former president of the Service Employees International Union (SEIU), successfully challenged the federation's incumbent leadership and became its president in 1995. Sweeny, born into a Catholic working-class family, learned about the papal encyclicals on justice in parochial school and, after college, went through a Catholic labor school organized by a Jesuit priest.[22] After his election, Sweeney worked hard, traveling the country, joining picket lines and delivering labor's message to union members, allies, politicians, and business opponents. Partly as a result of Sweeny's actions, the AFL-CIO and the labor movement built a stronger public presence.[23] In recent national elections, political organizing campaigns mounted by the AFL-CIO and its affiliate unions managed to win back an increasing number of union households (26 percent in 2000) to voting for labor-backed candidates. Organized labor persuaded the Democrats to pay more attention to bread-and-butter issues of concern to working families; they reversed their long-standing opposition to undocumented immigration, urging a broad amnesty for undocumented workers, and in 1999 the AFL-CIO actually had a vigorous presence at the Seattle protests against the World Trade Organization (WTO), none of which would have occurred in the past.[24]

Yet, the number of unionized workers has continued to decline. President George W. Bush's 2000 victory "exposed labor to untempered attacks by a Republican Party more right wing and pro-corporate than under President Reagan."[25] In 2003 Andy Stern, the president emeritus of SEIU and a Sweeney protégé, initiated a vigorous debate within the AFL-CIO on the relative importance of winning political reforms favorable to labor versus prioritizing new organizing. Stern called for a radical restructuring of the federation and its affiliate unions to enhance organizing. After a lengthy internal debate, several of the unions, which had most actively taken up new organizing, decided to leave the federation and form the Change to Win (CtW) federation, precipitating the largest split in organized labor since the 1930s.

As of 2010, the CtW includes the SEIU, the Laborers, the Teamsters, the United Food and Commercial Workers, and the United Farmworkers Union. With the exception of the Farm Workers, these are all older AFL unions, with origins in the early twentieth century. The sociologist, Ruth Milkman argues that in this current environment, which is indeed reminiscent of the early twentieth century, certain AFL unions have proven more effective at new organizing.[26] Furthermore, much of their work is now concentrated among immigrant workers where new strategies, which build worker participation, extensive community support, and legislative advocacy, have led to victories among workers who were previously considered too vulnerable to organize. It has also led to the creation of new organizational forms, which combine characteristics of unions, community outreach and service, and advocacy groups. These hybrid organizations often arise among groups of workers whom the existing unions remain uninterested in organizing, and yet it is these same workers who suffer the most egregious violations of their rights as workers.

In 2008, both the AFL-CIO and Change-to-Win endorsed Barack Obama after he secured the Democratic nomination, but it was the AFL-CIO that led the labor movement's work during the general election. Obama's strength among union voters helped the Democrats win in key midwestern battle-ground states. In exchange for their assistance, Obama promised to support their key legislative initiative, the Employee Free Choice Act (EFCA) once he was elected president. The EFCA is a long-overdue labor-law reform measure, which would greatly facilitate workplace elections for union recognition. However, the prospects for EFCA's enactment are uncertain since not all Democrats in Congress fully support it.

In this difficult context, active collaboration between worker-organizing campaigns and religiously inspired labor-support networks and worker's centers not only lend a crucial moral voice to workers' justice campaigns, but they also provide much needed material and spiritual sustenance. These organizing campaigns and their religious allies are crucibles of "insurgent citizenship" arising in response to global capital and American empire. They are also another example of the new types of hybrid organizations emerging in the borderlands as activists create innovative strategies for building power among people who lack basic citizenship rights.

The United Farm Worker Model

Much of the character of present-day organizing among low-wage workers draws on the legacy of the United Farm Workers' organizing campaigns and the work of the union's prophetic founder, César Chávez. Chávez's life was profoundly shaped by the borderlands context in which he grew up, having come from a family of Mexican American farmers in Yuma, Arizona. His parents were among the roughly 1 million Mexicans who constituted the backbone of wealth creation in the Southwest even as they faced new and enlarged forms of racial and class oppression.[27] As a Catholic, Chávez had read the social justice encyclicals, including those affirming the dignity of labor. He also read a biography of Mahatma Gandhi and is said to have been highly impressed by his use of nonviolence to achieve Indian independence. Nonviolence thus would become a central tenet of the farm workers' struggle.[28] Chávez's first experiences as an activist were as an organizer for the Community Service Organization (CSO), an Alinsky-style organization active among urban Mexican Americans in California. It spearheaded voter-registration drives and worked on urban issues such as police brutality, improved streets and sidewalks in the barrios, and greater Latino access to educational, housing, and medical facilities. Chávez eventually left the organization because of its reluctance to organize farmworkers and, in 1962, founded the National Farm Workers Association.

What became the United Farm Workers Union (UFW) never fit the traditional union paradigm. The organization was always a hybrid, combining elements of a community organization and those of a union. It offered services such as a credit union, a cooperative food store, gas station, and drug store, as well as burial insurance. The UFW resembled many of the mutual aid societies founded among earlier Mexican, Chinese, and European immigrants. The creation of a union was an outgrowth of the daily praxis of solidarity embedded in this form of mutual assistance. After three years as a community organization, its members began to ask: If unity could bring them cheaper automobile rims, why not better wages and working conditions?[29] The result was the decision to call a strike in 1968 against major table-grape growers in California's central valley in conjunction with a smaller union of Filipino workers. Supposedly, Saul Alinsky sought to dissuade Chávez from turning his community organization into a union, arguing that the community model was more appropriate for farmworkers. Chávez broke with Alinsky and proceeded to organize the first viable union of farmworkers in American agricultural history.[30] Yet, the union would retain elements of its original character as a community organization. Years later, many within the AFL-CIO would ridicule the UFW for not functioning as a bona fide union. According to Mgsr. George Higgins, this disdain was most evident at the annual AFL-CIO convention where Chávez, still dressed very much like a farmworker, stood out amid the sea of double-breasted suits.[31]

In the course of the five-year strike against the grape growers, Chávez pioneered many of the elements that still characterize low-wage worker organizing and religious activism. According to Dolores Huerta, one of the union's most respected leaders, "Religion was always part of the very fabric of the UFW."[32] So it is not surprising that as the strike dragged on, Chávez argued that the human dignity of the workers was at stake in the conflict, not just a union contract. To reinforce that point, the strike was infused with the twin symbols of Mexican national identity: the indigenous Aztec eagle and the Virgin of Guadalupe. Guadalupe is both a religious symbol as well as the representation of a distinctively Mexican national identity as a mestizo people. The biblical scholar David Sanchez contends that Chávez would have been well aware of the subversive manner in which a variety of Mexican and Chicano/a social revolutionaries had employed Guadalupe in earlier struggles for control of the land. In the case of the farmworkers, Guadalupe's iconography was used to argue for the humane treatment of those who worked the land.[33]

Recognizing that the union alone did not have sufficient power to force the wealthy growers to the bargaining table, Chávez strategically built both widespread religious and community support. Protestant clergy from the Farm Worker Ministry were the first to get involved.[34] The union later established extensive support networks among Catholics, Protestants, and Jews, all of whom turned out in large numbers to lend public backing to the union. According to Higgins's eyewitness account of the Catholic presence, "we did not enter the dispute to tell César Chávez or the growers how they should write their contracts. What we did tell the growers (and I think to some extent we helped the farmworkers merely through the respectability that comes with church backing) was that they had to recognize the rights of these men and women to organize and bargain collectively."[35] Since agricultural workers were not covered by the 1935 National Labor Relations Act that regularized union organizing among industrial workers, they were not bound by later amendments, which restricted the use of secondary boycotts. In this case, by standing outside of the regularized structures of union/employer relations, the union was able to make innovative use of a national and international boycott of table grapes. This expanded the locus of the conflict well beyond California's central valley. By the late 1960s farmworkers were dispatched to cities throughout the United States, Canada, and Europe, where they built widespread support for the boycott by retelling their stories. What had been a local labor dispute became an international justice cause. Various city councils and other local governing bodies throughout the country voted to endorse the boycott. The UFW also succeeded in mobilizing hundreds of high school and college students, many of them Latinos, to picket supermarkets in their own communities to convince consumers not to purchase the nonunion grapes. The impact of all these efforts was to build far more extensive solidarity for the farmworkers than the union could ever have done on its own. Furthermore, many of these same tactics are used by contemporary religious activists who support worker organizing.

Chávez also made extensive use of well-publicized public events, including marches and vigils, which were understood not only as political events but as a *peregrinación* or religious pilgrimage. Chávez lived within a Mexican Catholic worldview in which public pilgrimages and vigils were accepted as acts of penance. Huerta recalls, "César always wanted to hold a Mass first before the marches. The workers were given absolution."[36] One of the UFW's best-known examples was the 1966 march from Delano to California's state capitol in Sacramento. The idea of the march was undoubtedly influenced by its use in the civil rights movement. The marches from Selma to Montgomery in 1965 had created the necessary public pressure to enact national voting rights legislation. To mark the occasion, the UFW issued the "Plan of Delano," which emphasized the penance or suffering and sacrifice of the farmworkers' nonviolent struggle for their dignity and rights. The imperative of sacrificial love underpinned Chávez' own prophetic understanding of this struggle. To quote Chávez, "Love is the most important ingredient in nonviolent work—love the opponent—but we really haven't learned yet to love the growers. . . . If we're full of hatred, we can't really do our work." Here Chávez echoes both King and Gandhi in his articulation of prophetic activism.[37] Significant elements of the United Farmworkers' model reemerge in contemporary worker-justice organizing.

Contemporary Religious Support for Worker Justice

Today, building workers' rights requires the creation of new hybrid strategies, which bear more resemblance to the UFW's style of organizing than that of traditional union organizing. Organizing drives are now highly complex, risky affairs because even smaller subcontractors have no qualms in engaging in massive intimidation campaigns, including calling in ICE agents to deport undocumented workers. As was the case with the UFW, contemporary unions seeking to organize now recognize that they are not strong enough to win without successfully building broader community alliances, which can put public pressure on recalcitrant employers.

Just as was true for the farmworkers, one of the most important of those alliances is with religious communities. The election of John Sweeney as president of the AFL-CIO in 1995 created new openings for deeper collaborative relationships between organized labor and organized religion. Since then, religious supporters have become a critical expression of broader societal solidarity for workers engaged in union organizing campaigns. It is also apparent that at times, unions' priorities, organizational structures, and values are not in harmony with the needs of low-wage workers. There are also regions of the country where unions are virtually nonexistent. This is especially true in southern right-to-work states that prohibit unions from making membership a mandatory condition of employment. In response to such circumstances, religious worker-justice activists have also begun setting up workers' centers as a semi-union alternative. Workers' centers are typical borderlands organizations in their willingness to experiment with various innovative strategies to secure rights for marginalized workers. In the most comprehensive study of workers' centers to date, the political scientist Janice

Fine identified 137 such centers in existence as of May 2005. These included organizations working with immigrants, nonimmigrants, and workfare participants. As of May 2009 there were twenty-one worker centers affiliated with Interfaith Worker Justice's (IWJ) network, with the possibility of another nine centers being added.[38]

The first of these current religious worker-justice committees was founded in Chicago in 1991. Kim Bobo, who is IWJ's founder and current executive director learned how to organize religious communities as a staff member for Bread for the World, a Washington DC–based Christian advocacy organization that mobilizes cosmopolitans to support stronger domestic and global anti-hunger policies (see chapter 7). After leaving Bread, Bobo first sought to organize denominational support for a mineworker's strike. After discovering that denominations had no staff working on labor or economic justice issues, she built a mineworkers' support committee from the bottom up. That led her to found a local worker-justice committee in Chicago by bringing together several well-known religious activists, including Msgr. John J. Egan, the founder of Catholic urban ministry and a close associate of Saul Alinsky's, the United Methodist bishop Jesse DeWitt, a leader in Chicago's African American religious community, and Rabbi Robert J. Marx, who had marched with Dr. King during his 1966 Chicago campaign and was the founder and past president of the Jewish Council on Urban Affairs. Within two months Bobo had a steering committee of two dozen people. In 1996, following John Sweeney's election as president of the AFL-CLO, Bobo decided the time was right to launch the National Interfaith Committee for Worker Justice (NICWJ) as a national organization.[39] Today the organization is known by its shorter name, Interfaith Worker Justice (IWJ).

That same year, another highly respected group of activists came together in Los Angeles to form Clergy and Laity United for Economic Justice (CLUE). In 1996, Rev. James Lawson invited a group of interfaith religious leaders to join him at Holman United Methodist Church, the city's largest African American UMC congregation, where he was the senior pastor. Lawson, who had brought Gandhian nonviolence into the American civil rights movement, was already training members of the local Hotel Employers and Restaurant Employees union (HERE), in nonviolent organizing. Among the city's well-known religious leaders who attended this initial discussion was Rabbi Leonard Beerman, one of LA's towering Jewish leaders, and Father Dick Gillett, a well-respected Episcopal priest. The discussion was centered on how the religious community could respond to the city's burgeoning economic inequalities. Lawson also approached Maria Elena Durazo, who was then the president of HERE's Local 11, and asked her, "How do we do in LA what we did in Memphis—how do we engender church support for union organizing?"[40] Together this group of activists formed CLUE. Its first major breakthrough came quickly after it organized religious support for a living wage ordinance under consideration by the Los Angeles City Council. The ordinance, enacted in 1997, provided raises and health benefits to more than 10,000 workers.[41] It continues to serve as a platform for ongoing labor justice activism in LA. As a result of the campaign, Madeline Janis, the executive director of the Los Angeles Alliance for a New Economy (LAANE), also became a strong supporter of CLUE's vision. LAANE had led the campaign for the living-wage ordinance and remains the leading voice advocating for the creation of livable-wage jobs in the city's burgeoning service sector. According to Rev. Alexia Salvatierra, the executive director of CLUE-California, CLUE was created by LA's existing justice leadership to be the next step in the movement. Although CLUE is an IWJ affiliate, it has also built its own statewide structure in California with additional chapters in Orange and San Bernardino counties and in northern California.

While these two organizations have similar origins and continue to work cooperatively, there are both commonalities and distinctions in their approaches to organizing. For example, IWJ's trajectory continues to be influenced by Bobo's experiences in building religious support for Bread's national legislative advocacy campaigns, whereas in Los Angeles, LAANE takes the lead in the local legislative arena. In its early years, IWJ built a strong partnership with the AFL-CIO's new leadership; CLUE's most consistent local partner has been HERE, whose core leadership came out of the United Farm Workers and the 1980s struggles in Central America against the U.S.–backed contras. The board of directors of IWJ is made up of denominational and labor leaders; CLUE's board is made up of two elected representatives from each of its local chapters. The IWJ affiliates focus primarily on organizing clergy participation in their public actions; CLUE has encouraged the creation of economic justice committees within local congregations. Those committees are supposed to make sure that congregational employees are also earning livable wages.[42] CLUE also conceives of the work of its religious leaders as a form of chaplaincy, in which clergy give comfort and strength not only in their public presence but their one-on-one visits to workers' homes.[43] According to Salvatierra, CLUE's focus is on grassroots work, while IWJ combines grassroots work with advocacy campaigns. Since its early days, IWJ's national office has used public policy advocacy as an additional form of leverage against recalcitrant corporations. Six or seven years ago they added a public policy director position to their staff, and by 2008 they had two policy positions on a relatively small national staff. Through its experiences with its workers' centers, IWJ has gained firsthand knowledge of the weakened state of many of the federal regulatory agencies that were created to protect workers. In recent years, resuscitating these agencies has become the focal point of much of IWJ's advocacy efforts.

Conversely, CLUE's self-understanding is more as an heir to the theologies that informed the American civil rights movement and subsequent liberation struggles in Latin America and the Philippines, as well as the 1980s sanctuary movement. The organization seeks to bring the unique contributions of faith to social justice, which includes elements such as its vision, values, spiritual community building, and the use of texts, symbols, rituals, disciplines, practices, and the arts. While CLUE has developed a distinctly "faith rooted" model of organizing, it understands this as an alternative to Saul Alinsky's classic model, which Salvatierra regards as just "too dang western." Instead, CLUE has developed a methodology that blends groundedness in faith with the use of Freirean models of popular education. While in Alinsky's version of doing one-on-ones, everyone was equal, CLUE's faith roots and Freirean influences call for a prioritization of the marginalized. In doing power mapping, their goal is to enable people to realize the power they already have. Yet, in contrast to Alinsky, for CLUE the powerful are not just "the target" because, in a more Freirean sense, they too are seen as being capable of transformation. In addition, CLUE also disagrees with Alinsky's understanding of self-interest as people's chief motivator. Indeed, Alinsky's very utilitarian notion runs contrary to all faith traditions' embrace of love as a central motivator of human action. For Jews, this means being obligated, while Muslims, who emphasize a person's surrender to God, would seek the collective self-interest or the common good.[44] Given its location in Southern California, CLUE bears the imprint of the UFW's influences. Indeed, many older activists in Southern California's labor and religious community trace their activist roots back to the UFW's marches, pickets, and boycotts. Yet, CLUE has made adaptations to the traditional religious pilgrimages, which the UFW used so successfully to instill a deeper spiritual meaning into its public actions. Since CLUE has less of a specifically Roman Catholic identity than the UFW, it does not interpret its marches as acts of penance but as visible signs of the religious dimension of worker justice. They are forms of public liturgy in which clergy dress in their clerical robes and reenact well-known, symbolic religious rituals. During the campaigns in support of hotel workers, airport employees, janitors, and security officers, CLUE was able to organize between 200 and 250 clergy to participate in public liturgies, which were strongly interfaith. At first, these liturgies were headed by Catholic, Protestant, and Jewish clergy. Later, Muslims joined as well. Religious rituals familiar to both Christians and Jews, such as outdoor foot washings, the giving of milk and honey to pro-union employers and bitter herbs to those who remain intransigent, or a posada through Disneyland's hotels (as described at the beginning of chapter 1), serve as a powerful witness of the religious dimension of these workers' struggles.

Both organizations have strong commitments to be interreligious, which IWJ has embodied in its very name. CLUE understands its approach to interfaith work as a search for complementarity, for the common sacred ground in various religious traditions. It has more successfully drawn evangelicals into supporting worker justice, without necessarily expecting them to become members of CLUE since they would probably have difficulties embracing its interfaith dimension.[45] The IWJ's interreligious collaborations are primarily among Christians, Muslims, and Jews. Even though most of its activists are Christians, IWJ hires a religiously diverse staff, maintaining both prominent Jewish and Muslim board members, and invites leaders from a broad array of religious traditions to serve as keynote speakers at its public events and conferences. However, at perhaps an even more meaningful level, the organization has written and published study materials on the different religions' foundational understandings of worker justice as well as material that can be used in Christian, Jewish, and Muslim worship settings. In November 2001 the organization took on an even more noticeable role in nurturing its relationships with Muslim leaders by holding an "Islam and Labor: Forging Partnerships Conference" in Washington DC. The following March's newsletter contained four pages of study material on Qur'anic teachings concerning worker justice as a part of their Workers' Memorial Day materials.[46] Both CLUE and IWJ incorporate ritual practices from Catholic, Protestant, Jewish, and Islamic traditions into the public events they sponsor. In IWJ's early years, its work primarily revolved around supporting its expanding network of local affiliates, and it has had as many as sixty-three local affiliates across the country. Not surprisingly, these affiliates have proven to be easier to sustain in urban areas where one can draw from a larger, more diverse religious leadership. They serve as the physical connecting points between religious activists, union organizers, and the workers. According to Bobo, in some areas the work remains marginal because there is only a half-time staff person in place.[47] Under those circumstances, a major crisis, such as an ICE raid on a major local employer, can prove to be overwhelming. On the other hand, CLUE has focused on its local organizing work in the Los Angeles and San Francisco regions.

Both IWJ and CLUE bridge between the borderlands and cosmopolitan social locations.[48] The majority of the local religious leaders, whom both organizations engage in support of workers' rights, are cosmopolitans from positions of greater privilege, but who have chosen to become engaged in solidarity on behalf of the marginalized. Rev. David Farley's story is emblematic of cosmopolitans for whom a spiritual calling has led to commitment to work among the marginalized. Farley's father was a United Methodist pastor active in progressive Christian pacifist-socialist circles in the 1940s and '50s. "I grew up in middle-class realities with a sense of being other because my family always had a strong orientation to progressive politics and justice," stated Farley. He went to Chile in 1972 while in college and encountered liberation theology as a lived reality rather than as a subject taught in American seminaries. After returning to the United States, he was confronted with contradictions between the church's rhetoric and the reality of what the church actually does for the poor: "That is when I experienced my calling—it was a conviction by the spirit—burdened by Northern American guilt and offered grace by the people who were the victims." Farley has spent twenty-seven years pastoring a multiethnic church in Echo Park, close to downtown Los Angeles, that has a long history of justice activism. "What's unique about being at Echo Park is to be pastor of a people who are struggling, and from there and from them be a pastor who can access the levers of power." Farley became involved with the struggles of hotel workers and janitors in the late 1980s, and was active in CLUE, but he has become even more strongly reconnected to it through its recent work in the new sanctuary movement (see chap. 5).[49]

Certainly there are also religious leaders involved in this work who themselves come from borderlands social locations. Rev. Bridie Roberts, CLUE's Los Angeles program director, says they are working with clergy who grew up in the same displaced communities as many of the workers. "Some of them became radicalized in Central America and are now serving in embattled communities in Los Angeles."[50] Although they come from borderlands locations, by virtue of their education and present status many of these religious leaders have acquired elements of a cosmopolitan identity.

Collaboration with the Unions

In its early years, IWJ established a strong collaborative relationship with the AFL-CIO's new leadership that was embodied in a joint effort to promote a "Labor in the Pulpit" program as well as a "Forging Partnerships" conference that immediately preceded the 1999 AFL-CIO convention. Both of these collaborations were designed to strengthen emerging religious activism on behalf of worker rights by highlighting the presence of a shared set of values concerning the dignity of work and the rights of workers. Unions place those values into a secular framework of democratic rights, while religious supporters ground their beliefs in God's love of humanity, which leads to an insistence that humans act justly, especially to those on the margins.

"Labor in the Pulpit" exposes worshippers, in predominantly middle-class settings, to labor activists who are able to articulate their commitments to the labor movement in religious terms. Through "Labor in the Pulpit," local union members were recruited and trained by IWJ to speak at religious worship services marking the Labor Day weekend as a means of "celebrating the sacred link between faith and work." Together, IWJ and the AFL-CIO published a forty-two-page manual that offered extensive instructions to union members who were preparing to speak at one of the religious services. It contains a sample outline and tips for the speakers, suggested biblical passages on the value of work and just treatment of workers, and excerpts of official Catholic and Protestant denominational statements affirming the sacredness of work and the rights of workers, along with Islamic and Jewish statements on workers' rights. There are five sample presentations, examples of litanies, and even a hymn that can be used in the service. The affirmation of the religious commitment to the dignity of all humans and the call for justice runs as a thread through all five of the presentations. Several of the samples were used by labor activists who were also members of the congregations or temples to which they were speaking. For example, Tom Balanoff, who spoke at a Methodist Church, grew up as a Methodist and is now the president of a Service Employees International Union (SEIU) Local in Chicago. The congregation Balanoff addressed is located in the heart of the city's downtown and is well known as an activist congregation. In 2000, IWJ affiliates held "Labor in the Pulpit" services in thirty-seven states.[51]

The "Forging Partnerships" conference took place at the Biltmore Hotel in downtown Los Angeles in October 1999. The event, which embodied the emerging partnership between religious activists and the AFL-CIO, focused on religious leaders in local IWJ affiliates. It sought to inspire them through the keynote speakers who conveyed a strong sense of this movement's significance, deepen their ability to articulate the religious underpinnings of the movement, and create space where local activists could learn and strategize together. The event was sponsored by both IWJ and the AFL-CIO, and hosted by CLUE and LA's Central Labor Council. The opening speakers were John Sweeney, president of the AFL-CIO, and Roger Cardinal Mahoney, the archbishop of Los Angeles, who had worked on behalf of the UFW in the 1960s.

In a later panel discussion of the various faith traditions' perspectives on worker justice, Mahoney spoke of the way the first book of the Hebrew Bible, Genesis, speaks of God as a worker and that through our work we come to share in God's activity. He also reminded the audience that all Catholic social teaching rests on the belief in the sacredness of all human life; all of us are to be treated with the reverence and awe worthy of God's creation. Bishop McKinley Young from the African Methodist Episcopal Church called on the audience to stand against racism in all its forms. Rabbi Leonard Beerman, the vice president of the Jewish Peace Fellowship, told the audience that in the Talmud, biblical injunctions to pay workers on time were still further expanded to give preference to the rights of workers over those of employers. Speaking on the Islamic perspective, Dr. Muzzammel Siddiqui told the audience that the Qur'an maintains that a person is to stand as a witness to justice even against a member of one's own family. Islam regards all people as equal regardless of race or country of origin. Indeed, the prophet Muhammad spoke highly of workers so that Islam also affirms their dignity.[52]

The workshops that followed were used to strategize on how to build ongoing religion and labor partnerships in key sectors of the economy such as among farmworkers, poultry workers, hotel and restaurant workers, construction workers, health-care workers, and day laborers. Still other workshops strategized on how to get worker-justice issues into seminaries and congregations, how to respond to the legacy of racism, the challenge of union busting, and strengthening the network of interfaith committees. The conference concluded with participants joining the opening convocation of the AFL-CIO's 1999 national convention held at LA's Staples Center. The entire conference brought a spotlight onto the extent to which Los Angeles, long known as a "company town," was now at the forefront of national efforts to reenergize the labor movement by organizing low-wage service workers. It highlighted several recent difficult, but ultimately successful, organizing drives among low-wage workers, including workers at several luxury hotels in Beverly Hills and downtown LA, and for the 340 food service and housing workers at the University of Southern California.

TABLE 1
Interfaith Workers Justice's Funding Stream

	1999	2004	2005	2006	2007
Unions	17%	16%	18%	19%	12%
Religious Organizations	18%	11%	7%	11%	7%
Foundations	44%	59%	59%	56%	60%
Conferences	NA	2%	6%	NA	9%
Individuals	14%	7%	6%	8%	7%
Other	7%	3%	4%	6%	5%

All numbers given as percentages.

The 2005 breakup of the AFL-CIO into two competing federations has complicated IWJ's relationship with the AFL-CIO since the unions that were actually doing the most organizing pulled out to form Change to Win. An analysis of IWJ's funding streams as reported in the organization's annual reports suggests that the unions provide less financial support to IWJ since the 2005 split (see table 1).

Over the last nine years, foundations have consistently been the single largest category of the organization's funding. Yet in its early years, IWJ had a more balanced base of financial support from within its own core constituencies of organized labor, religious institutions, and individual supporters. In 1999 IWJ received 17 percent of its funding from unions, including from the AFL-CIO and a number of individual unions. Eighteen percent came from religious sources, many of them Roman Catholic, including the Catholic Campaign for Human Development. They also received funding from the Presbyterian Church USA Urban Ministry Office, the United Methodist Women, the Unitarian Universalist Veatch Program, and the United Church of Christ Board of Homeland Ministry. By 2005 the amounts received from religious institutions and individuals had declined by more than half, while foundation support had jumped to 59 percent of the organizations' income. No doubt the impact of the Catholic Church's massive settlements of clergy abuse cases have affected its ability to support IWJ, just as was the case with its support of congregational-based community organizing.

In 2005 foundations were the source of five out of six of IWJ's largest grants, while SEIU is the only union to have consistently donated between $100,000 and $200,000 to IWJ in the years since 2005. The AFL-CLO's contributions have fallen since the 2005 split, giving an amount between $25,000 and $50,000 in 2007. This is certainly no longer reflective of the strong part-nership evidenced by 1999 conference. By 2007, labor's total financial contri-bution had dropped to just 12 percent of IWJ's total income, while founda-tion support had grown to 60 percent of the organization's income. Although Kim Bobo is careful in protecting her relationships to the unions, when asked what impact the split between the AFL-CIO and Change to Win had on IWJ, she admitted that it had made fund-raising much more difficult.[53] On the ground, much of the work done by IWJ's various affiliates has been in conjunction with the CtW unions who are the most aggressive at grassroots organizing. In 2009, another messy divorce within the labor movement fur-ther threatened to disrupt relationships with one of IWJ's closest labor part-ners. In this case, the amalgamated union, UNITE-HERE, decided to split back into its two preexisting separate unions amid great acrimony. SEIU ini-tially entered the dispute by allowing several breakaway UNITE locals to join SEIU, thereby further complicating the religious community's collaboration with organized labor. SEIU's new president, Mary Kay Henry, finally resolved the dispute between SEIU and UNITE HERE in the summer of 2010.

Engagement by the Local Affiliates

The IWJ carries out all of its local work, including in Chicago, either through its affiliated interfaith groups or its network of workers' centers. By studying IWJ's newsletter, *Faith Works,* over a ten-year period from 1999 to 2009, it is possible to identify a number of areas of emphasis within their local work. Over these years, local affiliates have more frequently collaborated with locals of the unions that affiliated with CtW, such as the HERE and SEIU. Certain industries have repeatedly been the target of local campaigns—in some cases they are regionally based, such as the poultry industry; in others, they are national such as the hotel, restaurant, and hospital industries. Throughout the last decade, worker-justice activism has become increasingly intertwined with immigrant rights work. Not only do they engage the same population of new immigrants, but employers also frequently use U.S. Immigration and Customs Enforcement (ICE) to break strikes, while that agency chose to make low wage workplaces a focus of its enforcement efforts in the U.S. interior.

As of December 2000, IWJ was connected to sixty local interfaith affili-ates, covering every region of the United States. In some cases, new com-mittees began to form in cities that had very recently experienced an influx of new immigrants who were being hired into the low-paying service sector. For example, the Twin Cities Labor Religion Network in Minneapolis supported HERE's efforts to gain contracts for an ethnically diverse group of hotel workers, which included Latinos, Vietnamese, Oromos, Bosnians, and Somalis. To do so, they collaborated with the Hispanic Social Justice Committee of a local Catholic Church and with ISAIAH, a local congregational-based community organization that was affiliated with the Gamaliel Foundation. Ultimately, the union was able to secure a master contract covering nine hotels.[54] The following year, New York City's IWJ chapter also supported HERE's organizing campaign among immigrant cafeteria and executive dining room workers at the investment firm of Goldman-Sachs and at the Metropolitan Opera, all of whom worked for the same subcontractor.[55]

Since its founding in 1996, IWJ has given extensive support to a series of union-organizing campaigns among poultry workers in Delaware, Georgia, North Carolina, Mississippi, and Arkansas. Historically, the poultry industry had been dominated by African American workers, but in recent years the companies shifted to hiring increasing numbers of immigrants. This was, in part, a very conscious strategy because as citizens with an activist tradition, African Americans are much more willing to speak out against unfair labor practices and demand higher wages for such dangerous work. Not surprisingly, many employees regarded new immigrants are more compliant since they're perceived as having less experience with capitalist institutions. Under these circumstances, successful organizing campaigns need to develop strategies to bridge these ethnic divides by creating inter-ethnic dialogue among African- American and Latino/a workers.

The United Food and Commercial Workers, another CtW union, has spearheaded organizing campaigns against several giant poultry companies, including Tyson Foods and Purdue Farms. From its very beginnings, IWJ's support involved the pursuit of a multipronged strategy of fostering the development of local poultry justice alliances, and holding press conferences around the country highlighting the industry's abusive working conditions, while also engaging in an advocacy campaign that publicly called on the U.S. Department of Labor to investigate the industry. The IWJ advocacy work was strengthened by its direct connections to poultry workers through the work of its local affiliates who heard the workers' personal stories. After six years of community and congregational organizing by IWJ and its affiliates, the U.S. Department of Labor finally reached a settlement with Perdue Farms in May 2002 in which the company agreed to pay out $10 million to 25,000 of its workers in compensation for unpaid time worked. The ruling was one of the largest settlements ever brokered by the Department of Labor.[56]

Local interfaith committees have also extended historic links between the religious community and farmworker organizing. Religious labor activists gave extensive support to the national boycott against Taco Bell in support of the Coalition of Immokalee Workers who began their campaign against Florida growers' cuts in the tomato-picking piece rate in 1995. One of the organizers credited their religious supporters with being especially effective "translators" of the workers' message "to the non-farmworker community, helping thousands on people outside of Immokalee listen to and understand our message of fair wages and respect for the farmworkers for the first time."[57] The March 2002 edition of *Faith Works* announced an agreement between the Oregon Farmworkers Union (PCUN) and NORPAC Foods after a ten-year-long campaign that involved strikes, work stoppages, pickets, protests, religious delegations, arrests of clergy supporters, and a nationwide boycott of NORPAC products, all of which had been endorsed and actively supported by IWJ. Here again a consumer boycott (through which several of the nation's largest commercial food-service companies had finally agreed to sever their ties with NORPAC) was said to have been crucial in bringing the company to the bargaining table. In 2003, New York religious activists joined a 330-mile march starting at both ends of the state and converging in Albany, the state capital, for justice on behalf of farmworkers. Clearly echoing the UFW marches of the 1960s, the march started on Easter Sunday.[58] Local affiliates have also given various forms of support to the Farm Labor Organizing Committee (FLOC), a farmworkers' union that has organized fruit and vegetable pickers in the Midwest and in the Carolinas. After a seven-year-long battle, the union finally won bargaining rights over wages and working conditions for workers at Mount Olive Pickles in North Carolina in 2004 after the National Council of Churches, American Friends Services Committee (Quakers), and dozens of denominations had endorsed a boycott against the company.[59]

Additionally, the IWJ has also supported campaigns waged by the United Steelworkers Workers of America (USWA), by grocery workers in West Virginia, Ohio, Kentucky, and Southern California, and by hospital workers, janitors, and workers at several large corporations such as Cintas and Wal-Mart, both of which became the embodiment of corporate exploitation of their employees. In the aftermath of Hurricane Katrina, IWJ focused national attention on the unethical practices being employed by contractors who were overseeing the cleanup of the Gulf Coast.

The Emergence of Workers' Centers

While the work of IWJ's local affiliates is largely done among cosmopolitans, their workers' centers are clearly a form of borderlands work. The worker centers are characteristic of the hybridity present within most borderlands work. They assume a multiplicity of roles, serving as pseudo-unions, quasi-hiring halls, and community and advocacy organizations. As the U.S. economy rapidly shifted to the widespread use of subcontractors, these centers have filled a gap that the labor movement has been unable to address because unions continue to prioritize organizing drives in larger consolidated businesses. The political scientist Janice Fine characterizes workers' centers as "community-based mediating institutions that provide support to and organize among communities of low-wage workers."[60] Nationally workers' centers differ in how they conceive of their mission and carry out their work, yet, "in the combination of services, advocacy, and organizing they undertake, worker centers are playing a unique role in helping immigrants navigate life in the United States. They provide low-wage workers with a range of opportunities for expressing their 'collective voice' as well as taking collective action."[61] Workers' centers generally develop in response to two circumstances. First, existing unions frequently fail to organize adequately—or do not organize at all—among many workers who want representation. Those workers or their advocates begin building grassroots organizations that they believe will empower them. Given the increasing prevalence of temporary and contingent work, the broad-based, multi-occupational makeup of the resulting workers' centers is an appropriate form of organization. Second, sometimes the circumstances of employment make traditional union-organizing techniques difficult or ineffective. The broader strategies used by workers' centers have proven to be a much needed innovation under such circumstances.[62]

As was the case with congregational community organizing, these organizations are creating democratic rights for people who in many cases are not citizens and may never become citizens under current laws. They are doing so by creating spaces in which marginalized workers can gain power over their conditions of employment, thereby affirming their human dignity. In Southern California there are a number of worker centers rooted within Latino, Chinese, and Korean communities that provide strong examples of the potentials inherent in this model of organizing. One of these is IDEPCSA (Instituto de Educacion Popular del Sur de California), which operates six day-laborer centers primarily used by migrants from Latin America. This organization is strongly committed to the use of Freirean popular education models as a means of building up the day laborers' leadership. As Raul Arnova, IDEPSCA's executive director explains:

> For us, teaching literacy is a pretext that enables workers to understand the context in which they are living, how they can improve their lives while maintaining the little they already have. Workers are able to become very clear on their role and contributions to society. Popular education gives us the tools to see how the powers are affecting ordinary people's lives. We can see who our allies and who our opponents are and sometimes we can find ways of transforming our opponents into allies.[63]

The core strategy of IDEPSCA is to form workers' cooperatives where the workers become joint owners. By training workers how to do eco-friendly landscaping designs, they transformed day laborers who did gardening into part-owners of a landscaping cooperative, which is now a constituent organization within the environmental movement. Emphasizing gender equality in their work, IDEPSCA has consciously sought to invite women to be a part of their centers as well. According to Arnova, "everything we do has to go through a gender lens." As a result, IDEPSCA trains women in leadership, has established a women's council within the organization, and has created a house-cleaners cooperative, which is pioneering the use of green cleaning products.[64]

Raul Arnova effectively understands his organizing methodology as a means of building insurgent citizenship: IDEPSCA allows a group of marginalized workers to fully claim their humanness and use their new self-understanding to create a space for themselves within the larger civic and economic sphere from which they were previously excluded. Not unexpectedly, the UFW stands as a model for these workers' centers. As is true of the UFW, these centers serve the dual roles of community centers and bargaining agents, set up among groups of workers whom the existing unions consider to be too difficult to organize.

Among the twenty-one existing interfaith worker's centers, some were formed independently and, as they engaged with religious communities, chose to affiliate with IWJ. Others were intentionally set up by local interfaith committees, which were approached for assistance by workers after they had been treated unjustly by their employers. Kim Bobo says that IWJ cannot get unions to accept the workers that the IWJ has coming into their worker's centers. She offered the example of a group of car-wash workers in Nashville who had recently won a settlement of $130,000 in back wages after the local affiliate had helped file an unfair labor claim and held direct actions against the employer. Yet, according to Bobo, "no union will take these workers."[65]

The decision to encourage the formation of workers' centers comes directly out of IWJ's one-on-one interactions with low-wage workers. It demonstrates how this work continuously evolves in response to IWJ's ongoing interactions with marginalized workers themselves. The first three IWJ worker centers were started in Boston, Chicago, and Las Vegas in 2000. The Chicago worker center is a direct outgrowth of a workers' rights manual, published in 1998 by IWJ, which was translated into Spanish (and later into Polish) and distributed in the city's Latino immigrant neighborhoods.[66] Once the manual was in circulation, the Chicago Interfaith Committee on Worker Justice began getting calls from workers who had experienced the types of unfair treatment described in the manual. When the Chicago committee's staff funneled the complaints to various federal agencies, they proved to be of such little help that the committee decided to convene a meeting of all the agencies. This led to the creation of the Chicago Area Workers Rights Initiative. Working together with the agencies, they streamlined the complaint process by creating a single form. At this point, the Chicago Interfaith Committee on Workers Issues (CICWI) had primarily taken on the functions of a workers' service center. Yet it quickly became apparent that complaints rarely involved just one worker; soon they were meeting with groups of workers and asking them what they wanted to do collectively.[67] According to Jose Oliva, the former director of IWJ's network of worker centers, "It flies in the face of conventional wisdom, but 90 percent of time, the workers decided they wanted to organize a union. For them, the key principle is self-determination"[68]

Responding to the workers' desires for more systemic solutions to their grievances, CICWI envisioned the formation of a new Chicago Workers' Rights Center as a "safe haven where workers, people of faith, union organizers, Worker Rights Advocates, and others . . . can come together to learn and teach about workers' struggles and various actions that can be taken to correct violations of workers' rights." The new center "will not be a traditional legal services program;" instead it "will educate and organize workers to represent themselves and resolve workplace problems on their own, in collaboration with their co-workers, and with the support of religious, community, union, and legal partners."[69] The new center initially sought to connect workers who were interested in organizing to existing unions, but it soon realized that it could be more effective to use a combination of strategies. They began training worker rights' advocates, and connecting workers to unions whenever possible, while also taking workers' complaints to the appropriate government agencies, which in turn filed complaints against the employers. They also organized the workers' pastors, encouraging them to apply moral pressure on the employers.[70] Since 2000 the center has transformed itself into a membership organization, which has formalized relationships of mutual accountability and responsibility between worker/members and the staff. It has enabled workers to have a voice in an emerging public policy debate that links workers' rights to immigrant rights. These include defending workers against illegal uses of "no match" letters, which are sent to employers by the Social Security Administration when an employee's name does not match their social security number, convincing the Chicago congresswoman Jan Schakowsky to push for a moratorium on workplace raids against immigrant workers, and influencing the framing of then Senator Barack Obama's position on immigration reform as a labor issue.[71]

Since the creation of workers' centers represented a shift in IWJ's overall strategy, it has required some subtle adjustments in its understanding of its own mission. The opening of this new arena of borderlands work necessitated a strengthening of relationships with constituencies that had previously not been central to IWJ's work. Speaking at a 2005 IWJ Workers' Center Organizer Training conference, Kristi Sanford, the IWJ staff person who wrote much of the original Worker Rights Manual while working there as a Lutheran volunteer, spoke of the four legs on which the centers' work stands. These are (1) partnerships with government agencies, (2) with lawyers, (3) with unions, and (4) with faith communities. While IWJ certainly had earlier interactions with government agencies, these relationships are now central to the centers' work. Sanford offered examples of successful interactions with governmental agencies who have either sought to expedite wage-and-hour claims or have provided centers with funding for ESL classes. She then told stories of centers successfully drawing on the volunteer services of law school students, who have done research, helped to file claims, and served as a source of fund-raising. She went on to affirm IWJ's history of building labor and religion partnerships, saying that they were seeking to build centers that serve the needs of low-wage workers but still have good relations with unions. This is clearly a recognition that these centers are carving out a distinctive role that is independent of, yet in partnership with, the unions. Now, IWJ is choosing to support new forms of organizing among low-wage workers that do not necessarily result in unionization. Finally, Sanford said that IWJ's national staff is encouraging all of their local affiliates to partner with workers' centers in their area. "If a workers' center has policy goals, it gives the religion and labor coalitions something to focus on."[72] Situating the new workers' centers in relationship to the preexisting IWJ affiliates also necessitates a reframing of the larger organization's vision. Some of the religious members of IWJ's national board initially voiced concerns about IWJ's inclusion of the workers' centers within its existing network. The board came to embrace the new approach once they understood that workers can gain power not only by organizing themselves but by organizing their communities, of which religious institutions are a critical component.[73]

While the 2005 Workers' Center Organizer Training offered the staff of various workers' centers valuable opportunities to exchange stories of their work with one another, it was also designed to strengthen the centers' focus on empowering the workers themselves. In her presentation, Sanford affirmed that, "popular education is at the heart of the work," while also acknowledging that the centers are "at different stages of building worker leadership and ownership of the work." All of the IWJ-affiliated workers' centers that were interviewed expressed a strong desire to be places of empowerment for workers, even though several started out mainly as service centers. For those with very small staff this empowerment agenda remains a challenge because of the enormous amount of time consumed in filing individual unfair labor practices claims. Yet, each center has sought to increase worker participation at all levels of the organization, including as active members of the boards of directors. The Organizer Training highlighted the work of New Labor in New Jersey, which has since become an IWJ affiliate. New Labor successfully transformed itself into a membership organization within a year of its founding in 1999. At any given time, they had roughly 350 active members. Rich Cunningham, New Labor's director, told the assembled leaders, "I come out of the labor movement and was taught by someone from the farmworkers union where membership was very important." Thus, New Labor functions as a "pay-to-play organization" Once they become members, workers gain a right to vote on organizational decisions. They can access leadership training, along with ESL, computer, and occupational health and safety classes. They are each given a member ID card with a bar code on the back.[74] Since the 2005 training, other centers have moved towards becoming membership organizations as well.

Interviews with staff from a number of the IWJ workers' centers confirm an emphasis on worker empowerment. For example, Jeanne Geraci from the Milwaukee workers' center asserted that empowering workers is "the main reason we are here. We are trying to train the members to take roles in organizing and running the centers. We want them to be able to train others, recruit other workers, and be able to speak in public. We believe that empowerment comes from identifying the injustice and seeing that when we unite we can change the system."[75] At the time of this interview, the Milwaukee center had placed far more of its energies into advocacy work because of the immediate threat posed by the highly punitive Sensenbrenner bill, known as HR 4437. This bill threatened to make any assistance provided to undocumented immigrants a felony, thus posing an immediate threat to all immigrant justice work. For Milwaukee it was also a local issue since James Sensenbrenner is the U.S. Senator (R) from Wisconsin.

Several workers' centers use Freirean popular education models as the basis of their workers' training classes. At the Workers' Defense Project (*Proyecto Defensa Laboral)* or PDL in Austin, Texas, the staff created classes on worker rights, the history of the labor movement, and the effects of globalization on poor workers.[76] A membership-based workers' center in Mississippi, MPower, describes itself as a collaboration among poultry workers of diverse backgrounds, civil rights and immigrants' rights organizations, religious leaders, labor unions, employment justice groups, and other community partners. In a very Freirean fashion, it offers both Spanish- and English-language classes that teach members about their rights in the poultry plants.[77] MPower is one of several workers' centers located in the South that have created training workshops aimed at building cross-racial solidarity between Hispanics and African Americans. The agency developed a four-part workshop titled "Valuing our Difference, Envisioning our Common Struggle" through which poultry workers learn about "co-workers' backgrounds, histories, and cultures and discover how oppression and discrimination have impacted our diverse communities."[78]

Building alliances between African Americans and Latino/a immigrants has also become a focal point of the Beloved Community Center in Greensboro, North Carolina. The Beloved Community Center takes it name from Dr. King's expression for God's reign in which all people will truly love their neighbors as themselves. It is a predominantly African American organization, which has taken the lead in a wide range of justice issues in Greensboro, including the convening of the first Truth and Reconciliation Commission ever to function within the borders of the United States. Its executive director, Rev. Nelson Johnson, is a well-known civil rights activist in Greensboro who also served on the board of directors of IWJ for nine years, including a term as president of the board. In 2006, the Beloved Community Center decided to make black-brown unity one of its priorities. Rev Johnson explains the decision:

Our popular culture is built on an attitude of us against others. We value ourselves over against others. This has an economic dimension as well. We saw two people of color with a shared history caught in a collapsing economy where both groups were striving for work. One group has fewer rights than the other, so they drive down wages. The other group sees the first group as the problem. The result is that the two groups are set on a track headed towards each other.[79]

The Beloved Community Center had already supported FLOC's organizing efforts among pickle growers in North Carolina as well as organizing efforts by five thousand workers (60 percent were Latino) at Smithfield, Virginia, a large international corporate hog grower. Smithfield had a long history of inviting ICE raids in response to workers' efforts to unionize. In 2004, the Beloved Community Center supported the establishment of the Southern Faith and Labor Alliance which invited "our Latino brothers and sisters to our churches. We framed it as a spiritual question. We must speak out whenever anyone human has lost their dignity, no matter how they came here. This has been an enormous help to our clergy."[80]

In Southern California, which is also a site of strong tensions between a more well-established but numerically shrinking African American community and a burgeoning Latino/a population, CLUE California in collaboration with CLUE-LA and La Red de Pastores del Sur de California are facilitating a similar black/brown dialogue. In mid-June 2009, the California Community Foundation awarded CLUE California a $100,000 grant to further its ties among evangelicals and to strengthen its efforts to build a dialogue between black and brown clergy.[81] As we have seen in other grassroots efforts to build interracial unity, CLUE's work centers on a mutual exchange of each community's stories of suffering. According to CLUE California's executive director Alexia Salvatierra, "immigrant pastors have shared stories about the wrenching impact of deportations on families, while African Americans have described the pain of violence among their youth."

Producing Worker-Justice Pedagogies

The emerging workers' rights movement faces multiple challenges. While it continues to strengthen the empowerment pedagogies used within its workers' centers, it must develop an alternate set of educational tools for use among the cosmopolitan activists who are being drawn to the work. Given organized labor's decline, many middle-class clergy and young adult leaders have little direct experience with unions. Some may even have negative opinions based on periodic press coverage of union corruption or personal experiences with someone who is dissatisfied with the union to which they belong. Leaders of the national movement for worker justice are therefore faced with the challenge of educating a new generation of religious worker activists. As with all forms of religiously inspired social activism, leaders use various avenues through which to educate their fellow activists. Yet, once again, one of the most commonly used pedagogies is the creation of events at which cosmopolitan religious activists have opportunities to hear the personal stories or testimonies of the borderlands workers who are in the forefront of various union organizing campaigns. These experiences are deeply meaningful both for the workers and for those in the audience. The workers give firsthand accounts of their personal experiences with their employers and in many cases also offer glimpses of their own spirituality, which sustains them. The sociologist Pierrette Hondagneu-Soleto captures the impact of such storytelling on an audience of pastors at a CLUE breakfast in Los Angeles:

> The testimonials establish a shared understanding of what is unjust and a shared emotional response. When the workers were testifying, the clergy had empathetic expressions on their face, and some shook their heads in visible signs of disapproval. They signaled this to one another and back to the workers. A few shed tears and on several occasions, both workers giving testimonials and clergy in the audience wept. Compassion is the central shared emotional response to the worker testimonials. And compassion deepens the clergy's commitment and resolve to pursue social justice activism as an expression of faith.[82]

The workers' opportunity to tell their stories in front of a respectful audience enables them to gain a sense of their own stories' power. According to Rev. Bridie Roberts, CLUE-LA's program director, "For a worker to tell their story in front of a two-hundred-member congregation during a 'Labor in the Pulpit' service is an empowering experience."[83] During the car-wash workers campaign in the summer of 2008, the ability of the workers to tell their stories of abuse at the hands of their employers changed how many Angelenos thought about them.[84]

The national office of IWJ has invested considerable resources in the production of various written materials designed to deepen activists' ability to articulate the biblical and theological underpinnings of the work in which they are engaged. They recognize that many religious people become con-

vinced of the righteousness of a particular cause when they are able to connect contemporary forms of injustice to the scriptural prophetic tradition.
This connection enables them to act against injustice out of an embrace of
a scriptural mandate to do so. Furthermore, they recognize that clergy also
need resources to aid them in connecting biblical texts to the injustices experienced by present-day workers. While the majority of the Christian clergy
involved in this work are likely to have some formal biblical and theological
training, it does not necessarily give them an understanding of the prophetic
tradition in relation to these very contemporary sorts of justice issues. At the
more conservative Christian seminaries, the emphasis is on the teaching of
"classic" interpretations of Scripture with special attention given to the New
Testament. The Hebrew Bible is largely treated as a foreshadowing of the full
revelation contained in the New Testament. The more liberal seminaries do
incorporate the study of contextualized theology into their curriculum, offering courses on black, feminist, and gay theologies as well as various liberation-
ist theologies. They may also offer courses related to the civil rights movement
and the work of other historic prophetic activists such as Dorothy Day, yet
these courses tend to remain disconnected from the contemporary struggles
for justice within marginalized communities. Furthermore, many clergy rely
on an assortment of lectionaries that provide interpretations of whatever texts
they are planning to use as the starting point of their weekly sermon.

In preparation for "Labor in the Pulpit" over Labor Day weekend in 2001,
IWJ published an insert in its newsletter, *Faith Works*, that included a sample
of a litany titled "Remember the Immigrant" to be used as a responsive reading in a worship service. The litany itself included several of the best-known
passages in the Hebrew Bible that call for equal protection of immigrants.
The next page contains two sample reflections on worker justice based on
the readings from the Common Lectionary, which is used by most Roman
Catholic and many Protestant churches. However, the reflections are written
in such a way that they could be used in "most religious settings, including
Jewish and Muslim."[85] Later that same year, IWJ published another insert on
understanding Islam, which contained answers to some of the most common questions about Islam and tips on how to reach out to the Islamic community. In 2003, prior to the national Immigrant Freedom Rides, which IWJ
supported, *Faith Works* published another "Labor in the Pulpit" insert that
focused on what various faith traditions say about the treatment of immigrants along with a brief history of the earlier freedom rides, organized in
opposition to the segregation of public transportation. In preparation for
the 2004 presidential elections, IWJ published a separate booklet containing

instructions for religious congregations on how they could do nonpartisan voter registration work.

In what is certainly IWJ's single most ambitious educational effort to date, Kim Bobo took at three-month leave of absence in 2008 to write a book titled *Wage Theft in America*.[86] The book has become the focal point of a major advocacy campaign that has Bobo speaking around the country as well as testifying before Congress. The combined effort has placed a spotlight onto IWJ's workers centers, since the focus on wage theft emerged out of IWJ's direct engagement with workers at its affiliated workers centers. In the book's introduction, Bobo writes, "my experience from Interfaith Worker Justice and particularly the workers' centers provides a disheartening view of the underbelly of the economy. Millions of workers are having billions of dollars of wages stolen each and every year."[87] The book targets the U.S. Department of Labor's Wage and Hour Division as the primary federal agency responsible for enforcing wage payment laws. As we read earlier, this agency's staff has been gutted as a result of repeated budget cuts. Consequently, protections are either inadequate or not enforced. By naming wage theft as a crime that hurts both middle- and lower-income workers, IWJ is consciously seeking to shift the terms of the discussion surrounding low-wage workers. Bobo explained that it is "easier to get affluent congregations on board on wage theft than it is to get them to support unions."[88] While written in part as a policy study, it is nonetheless clearly aimed at IWJ's religious audience. Throughout the book Bobo integrates Hebrew, Christian, and Muslim Scriptures, thereby grounding the struggle against wage theft within the prophetic tradition. She writes, "These references are not intended to be used as "proof texts" but as a way to illume how the religious texts speak to the matter of wage theft that transcends time and culture."[89]

Another significant pedagogical tool used extensively by IWJ and CLUE are internship programs, which have proven to be one of the most singularly effective means of training future staff. Both organizations have been able to secure outside funding to train and deploy college and seminary students: IWJ received funding from the AFL-CIO for a number of years to run what it calls "Seminary Summer," and CLUE has its own program called the "Young Religious Leaders Project," which accepts students from California high schools, colleges, seminaries, and rabbinical schools, as well as young adults at large. These young interns have been vital contributors to both organizations' work, at times taking on new projects to which a regular staff member has not yet been assigned. The programs have a week-long orientation process during which students are given a basic overview of the work and its religious underpinnings. The programs have been highly successful in identifying and then educating a new generation of justice leaders. Prior to enrolling in the Pacific School of Religion, Rev. Andrew Schwiebert attended Seminary Summer in 2003. He had spent a semester in Chile while in college, after which he worked for Witness For Peace in Mexico for two years and in Colombia for another year. These experiences profoundly reshaped his worldview, leading him to decide that he would either go to seminary or work for a union as a way "of helping get people out of bondage." Seminary Summer proved to be Schwiebert's opportunity to connect to organizations that he could relate throughout his seminary studies.[90] While some of Seminary Summer alumni have taken jobs with either IWJ or CLUE, many others have become pastors. Their experiences will gradually enlarge the pool of clergy whose worldviews have been transformed by engaging in borderlands justice activism, leading them to make solidarity with the *other* a central element of their ministry.

Concluding Remarks

We have seen the extensive bridging work being done by both IWJ and CLUE as they serve as intermediaries between low-wage workers and their cosmopolitan religious supporters. Remarkably, CLUE has even been able to extend its reach to evangelicals who are rarely involved in these broad, inclusive, borderlands religious justice organizations. Although the two organizations have distinct origins, the nature of their work within borderlands settings determines their common use of various liberative pedagogies, to both empower workers and enable them tell their stories before cosmopolitan audiences. Both organizations are heirs to the legacy of the UFW, which continues to stand as a model of the hybridity necessary for successful borderlands organizing. Both organizations have interreligious origins and continue to invest in the resources needed to explain worker justice within multiple religious traditions. Even IWJ, which initially had a close relationship with the AFL-CIO's new leadership, has at times had to navigate through organized labor's tumultuous internal disputes over strategy. The 2005 departure of the Change to Win unions forced IWJ to develop new funding streams. However, it has perhaps also freed the organization to shift more decisively toward a greater focus on establishing workers' centers, which are more clearly a form of borderlands work. Throughout its existence, IWJ has consistently produced a broad array of educational material for its interreligious activist audiences. Its most recent book on wage theft reframes IWJ's emphasis from unionization onto the crime of wage theft, giving it access to still broader audiences, both within congregations and within policymaking circles.

5

Immigrant Rights Activism

During a meeting of a small group of religious activists in attendance at a national conference on immigrant rights sponsored by the National Network for Immigrant and Refugee Rights (NNIRR) the discussion centered on the emerging "New Sanctuary Movement." During the gathering, Flor Crisóstomo, a young Mexican woman, stood up and spoke tearfully of her decision to enter sanctuary at Adalberto United Methodist Church in Chicago. "I just want to be an instrument and send a message. Elvira [Arellano] left this movement in my hands. My children are fine—they're with my mother in a free country. I ask you to open your churches to help parents who are like you—we are here out of necessity to care for our children."[1] Like millions of others, Flor had entered the United States without a legal visa so that she could find work to send money to her two daughters in Mexico. Flor's work had provided the income to pay her daughters' school tuition, books, and uniforms. She became the second person to enter sanctuary at Adalberto, a small, predominantly Latino, storefront church on Chicago's Westside. More than a year earlier, in August 2006, Elvira Arellano had entered that same church, becoming the first person to enter sanctuary in what was being called the new sanctuary movement. Elvira, along with her American-born son, Saul, had chosen to enter sanctuary as a means of highlighting the injustice of an immigration system that was ripping apart immigrant families. Elvira understood this issue deeply, not only out of her own experience but because she had served as the first president of *La Familia Latina Unida*, a community-based organization that focused its organizing on highlighting the trauma that deportations were imposing upon another group of people with hybrid identities, families composed of both undocumented and documented members.

By making their pending deportations public, Elvira and Flor chose to engage in a form of civil disobedience. Rather than allowing themselves to be victims, they hoped to "become instruments" by showing the nation that immigrants would not willingly self-deport. As undocumented immigrants, they were engaging in prophetic activism by choosing to turn their deportation orders into an indictment of a broken immigration system that had labeled them as criminals. After spending a year in sanctuary, Elvira finally decided to leave in August of 2007 after congressional Democrats abandoned their efforts to enact immigration reform legislation until after the 2008 presidential election. After speaking at several sanctuary churches in Los Angeles, Elvira was arrested at gunpoint by a team of Immigration Control and Enforcement (ICE) agents, separated from her son, and quickly deported to Mexico. From there she has continued her activism, writing regular newspaper columns in the Mexican and Latino American press, meeting with Felipe Calderón, Mexico's president, and addressing both houses of the Mexican Congress. From Mexico she wrote, "I am still in Sanctuary because Sanctuary is the faith and solidarity we share as people and as families in the struggle for justice." By speaking out and telling their stories, Flor, Elvira, and many other immigrant activists are putting a human face to one of the most controversial national policy issues facing the United States.

There are hundreds of organizations working on various aspects of immigrant rights, from humanitarian groups, lobbying organizations, and legal defense organizations to community-based justice organizations. Today much of this work is rooted within immigrant communities and the various organizations and networks that they have established. Many of its leaders are second- and third-generation people, raised in the United States with hybrid identities, enabling them to bridge between first-generation immigrants and native-born Americans. These leaders generally recognize that immigrant rights are intertwined with larger movements for civil rights and racial justice. They are aware of this nation's history of dehumanizing people of color, engaging in acts of genocide against native peoples, and denying them access to full citizenship rights. Many also conceive of themselves as the inheritors of the civil rights movement and participants in a global human rights movement among people of color. Those doing grassroots work in immigrant communities are reconceptualizing the meaning of leadership by building various processes of consultation and popular education models into their work.

Religiously grounded activism is a distinctive component of the larger immigrant rights universe, yet its significance is widely acknowledged even by the ostensibly secular justice organizations. In part this stems from a recognition that many immigrants are religious believers, whose faith communities play a vital role in reconstructing their lives in the United States. Secular activists also realize that religious communities' moral voice has the potential to resonate with many native-born Americans who are also religious. Finally, some religious people have a greater willingness to engage in varying forms of civil disobedience in defiance of laws that they consider as unjust. Religious activism on immigration also has the ability to straddle between borderlands and cosmopolitan social locations (see chap. 2).

Despite Arizona's 2010 attempt to legislate immigration policy, this remains primarily a national policy issue. In recent years national policymakers have created new incentives for local governments, especially police and sheriffs' departments, to become involved in immigration enforcement. Although there is a great deal of local activism in support of immigrants' rights, much of it is aimed at either building support for national reforms or mitigating the increasingly negative consequences of existing laws and their enforcement on the lives of immigrants and their families. For the estimated 12 million immigrants who are living in this country without legal visas, their lack of legal status defines their marginalization. Their very presence in the United States is a form of civil disobedience. Their lack of legal status makes them uniquely vulnerable to exploitation by employers, denies them access to full legal rights, restricts them from accessing federally funded social services, and in many states prevents them from legally obtaining drivers' licenses. For immigrants without documents, the border is always present, not only at the immediate entry points but within the larger borderlands spaces and, increasingly, in the small towns of the Midwest and the South where immigrants began to settle in larger numbers during the 1990s.

Following 9/11, immigrants were quickly recast as potential national security threats. Muslim immigrants were the immediate post-9/11 targets of a government crackdown on undocumented immigrants. Thousands were deported in the months immediately following the attacks. Since then, attention has shifted to the U.S. border with Mexico, which has been reconstructed as a potential terrorist threat. The reframing of the border was spurred on by unrelenting attacks on "illegals" by various conservative TV commentators. They helped popularize a variety of negative myths to support their contentions that immigrants are threats to American citizens.[2] In April 2005, the Minutemen, who claimed to be a citizens' army, began patrolling the U.S. border south of Tucson, Arizona, on the assertion that it had been surrendered to illegal immigrants. Duncan Hunter, a member of the U.S. House of Representatives (R-CA), declared that the country was under siege and demanded funds to erect a fifteen-foot-high wall, which would separate the two countries.[3] The continuous media attention on the alleged dangers posed by undocumented immigrants serves as a handy recruiting tool for the major anti-immigrant organizations such as NumbersUSA and the Federation for American Immigration Reform (FAIR). As of 2006, NumbersUSA claimed to have 237,000 members who were regularly being urged to email and fax their members of Congress as they deliberated on immigration reform.[4]

In a surprise move, shortly before Christmas 2005, the U.S. House of Representatives passed one of the most vicious anti-immigrant bills in more than a decade. Had it been enacted into law, the Border Protection, Antiterrorism, and Illegal Immigration Control Act of 2005 (also known as the Sensenbrenner bill), would have made it a federal crime to live in the United States illegally, thus turning those 12 million undocumented immigrants into felons. The bill would also make it a crime for social service agencies or church groups to shield or offer support to undocumented immigrants. News of the legislation quickly spread fear through immigrant communities. In an interview shortly after the bill's passage, Fr. Brendan Curran, a priest at St. Pius V Catholic Church in the heart of Chicago's Mexican community, reported that "there so much fear people won't even call the police or fire department if something is going on next door. If this becomes law nurses and priests will not be able to do their work."[5]

Ultimately, the bill galvanized immigrant communities and others who stood in solidarity with them, giving rise to what became a very broad-based immigrant rights movement in the United States. Sweeping aside their fears, several million immigrants and their supporters responded to calls for mass action and marched in cities across the country. In March 2006 more than 100,000 people marched in Chicago.[6] In April there were rallies in 140 cities, including Washington DC where 500,000 turned out and Phoenix, Arizona, where another 200,000 showed up; in May another set of rallies turned out even larger numbers. According to Arnoldo Garcia from the NNIRR, "immigrant communities self-organized."[7] People were primarily mobilized through Spanish-language radio stations and various diasporic organizations such as U.S.–based branches of Mexico's three major political parties and hundreds of Mexican hometown organizations.[8] Rally participants were hoping that Congress would pass an immigration bill containing some form of amnesty, but Congress was unable to reach consensus on a proposed bipartisan reform bill. When the bill was resurrected in 2007, the voices calling for tougher border enforcement had grown even stronger. As negotiations proceeded, conservative legislators kept adding increasingly onerous requirements for those who were hoping for a pathway to citizenship. Finally, supporters of the Democratic version of the bill pulled out, and hopes for legislation were postponed until after the 2008 presidential election.

The Bush administration responded to the congressional failure by further stepping up its enforcement efforts. It ramped up the use of "Operation Streamline," an ICE policy enacted in late 2005, which increased the legal punishment for those caught in the United States without proper visa documents, arguing this would act as a deterrent to future attempts to enter. Normally, the lack of a proper visa is treated as a misdemeanor resulting in deportation. Under "Operation Streamline," a skyrocketing number of undocumented immigrants are fast-tracked through special courts where federal prosecutors routinely add additional criminal charges, which result in prison sentences prior to deportation. On an average day, roughly sixty immigrants, mostly from indigenous regions in Mexico and Central America, are selected for this type of prosecution in Tucson's federal court. Shackled at their wrists, waists, and ankles, they are brought before the judge in groups of eight to ten. Every one of them pleads guilty to the charge of crossing without a visa, but roughly one-third are sentenced to as much as six months in prison. The rest are put on buses and dropped off at the border within hours. Immigrants who have gone through detention and court experiences report often being held in cells for three or four days with little food and water, without medical attention, or basic hygiene products, including sanitary napkins.[9]

Workers caught in workplace raids who had used fake Social Security numbers were being threatened with felony charges of identity theft. Under the threat of spending two years in prison, many "chose" to plead to a lesser charge of document fraud, which resulted in a five-month prison sentence prior to deportation. Federal prosecutors first tested this particular tactic during the 2008 ICE raid at Agriprocessors in Postville, Iowa, in which 389 workers were arrested.[10] These tactics resulted in enormous increases in federal immigration prosecutions. As of March 2009, the Transactional Records Access Clearinghouse (TRAC) found that federal immigration prosecutions were up by 189.2 percent from their 2004 levels.[11] In May 2009, in a case stemming from the Postville arrests, the U.S. Supreme Court finally ruled against this practice and concluded that "an immigrant who uses a false Social Security number to get a job doesn't intend to harm anyone."[12] These prosecutions, combined with large-scale raids and random ICE checks of thousands of otherwise innocent people, spread a climate of deep-seated fear and anxiety throughout immigrant communities. While activists continue to protest these tactics, full democratic rights for the undocumented can be achieved only through national legislative reform that includes a realistic means of gaining permanent residency and eventually citizenship.

Migration in a Globalized World

One of the greatest flaws in the current globalized world is the reality that capital and goods can cross borders much more freely than humans can. All sovereign nation-states reserve the right to exert control over their borders; yet, contemporary forms of national sovereignty ought to take the new realities of global interdependence into account. The universal declaration of human rights recognizes the freedom of movement across national borders as a fundamental right. It also grants every human being a right to a nationality.[13] While the declaration effectively grants all humans a "right to have rights," in reality those rights are circumscribed by the existence of nation-states that by their very nature include some people and exclude others. To address this dilemma, the political scientist Seyla Benhabib argues for a cosmopolitan perspective on sovereignty, which takes as its starting point the Kantian view that "'if the actions of one can affect the actions of another,' then we have an obligation to regulate our actions under a common law of freedom which respects our equality as moral agents. The consequences of our actions generate moral obligations; once we become aware of how they influence the well-being and freedom of others, we must assume responsibility for the unintended and invisible consequences of our individual and collective doings."[14] These moral obligations can take multiple forms, including commitments by wealthy nations to assist in a process of global income redistribution. It can also lead to an acknowledgment of an obligation to open one's borders, especially to groups of people who are suffering the negative consequences of one's own nation's economic and political policies. Within liberal democracies, this requires an electorate's willingness to support policies that accept responsibility for the consequences of global interdependence.

For nation-states to recognize that every human has a *right to have rights* would require that they make sure that no human being is permanently barred from citizenship. It also necessitates an acknowledgment that all people have a right to leave the country in which they were born and to choose another country in which they wish to live. Nation-states certainly have the right to erect criteria for granting citizenship, but here again, drawing on Benhabib, the reasons must be reciprocally acceptable: they must apply to each person equally. One cannot be denied citizenship based on one's ascriptive, nonelective attributes such as race, gender, religion, ethnicity, sexuality, or language community. Citizenship criteria can stipulate certain qualifications, skills and competencies such as marketable skills, length of residence, and language proficiency.[15]

American immigration policies have indeed largely been driven by ascriptive judgments of entire categories of people who were either deemed to be desirable or not. The United States systemically made use of immigration policies to shape its national identity. Despite the national myth of being a welcoming refuge, there has been a nativist strand throughout much of American history that regarded certain types of people as unassimilatable, primarily because they were ethnically or religiously distinct from the majority of citizens. Euro-Americans who oppose the entry of present-day immigrants often assert that their ancestors arrived legally, while current immigrants are breaking the law. Yet, the modern categories of "legal" and "illegal" were introduced only in 1924, making the category of "illegal immigrant" a twentieth-century political construction. It was first used against "undesirable" Europeans and later against people of color coming from the Southern and Eastern Hemispheres. Thus, the category of illegal has almost exclusively been used against non-Europeans as one element of this country's racially biased policies. The historian Mai Ngai maintains that "the passage of the 1924 law marked a turn in both the volume and nature of unlawful entry, and in the philosophy and practice of deportation."[16] To enforce this new understanding of illegality the jurisdiction of the Border Patrol was extended well into the interior of United States, thereby reconstructing the meaning of borders while simultaneously destabilizing them.[17]

The entire Western Hemisphere was excluded from the 1924 law, largely at the behest of southern and western growers who wanted uninterrupted access to seasonal Mexican labor.[18] Prior to World War I, immigration procedures along the still-contested U.S.–Mexico border were lax. By the 1920s the U.S.–Mexico border was rearticulated "as a cultural and racial boundary, as a creator of illegal immigration. Federal officials self-consciously understood their task as creating a barrier where, in a practical sense, none had existed before."[19] The Border Patrol's work assumed the character of criminal pursuit and apprehension even though officially it was enforcing civil, not criminal, laws.[20] Increased enforcement notwithstanding, until quite recently many Mexicans continued to pass across the border relatively unimpeded to work as seasonal agricultural laborers.

As the last wave of early twentieth-century immigrants were assimilated, these highly restrictive immigration policies gradually transformed the dominant Euro-American populace into a fairly homogenous population. The virtual shutting down of immigration from outside of Western Europe and the Americas effectively postponed the country's religious diversification for two generations. For example, the banning of all Asian immigration excluded the practitioners of most Eastern religions. And throughout World War II, the United States remained unwilling to grant exceptions to its strict immigration quotas on Jews, despite mounting evidence of Nazi genocide. Finally, in the immediate postwar years special exemptions were granted to allow Eastern European refugees, including Jewish survivors of the Holocaust, to enter the United States.

President John F. Kennedy, who had a long-standing interest in immigration policy, initiated the reforms that finally ended the highly restrictive immigration laws. As was true of the civil rights legislation, the immigration proposals were replete with compromises given the deep internal divisions within the Democratic Party between those who supported an expansion of citizenship rights and those who remained staunchly opposed. Seeking to appease its opponents by downplaying the significance of the new immigration law, Senator Robert Kennedy claimed it would "have no significant effect on the ethnic balance of the United States."[21] After President Kennedy's untimely death, Lyndon Johnson ultimately pushed the 1965 immigration reforms through Congress. According to Jack Valenti, one of Johnson's closest advisors, "The president eventually recognized that existing immigration law, and in particular, national origins quotas created many decades before on racist grounds, as inconsistent with civil rights and racial justice."[22]

The new legislation allowed for modest increases in immigration as family reunification became the centerpiece of the new system. Yet, for the first time, countries in the Western Hemisphere were placed under the quotas. No more than 120,000 immigrants would be admitted annually, which represented a 40 percent reduction from the pre-1965 levels.[23] Since Congress had already eliminated the controversial Bracero program (a guest worker program aimed as seasonal agricultural workers), the new ceiling ensured that the flow of illegal immigrants from Latin America would continue and in fact increase. In 1976, Congress amended the law by placing a 20,000 visa limit on all countries, thereby creating ten- to twenty-year waiting lists for those from high demand countries who sought legal visas for immediate family members. Such horrendous backlogs effectively drive people into seeking illegal routes into the country. Immigration from Asia and Latin America has surged in the aftermath of the 1965 immigration reforms. As of 2000, immigrants and their children made up 20 percent of the American population; Asians and Latinos constitute roughly 75 percent of all immigrants living in the United States. In 2000, 41 percent of all Latinos living in the United States were immigrants, while among Asians 68.9 percent were foreign born.[24] Even though Mexicans account for one-half of all Latin American immigrants, there is far more heterogeneity among Asians in terms of their countries of origin. According to the 2000 census, the five largest contributors to the Asian-born population in the United States were China, India, Korea, the Philippines, and Vietnam.[25]

Given the global character of recent migration, religion in the United States has become far more heterogeneous. Not only have immigrants built new places of worship, they have also impacted long-standing American religious institutions. There are now large numbers of Latino, Filipino, and Vietnamese Catholics because that religion accompanied the European colonization of those countries.[26] Latinos are also joining smaller evangelical and Pentecostal churches, which are often affiliated with Latino denominations founded in reaction to the racism of traditional American denominations. These churches offer worshippers a more contextualized worship experience: the services are in Spanish and are led "by Latinos rather than Irish or Polish-American priests, with the cadences, rhythms, innuendos and flow familiar from the mother country." The services also tend to be livelier and last longer than the usual Roman Catholic liturgy. Women play greater roles and there are fewer parishioners for each pastor.[27] Most Latino Protestants hold moderate to conservative views on a host of social issues such as abortion and same-sex marriage, but there is broad agreement on the need for immigration reform. "Latino churches have a global ecclesiology, we don't have a citizen test to be a part of the church, we don't ask for a Green Card" says the Rev. Gabriel Salguero.[28]

Because of the immediacy of immigration among these predominantly immigrant religious institutions, it is not surprising that many of them are heavily invested in protecting immigrant rights, including the ongoing fight for fair immigration reform. At the same time, many immigrant congregations have a mixture of members with legal visas and those without, making them prone to being cautious about the positions they take and the types of activism in which they engage. In many cases immigrant religious institutions act quietly, providing hospitality to those who come to their doorsteps, while not speaking out in public so as to not endanger their own members. The American Roman Catholic church has long held pro-immigration positions, yet had done little to mobilize on these issues within its Latino parishes prior to immigration reform's emergence as a major national policy issue in 2006.[29] Although the 9 million Latino evangelicals are not a monolith, "there is now almost unanimous agreement that the immigration system is broken and that it is tearing apart families."[30] For their churches, it is a both a pastoral and a moral issue. This put them well ahead of the public stance of the National Association of Evangelicals, which did not endorse comprehensive immigration reform until 2009.[31]

Acting as the Good Samaritan

The story of the Good Samaritan is one of the New Testament's best-known lessons. Here, Jesus responds to a lawyer's questions concerning who the neighbor is in the commandment that says "you shall love the Lord your God with all your heart, and with all your soul, and with all your strength, and with all your mind; and your neighbor as yourself." After telling the story of a Samaritan who rescued a man left beaten and nearly dead at the side of the road, Jesus tells the lawyer to go and do likewise (Luke 10:25–37). This story is particularly provocative because the Israelites were antagonistic toward the Samaritans. It is an embodiment of Jesus' boundary-crossing vision of God's reign and continues to stand as a great challenge for all who profess to be followers of Jesus. For centuries this story has served as the theological basis for multiple forms of Christian humanitarian work. At present, it is embodied in the work of several Christian organizations working in southern Arizona to save the lives of migrants attempting to cross into the United States through the desert.

Beginning in late 1994, coinciding with the enactment of North American Free Trade Agreement (NAFTA) that eliminated all tariffs between the United States and Mexico, the Clinton administration authorized the construction of a wall along the most urbanized sections of the U.S.–Mexico border. By closing off the easiest crossing points, migrants were forced into the far more dangerous and harsh desert terrain in southern Arizona. As a result, the migrant death rate began to mount. By 2000, migrant deaths along the Arizona border were four times higher than in 1998. Most of these were from exposure or dehydration.[32] Activists point out that the actual numbers are still much higher since the remains of many of the dead are never found.

Tucson, Arizona, is a borderlands city. Although situated in the United States, it has strong Mexican cultural characteristics. Many of the residents, especially the Latinos who have lived in the area for generations, are deeply respectful and hospitable to those who are crossing. Latino churches provide a great deal of informal assistance to migrants who often show up unexpectedly. They also take clothing and other goods to churches in Mexico that receive migrants both before they enter and after they are deported from the United States.[33] Yet, there is also a sizeable number of residents who are deeply hostile toward the migrants. As the deaths in the desert south of Tucson mounted, a number of the area's religious activist leaders called for a rethinking of the government's border policies, which they held as at least partly responsible for the fatalities. They argued that while poor migrants were being lured by American employers who were advertising jobs in Mexico, those who responded were being forced to run a gauntlet of death in the desert. On Pentecost Sunday in 2000, ten churches from the Tucson area gathered to discuss what they could do. Many of the churches in attendance had been active in the 1980s sanctuary movement. The Reverend John Fife, one of the sanctuary movement's national leaders, was present at the meeting, as were several other pastors. At the time, the public was hearing only from the Border Patrol. One pastor, Randy Mayer, stated, "We wanted to be an alternate voice and give direct service to the migrants. We said, let's put water in the desert."[34] They formed a new organization called Humane Borders, choosing a drinking gourd as its symbol, thereby tying it to the Underground Railroad and the first sanctuary movement, which had also originated in Tucson.

Because of its strategic location as a borderlands city, Tucson's religious community has had a long history of aiding border crossers. In the early 1980s, Tucson's religious community birthed the first national sanctuary movement in support of refugees from Central America. At that time, Rev. John Fife, then the pastor of Southside Presbyterian Church in the multi-ethnic community of south Tucson, and others began hearing stories of mounting deaths through their "reporting network," which consisted of American priests and nuns working in Central America. As people began to flee the violence, Tucson, along with Los Angeles and south Texas, became one of their principal destinations. Between 1980 and 1983 an estimated 1–1.5 million people fled their homes as a result of civil wars in Central America.[35] In the initial stages of the sanctuary movement, the churches sought legal permission for the refugees to remain in the United States by filing asylum claims on refugees' behalf. Yet the Reagan administration, which backed the counterinsurgency in Central America, denied virtually every single petition, placing the refugees in danger of deportation back to the countries from which they had fled. In response, Jim Corbitt, a Quaker rancher in the Tucson area, envisioned the creation of a network of safe houses modeled on the Underground Railroad, which would move refugees to greater safety in the interior of the United States.[36] The resultant establishment of sanctuary churches was a political strategy designed to highlight religious opposition to the Reagan administration's foreign policy in Central America.

Humane Borders is another manifestation of the Tucson religious community's tradition of providing humanitarian aid. The organization's first relief station was set up in late 2000, placing water jugs along with food and clothing underneath a thirty-foot-high flagpole flying the symbol of water pouring out of the Big Dipper into a drinking gourd.[37] Soon they were erecting water stations consisting of large 130-gallon barrels. Robin Hoover, the pastor of a Disciples of Christ congregation in Tucson, became Humane Borders' first executive director. His church's parking lot came to serve as home to several trucks that have been outfitted with large water tanks used to refill the barrels situated in various locations out in the desert. Speaking at a 2007 memorial and march for migrants, Hoover described the organization's purpose:

> We are here because migrants are systematically being herded onto death trails. The immigration policy of the United States is fatally flawed. Some of America's most eager and desperate workers are having trouble getting to work. Far too many people have died crossing the deserts, canals, and rivers. Now is the time to take death out of the immigration equation.[38]

By the end of 2009 the organization had 115 water stations. Each new station is the result of complex negotiations with various local, county, state, federal, and private landowners to gain access to the sites along key migrant paths through the desert. Certain stations have been prone to repeated vandalism by both hostile ranchers and Minutemen. The organization relies on an ever-expanding group of dedicated volunteers to replenish the water and otherwise service each of the barrels, some of which are now located in increasingly remote regions.

In 2005 Humane Borders acquired GPS equipment that enabled it to begin mapping the exact locations of reported migrant deaths, allowing the organization to become more strategic in choosing sites for new water stations. They also used the data to produce poster-sized maps of southern Arizona on which each reported death was marked by a red circle. The multiple clusters of red dots on the maps provide a graphic reminder of the extent of the deaths in the desert. The maps, which are also marked with the positions of each of the water stations, are regularly distributed on the Mexican side of the border so that people intending to cross can be better informed about the routes that have proven to be the most treacherous. Despite these efforts, one of the organization's 2007 newsletters reported that "migrants continue to die in the same areas, in the same basic patterns, and in at least the same numbers as in the years before." Border Patrol enforcement strategies were forcing the migrants' trails farther away from the safe places so that in "each of the last seven years, on average, the distance from a recovered body to the nearest road is up."[39]

As Humane Borders became nationally known, it broadened its base of supporters, while also hosting countless groups of student and church volunteers, university researchers, and media workers, including several documentary filmmakers. By taking groups into the desert, enabling them to walk along the migrant paths, assist in refilling the water tanks, pick up trash left behind by the migrants, and visit makeshift shrines that commemorate those who have died, Humane Borders allows North Americans to visualize the travails facing migrants crossing the desert. In some cases they also take groups across the border into Mexico to visit the aid stations set up to provide first aid and hot meals to those who have been deported. To the extent to which these experiences uncover the underlying causes, such as the impact of free trade policies and U.S. immigration policies that are leading to the deaths in the desert, they become a form of popular education.

Humane Borders has never seen itself as only a humanitarian organization, even though that is clearly its primary focus. Hoover consistently advocated for a more humane and rational border policy. During the 2006 congressional debate over comprehensive immigration reform, Hoover advocated for a new guest-worker program, under which Mexico would approve workers to work in the United States on one- or two-year guest-worker visas. Guest workers would be allowed to move from job to job and to organize, thus avoiding the pitfalls of the earlier Bracero program. Hoover said that as a pastor, he was concerned about the number of migrants who are abandoning families in Mexico and Central America while starting new ones in the United States. He believed that requiring migrants to return home after a couple of years would help preserve families.⁴⁰ Following the collapse of national legislative reform efforts in 2007, Hoover publicly criticized the Bush administration's "unrestrained funding with virtually no oversight or accountability" for new fences, towers, and aircraft along the border. Conceding the need for increased national security, he continued to advocate for the creation of a stable legal workforce and the extension of human rights along the border.⁴¹

Recognizing that the desert continued to claim migrant lives, in 2002 a group of Tucson's religious activists decided to become a presence in the desert, giving medical assistance to those suffering from heat stroke and exhaustion. This led to the creation of a volunteer organization that calls itself Samaritans, in direct reference to the story of the Good Samaritan in Luke 10. Starting in the summer of 2002, the group sent daily patrols out into the desert, seeking to provide aid directly to migrants. Every patrol includes a Spanish speaker and, ideally, a medical professional. Following in the tradition of Tucson's earlier sanctuary movement, they consider their work as a form of civil initiative. Using a quote from Jim Corbett, one of the sanctuary movement's founders, the Samaritans define civil initiative as action that "maintains and extends the rule of law—unlike civil disobedience, which breaks it, and civil obedience which lets the government break it. . . . While openly submitting to the trials and penalties imposed by government, the free community refuses to be coerced into collaborating with violations of the law (that is, of right). Rather, it exercises its rights and protects the violated."[42] Reminiscent of the earlier sanctuary movement, these contemporary activists ground their work in international human rights laws, which the United States does not recognize within its own borders.[43] As one member of Samaritans explained the decision to leave water in a restricted federal wildlife refuge, "What the feds want may not be the way we want to do it—we tell them, 'That's your policy, not our policy.' People are dying on the refuge and we'll leave water there until it goes away."[44]

The Samaritans leave packs of food and water along the desert migrant trails. Although they generally work with the permission of the Border Patrol, they do provide assistance, including first aid, directly to migrants whom they encounter in the desert. Since their founding they have aided hundreds of migrants in distress by providing water to those suffering from dehydration, treating severe sprains and other injuries, and bandaging severely blistered feet, which can be life threatening if the migrant can no longer walk and is left behind. Initially, Samaritans would routinely evacuate weakened, lost, or dehydrated migrants. However, in the summer of 2005 the Border Patrol arrested two young volunteers working with No More Deaths (NMD), another humanitarian group that sets up camp along migrant trails during the summer months. Santi Sellz and Daniel Strauss had gone out into the desert with the Samaritans where they encountered three seriously ill migrants. After consulting with two doctors and a nurse, Sellz and Strauss realized the third individual was in danger of liver failure and death, and that all three were in need of immediate medical attention. The volunteers then consulted an attorney and were advised to take the migrants to the nearest medical facility. While en route, they were pulled over and arrested by the Border Patrol. Both were incarcerated and charged with two felony counts of aiding and abetting as well as conspiracy. In September 2006, a U.S. District Court judge finally dismissed the indictments against the two, saying that they were following guidelines that border volunteers had been using for several years without being arrested. All three migrants were eventually deported back to Mexico.[45]

When the Samaritans started up in 2002, they had approximately thirty volunteers. By the summer of 2006 that number had grown to three hundred, including a core group of seventy who go out on the desert patrols. In addition to the original Samaritans group in Tucson, new chapters have formed in the retirement community of Green Valley and in neighboring Sahuarita.[46] Randy Mayer, who pastors a United Church of Christ congregation roughly thirty miles north of the border, is the co-chair of Samaritans as well as a member of Humane Borders' board of directors. His church is one of four in southern Arizona that are thoroughly involved in border justice ministry. Randy's own story mirrors that of other cosmopolitans who have become committed to borderlands work. He grew up in Montana, yet his father regularly took the family to Mexico. While in college, Randy spent a year working with street kids in Costa Rica. He later spent another year studying at a seminary in Costa Rica, which was then the Protestant center of liberation theology in Latin America. When he returned to the United States he sought to put what he had learned into practice within a context of privilege. After asking for a pastorate close to the border, he was sent to his present church. There was little border work taking place at the church when he first arrived, but as the church gradually became involved in border justice work, it attracted new members who shared that interest. Mayer believes that the church has a role in doing public theology. He has seen that when controversial issues are placed with the context of faith, they can be pushed a littler farther.[47]

No More Deaths or *No Más Muertes* was formed in 2003 as migrant deaths in the desert continued to climb. Established as a coalition of Tucson's existing humanitarian border organizations, No More Deaths is an all-volunteer organization that has no board of directors and operates without federal non-for-profit status. It draws its theological vision from the passages in the Hebrew Scripture where God instructs the Israelites to care for the stranger because they too were once strangers in a foreign land. When NMD began its work in the summer of 2004, it had one hundred volunteers. After garnering nationwide attention as a result of its organizing work prior to Sellz and Strauss's trial, thousands of new volunteers offered to work with the organization. In response to the two activists' 2005 arrests, the organization had launched a campaign called "Humanitarian Aid is never a Crime." They sent more than 30,000 signatures on petitions to the U.S. prosecutor in charge of the case asking him to drop the charges, distributed more than 7,000 yard signs throughout southern Arizona, and also hosted several press conferences in which community leaders and groups voiced their support.

Among the organizations working in southern Arizona, NMD is clearly the most inclined to push against the boundaries of policies governing permissible aid to the migrants who have entered the United States without a visa. Its work is focused on maintaining a twenty-four-hour presence in the desert during the four deadliest months of the year, staffing three first-aid stations on the Mexican side of the border, and increasing its human rights advocacy work. Like the Samaritans, NMD conceptualizes its work as a form of civil initiative. Maryada Vallet, an NMD volunteer since 2005, believes that

> Civil initiative as a principle is very alive even though it's easier to see how it made sense in the sanctuary movement. Leaving water where you know it's needed is our presence in the middle of a low-grade war zone. Water is simple and symbolic. Civil initiative is not only a nonviolent and transparent process; it is also a willingness to sit down with people in power, although it doesn't mean bargaining with them. We just try to live it week to week by trying to hold the government accountable for what is going on in the desert."[48]

The organization recruits volunteers who are willing to spend at least one week in their camp, known as the Ark of the Covenant, set up in the desert twelve miles north of the border with Mexico. Volunteers set out from the camp each day, first by truck, and then by foot along the rough migrant trails, each carrying a gallon of water and some "migrant packs," small bags containing granola bars and crackers. Although they rarely encounter migrants directly, occasionally they do find someone who has been left behind by the group they were traveling with.[49] Most of the volunteers are young, although they do also attract people of all ages, who come from a wide variety of religious backgrounds. For many, like Maryada who came to Tucson after graduating from a Christian college, it becomes a place where they discover a sense of calling. When asked how she understands her involvement in this form of solidarity work, Maryada responded by saying, "a lot of what I understand of who Jesus was, has to do with taking risks—so I ask myself, what do I have to do to do what I know is right and to be in solidarity with others."[50]

All NMD's volunteers, who are mostly cosmopolitans, are required to go through a training that includes a 154-page packet of readings covering the history of immigration, descriptions of who the migrants are, articles on border-enforcement policies, a lengthy section on NAFTA, and a few of articles on white privilege. Emrys Staton, who has worked with NMD since 2004, says, "We really need to have conversations with our new volunteers about privilege because otherwise volunteers can build themselves up as superhero saviors and treat the migrants as objects of their life-saving efforts."[51]

The NMD training session in Tucson includes a presentation from a lawyer who gives legal instructions on what *not* to do while in the desert. Nonetheless, its volunteers are willing to risk getting arrested while placing water along migrant paths in the desert. As a result, the organization has had an escalating number of confrontations with federal officials. In early 2008, Dan Millis, an NMD volunteer, was charged with a misdemeanor offense for littering in the Buenos Aires National Wildlife Refuge after he had left jugs of water and picked up trash in the refuge without a permit to do so. According to Millis, he felt especially compelled to leave drinking water that day, because only two days earlier he had found the body of a fourteen-year-old girl in the desert.[52] John Fife responded to Millis's arrest by saying, "Regardless of the outcome of this trial, we're going to continue our humanitarian aid work whenever and wherever it is needed, until there are no more deaths in the desert." Fife is affirming the organization's commitment to act according to the concept of civil initiative. Millis was later found guilty, but had his sentence suspended.

In a further escalation of government harassment of humanitarian workers, in June 2009, Emrys Staton became the second NMD volunteer to be found guilty of littering in a federal wildlife refuge. Staton had been arrested six months earlier while leaving jugs of water just within the boundaries of the Buenos Aires Wildlife Refuge. Staton had been regularly leaving water in the refuge ever since he started volunteering with NMD in 2004. According to Emrys, "The wildlife refuge has always had a humanitarian presence because historically it was one of the most active migration corridors. You have to remember that people have been migrating across this land for centuries."[53] In response to the ongoing harassment, in July 2009, a group of forty NMD volunteers publicly announced their intentions of placing more gallon jugs of water in the same refuge. They hoped that by intentionally provoking further arrests, they would bring greater national attention to the growing conflict between humanitarian workers and the federal Fish and Wildlife agents. Thirteen people were arrested, including Fife, who serves as a mentor and inspiration to the younger activists. Following these arrests, seven representatives of NMD, Samaritans, and Humane Borders were invited to meet with the newly appointed secretary of the interior Ken Salazar and his staff to discuss possible resolutions to the restricted access to these public lands. Salazar's staff had thus far gotten information on the conflict only from the land manager in southern Arizona, so the meeting enabled Salazar's staff to see that the humanitarian activists were not just a bunch of renegades. "They took us much more seriously when we told them we just wanted the space to do our work, and we showed them our GPS data and the maps we have developed over the years."[54]

Alongside its efforts to maintain a human presence in the desert, NMD is also actively engaged in providing humanitarian relief to migrants who have been deported back to Mexico. In 2006 they partnered with several other humanitarian organizations to set up relief stations at the Nogales and Naco, Arizona, crossings. The Nogales station is located just past the Mexican border control station at the Mariposa crossing. Here, first aid workers, including volunteer doctors, attend to migrants who have just been dropped off at the border after being released from custody by the Border Patrol. The majority of the migrants were arrested while seeking to cross the desert; others were picked up in the interior and brought to the border for deportation back to Mexico. Many arrive without any possessions since their belongings were confiscated at the time of their arrest and frequently not returned. At times, family members have been separated from each other while in custody and are then repatriated at different border crossings. Many of the migrants are still visibly traumatized by their experiences in custody. Quite a few have stories of verbal and physical abuse while in the Border Patrol's custody. In its first two years of existence, the Nogales station alone has served 250,000 people. Volunteers from local churches on the Mexican side of the border supply the aid station with food they have prepared, while doctors tend to the immediate medical needs of those who have just been returned.[55]

In this context, NMD undertook a two-year project of documenting evidence of human rights abuses by collecting the stories of the returnees' treatment while in custody. The result was the publication of a report titled "Crossing the Line," which is the most recent in a long series of reports documenting human rights abuses at the border. Already in the late 1980s, following the passage of the 1986 Immigration Reform and Control Act (IRCA), the American Friends Service Committee reported over twelve hundred instances of abuse, including sexual, verbal, and physical abuse, false arrests, and illegal deportations. In 1998 Amnesty International again substantiated the routine deprivation of water, food, and medical attention, theft, and verbal, psychological, and physical abuse by the Border Patrol. There have been other reports since that time, demonstrating that the Border Patrol has continued its historic patterns of abuse dating back to the late 1920s, which systematically dehumanize migrants arriving from Mexico and Central America.[56] No More Deaths formally submitted its report to the Department of Homeland Security (DHS) as well as members of the congressional committees that oversee DHS's work.

There is no doubt that the thousands of American citizens who have spent time along the border, volunteering to provide aid, experiencing firsthand the militarization of the region, and hearing the stories of the humanitarian activists, are deeply impacted by the experience. The complexities of the global economy are laid bare, exposing its harsh human consequences that overwhelmingly affect the lives of poor, indigenous people who are leaving their homes, risking death to provide for their families. The volunteers are also asked to confront their own privileges as American citizens. This is especially true for those whose white skin gives them an automatic pass through the interior checkpoints, while every dark-skinned person is stopped and inspected. All the rhetoric about American commitments to fairness and justice are challenged by the shocking stories of human tragedy they encounter. One NMD volunteer describes the impact of his time in the desert:

> All things political, economic, social, and historical intersect here. They crash into each other, they try to overpower one another. This is where the global economy and everything that supports it is stripped of its rhetoric and shields, of its disguises and glossy advertisements and decontextualized economic statistics. It is a complicated war in which individual people are struggling against an entire system that wants to make them disappear. Men, women, and children trying to pay their bills and see their families are left standing alone, burning up in the desert's harsh heat and light.[57]

These three humanitarian organizations are by no means the only religious presence along the long border that stretches from Texas to the Pacific Ocean. The urgency of saving lives has also strengthened ties between American churches and their Mexican counterparts. For example, recognizing that the two denominations must work as partners, the United Methodist Church has developed an official cross-border collaboration with the Mexican Methodist Church. Bishop Minerva Carcaño, one of the co-chairs of the effort, says the Mexican church leaders "have taught us the whys of immigration and how we can work with people who are migrants."[58] Thus, instead of serving as a dividing line between two denominations that share a common religious heritage, the border is becoming a common space where they can share ideas and work on the basis of mutual respect.

The Call for Sanctuary

The provision of sanctuary has historically been a distinctively religious response to the government's unjust treatment of immigrants who have entered the United States without legal visas. Within the Jewish and Christian traditions, the right to sanctuary is grounded in Moses' designation of six cities of refugee out of the land given to the Levitical tribes (Num. 35:6–15). Anyone, Israelite and foreigner alike, who had committed a murder without intent, could seek refuge in one of these cities. During the 1980s Central American sanctuary movement, religious activists further elaborated the theological underpinning of their work by documenting historic Greek, Roman, Anglo-Saxon, and Christian practices of granting asylum under certain circumstances.[59] They also cited historic examples of American churches whose consciences had led them to provide sanctuary in defiance of existing laws. This included churches and religious communities who, in defiance of the Fugitive Slave Act of 1850, had participated in the Underground Railroad, smuggling fugitive slaves who were fleeing their southern masters. During the Vietnam War there were also churches that gave refuge to draft resisters.

While Elvira Arellano's decision to seek sanctuary at Adalberto Church had been a personal one, it served as an inspiration for the creation of a broader sanctuary movement. In November 2006, the Mexican American Cultural Center (MACC) in San Antonio, Texas, once again played a catalytic role by convening a meeting of a small number of Latino activists to discuss their communities' responses to immigration. During the course of three days of intense discussion, participants decided that it was necessary to do more than just *acompañamiento* or accompaniment with immigrants. Instead, some resistance was needed; some form of active nonviolence that would unleash the transforming power of love. The group decided to duplicate the example of Elvira Arellano's witness in sanctuary. Alexia Salvatierra from CLUE California and Juan Carlos Ruiz from New York City agreed to start talking to people who might be interested.[60] By the end of the year, CLUE California was circulating a proposal calling for the creation of the "New Sanctuary Movement." It envisioned a new movement that would take a united, public, and moral stand for immigrant rights.[61] To highlight the threat that aggressive deportations were posing to families, the new movement sought to focus on those that included citizen children as well as at least one member who had received a final order of deportation, yet had a potential case under current law.

In late January 2007, religious leaders from eighteen cities convened in Washington DC. The gathering was broadly interfaith, consisting of representatives from Catholic, mainline Protestant, and evangelical churches, Unitarians, the Union of Reform Judaism, Muslims, and Sikhs, along with religious justice organizations such as Interfaith Worker Justice and the American Friends Service Committee. After listening to the experiences of immigrant families fighting deportation, the group embraced the call to form a new sanctuary movement, stating that its goals were "protecting immigrant families from unjust deportation, affirming and making visible these families as children of God and awakening the moral imagination of the country through prayer and witness." Participants committed to continue this work until Congress finally passed just comprehensive immigration reform, acknowledging that "their support for immigrants might include physical sanctuary at some point."[62]

By May 2007, churches in five major U.S. cities announced that they would provide sanctuary to immigrant families in which a member had received a deportation order. Among the churches were several in Los Angeles that had chosen to collaborate in their provision of sanctuary. One of them was Our Lady Queen of Angels Church, a historic Latino church located in what had been the city's central plaza during Spanish colonial times. Fr. Richard Estrada announced, "We want to put a human face to very complex immigration laws and awaken the consciousness of the human spirit." The organizers announced that there were churches in fifty other cities planning to join the sanctuary movement.[63] Initially, national organizers had envisioned that churches would agree to care and support the families since the member facing deportation usually can no longer work to earn a living. In many cases, the person under deportation orders is fitted with an ankle GPS system. They are also required to report to a monitoring office on a regular basis to make sure that authorities know of their whereabouts.

The actual practice of sanctuary has been constructed differently by various local groups throughout the country. In the 1980s sanctuary movement, refugee families who had recently arrived in the United States were given shelter within churches. The churches then took responsibility for meeting all of the refugees' needs. In some parts of the country that same model was initially replicated, yet, there is a risk of paternalism. The families facing deportation today are generally well established with deep community roots and extensive personal ties of their own. Thus, the response of the new sanctuary movement can be quite different. The New Sanctuary Coalition of New York City, which coordinates the congregations' involvement in the sanctuary movement, has chosen to prioritize the families' legal defense. Defense committees that work on each family's legal defense constitute the basic building blocks of their work with the families. According to Amy Dalton, a Union Theological Seminary student and activist, all of the families they work with had previous problems with their lawyers. However, only a small subset of the New York City churches and synagogues actively participate in a defense committee.[64] Judson Memorial Church, which is one of the city's oldest activist churches, has a defense committee that oversees the congregation's "moral and legal support for a Haitian family threatened with unjust deportation."[65] At Judson there is a staffperson who assists the task force, while in other cases, the work is done solely by lay members.

There has always been a political dimension to the work of sanctuary in which the families' own stories serve as illustrations of the institutionalized forms of injustice against which activists are protesting. In the 1980s, the political goal was to end U.S. support of the military juntas in Central America. Today, the goal is to reform a broken immigration system that defines certain immigrants who have committed even minor infractions of the law as "bad" and therefore deportable. This profiling can occur even to a person who has been living in the United States legally. New York City's New Sanctuary Coalition agreed that they could not just denounce the injustice of the present system but needed to propose alternatives. Consequently they have chosen to focus on the passage of the Child Citizens Protection Act and on the implementation of an ICE-sponsored program (287g), which grants local police departments the powers to arrest undocumented immigrants, The Sanctuary Coalition believes it is a violation of human rights for the DHS to maintain an office at Riker's Island, New York City's massive 20,000-bed prison, that checks the immigration status of every person passing through there, even those who are later found innocent of any crime.

As was true in congregational community organizing and worker-justice activism, once again the personal stories of sanctuary families become a powerful means of unmasking injustice and proclaiming the families' dignity. The sanctuary activists see the storytelling as a form of popular education. Juan Carlos Ruiz, one of the coalition's leaders, says, "There has been a concrete effect from the stories of our families. We have humanized our families and the old charity poster of the good immigrant has been done away with. We need to talk more about dignity and less about status."[66]

New York City's sanctuary movement is mostly driven by Christian religious institutions. This is partly because most of the families are Christians, although there is one Muslim family from West Africa.

There has been some Jewish support, yet Jewish congregations have a lengthy discernment process, which means that they tend to respond more slowly. Muslims have largely been too afraid to become involved because of the heavy profiling they have endured since 9/11. Nonetheless, the coalition has a good relationship with Desis Rising Up and Moving (DRUM), a grassroots organization based in the borough of Queens, which seeks to build the power of South Asian low-wage immigrant workers, families fighting deportation, and youth in New York City.

Although a discussion of the sanctuary movement was not officially on the NNIRR's formal conference agenda at their January 2008 conference in Houston, it was the central topic among the religious activists in attendance who sought to strengthen what was still an emerging movement. Yet, just a few months later, the nascent sanctuary movement that focused its work on a small number of families was overshadowed by the massive ICE workplace raid on Agriprocessors in Postville, Iowa. Suddenly, workplace raids were being carried out on a massive scale. The raid in Postville on May 12, 2008, represented a dramatic escalation of the Bush administration's renewed emphasis on enforcement. The ICE raid at a kosher meat processing plant, where 389 workers were arrested, represented the single largest workplace raid in history.

As a result, the push to extend the new national sanctuary movement quieted down, and some churches pulled out of the work. In New York City, which has not experienced the same large-scale raids that occurred elsewhere, the New Sanctuary Coalition continues to support five families. Through their intimate connections to a small number of families, these faith communities are connected to a much larger universe of families facing the same dilemma. This bond to specific people and their stories of suffering provides the impetus to engage in broader advocacy campaigns. Now, when they appear before city council, it is not an abstract call for justice but a call aimed at transforming the futures of very particular families who are living among these activists.

A Broadening of Religious Support

Following the 2007 collapse of congressional immigration reform legislation, an unrelenting barrage of anti-immigrant propaganda created such a highly charged environment that even swing voters, including African Americans, native-born Latinos, and white progressives, were increasingly convinced that undocumented immigrants were bad for the county. Public opinion had shifted toward enforcement, giving the federal government the cover it needed to forge ahead on implementing its strategy of massive deportations. By 2008 the full effects of the DHS's new enforcement strategy were being felt in immigrant communities throughout the United States. The military tactics that had long been present on the border now became visible in the interior.

The DHS stepped up its use of the 287g program through which local police departments were empowered to act as immigration officials. Intended to catch serious criminals, the program allowed police to check the immigration status of anyone they apprehended, resulting in the deportations of thousands of people who were arrested for minor offenses. Since the federal government reimbursed local police for people held on visas violations, its expansion quickly led to increased racial profiling. Numerous Latino citizens who were unable to quickly produce proof of U.S. citizenship were deported. Among the most egregious examples of 287g's impact was the February 2008 arrest of Juana Villegas during a minor traffic stop. The mother of three young children, who were in the car with her, was nine months pregnant at the time of her arrest. On her second day in jail she went into labor. Her hands and feet were shackled for transportation to the hospital. One hand and one foot remained shackled to the hospital bed until shortly before she gave birth, and she was then reshackled following the birth. The case garnered international media attention including coverage by the *Washington Post*, the *Boston Globe,* and the *New York Times*, as well as the concern of global human rights advocacy organizations such as Amnesty International and the American Civil Liberties Union.[67] The cumulative effect of these new policies was a significant increase in deportations. Between 2007 and 2008, the escalating enforcement strategies led to a 20 percent increase in deportations. Of these totals, roughly 2 percent were the result of workplace raids; the rest resulted from increased collaboration with local police.[68]

The full impact of the government's new enforcement measures were not yet visible in January of 2008 when 650 highly committed immigrant rights activists gathered in Houston for NNIRR's national conference. As the oldest national network of grassroots immigrant rights organizations, NNIRR traces its origins back to various local Mexican and Asian community-based immigrant rights groups that coalesced over the fight to enact what became the Immigration Reform and Control Act of 1986 (IRCA).[69] As a network NNIRR has a long-standing commitment to the use of popular education as a tool, which enables grassroots activists to uncover the root causes of immigration and its impact on a wide variety of communities. The results were evidenced by the high level of sophistication among the conference's plenary and workshop presenters. The diverse, mostly young, multi-ethnic activists who assembled in Houston came from a broad array of organizations including immigrant, labor, human, civil, and LGBTQ rights organizations "rooted in indigenous peoples, Latino, Arab, Muslim, South Asian, Asian Pacific Islanders, African and African American communities."[70] The NNIRR's emphasis on inclusivity was on display as the conference opened with a blessing and spiritual orientation given by an indigenous woman whose people's tribal land straddles the border between Texas, New Mexico, and Mexico. It was further reflected in their provision of a completely multilingual event that provided translation to anyone who was monolingual. The NNIRR is also conscious of the critical need to build alliances between Latino and African and African American communities and, to that end, gives high visibility to the work of the Black Alliance for Just Immigration (BAJI).

In the months following the NNIRR conference, the enormity of the Postville raid coupled with the highly visible use of 287g slowly began to trigger new activism within a broader array of local communities. The Bush administration's stepped-up enforcement actions led to significant increases in Latino voter registration, which ultimately contributed to turning several formerly red states blue in the 2008 presidential election. Reflecting the larger community's great sense of urgency as well as the centrality of the family within Latino cultures, both Latino Catholics and Protestants have made family unity the focal point of their campaigns for immigration reform.

In early 2009, families who were under threat of deportation also became the focal point of the *Familias Unidas* (Family Unity Tour) that held large public events at Latino churches in twenty-two cities. While the events brought together Latinos from a broad spectrum of Christian traditions, including evangelicals and Pentecostals, Methodists, and Catholics, they were targeted at members of the Congressional Hispanic Caucus (CHC). Attendance at events in each of the cities ranged from one thousand to five thousand people.[71] According to Rev. Walter Coleman, one of the tour's organizers, the tour went into every congressional district that had a Hispanic congressperson.[72] Each event consisted of a complete worship service with choirs and preaching, and ended with an "altar call" at which U.S. citizens with an undocumented family member were asked to come forward and fill out a statement to be delivered to President Obama. At Pius V Catholic Church in Chicago, six hundred people came forward. One of the events held in Harlem welcomed two thousand people. Both Rep. Nydia Velázquez, chairwoman of the CHC, and Rep. Charles Rangel, a founding member of the Congressional Black Caucus and current chair of the House Ways and Means Committee, were present.[73] Speaking at one of the events held in California, Speaker of the House of Representatives Nancy Pelosi told the audience, "this separation of families is un-American and must be stopped immediately." At another event, Rep. John Lewis, a veteran of the civil rights movement, called immigration reform the civil rights movement of this decade and committed himself to "make trouble" until it is resolved.[74]

These events were clearly designed to showcase the abilities of Latino religious leaders to mobilize their members, as well as the strength of their ties to the CHC. The events were also evidence of a growing nexus between national lobbying and grassroots movement-building that had been lacking in the failed 2007 efforts to enact comprehensive immigration reform. Following the tour, the CHC took the signed petitions to President Obama and asked that he honor his campaign promise to pass comprehensive immigration reform during his first year in office and to stop the raids, deportations, and separation of families. They reminded him of the statement he made in accepting his nomination, that the separation of a mother from her child must be unacceptable in the United States. They also reminded him of the overwhelming and decisive support he received from Latino/as in the last election because of that same campaign promise.[75] The caucus has also flexed its power as a voting block to prod Obama into taking tangible steps in moving the legislation forward. In June 2009, after Obama twice cancelled a promised White House meeting on immigration reform, the CHC withheld their votes on a bill dealing with the war in Iraq. The day after Obama finally convened the meeting on June 25, an energy bill passed in the House by seven votes. Those seven votes came from caucus members.

The increasingly harsh enforcement measures also began to activate a broader grassroots interfaith movement, reaching well beyond the many long-time immigrant and cosmopolitan activists who are already deeply committed to immigrant rights. In Iowa, Rev. Jim Perdue, a United Methodist missionary for immigration, stated that "Postville awakened the center of the church. People now saw the human dimensions of immigration."[76] Postville proved to be such a powerful catalyst because the ICE raid devastated the small town, arresting one out of every four of its residents.[77] Stories emerged of the ways workers were dehumanized, denied their rights, and how the workers' families had fled into hiding at a local church. The whole town was traumatized and continued to suffer from its after-shocks. Writing on the occasion of the raid's first anniversary, Perdue reflects on the reaction to the raid within Iowa:

Afterwards there was some speculation as to why ICE had chosen to conduct the first such a large-scale raid in a farmbelt state deep in the interior of the U.S., far removed from more urbanized borderlands space. Perhaps they had anticipated receiving a more sympathetic response, yet in the raid's aftermath, there was a tremendous outpouring of support from the surrounding community for the roughly sixty mothers who remain under house arrest, wearing ankle bracelets, while their husbands have vanished into the vast network of private ICE detention centers.[78]

St. Bridget's Catholic Church in Postville instantly became the center of what can only be characterized as a disaster relief effort. St. Bridget's is a small church with no more than one hundred members, yet in the aftermath of the raid, it became the center of a nationwide outpouring of emergency aid. Immediately after the raid four hundred to five hundred people took shelter in the church. Fearful that ICE was still looking for them, they stayed there day and night for an entire week after the raid. Initially, ICE had made no provisions for the care of the minor children whose parents had been arrested. Then, after spending several days in detention, forty-two women who had young American-citizen children were released on humanitarian grounds. Each woman had a GPS monitor, which had to be recharged for two hours each day, placed on one of her ankles. The women were prohibited from working or leaving the area. Suddenly, St Bridget's was called to care for these families and others who no longer had any other means of survival. During the first year after the raid, St Bridget's, along with other faith communities in Iowa and beyond, raised over $1.2 million to support the families. The United Methodist Committee on Relief (UMCOR) donated the funds to hire a half-time coordinator just to care for the American-born children.

The American Jewish religious community was also deeply impacted by the Postville raid and the revelations that followed. Agriprocessors' owners were Jewish; the plant had been producing more than half of all the kosher meat sold in the United States. There had already been long-standing debates over a broadening of the definition of the word "kosher," beginning with efforts in the early 1970s to persuade Jews not to eat nonunion grapes. According to Jewish law, "kosher" designates meat from animals that have been slaughtered in a ritual fashion intended to be painless and to minimize the presence of blood in the resulting meat. In the 1970s there were calls to also include the ethical treatment of the workers who had prepared the food and still more recently to include foods that had been grown organically. The Postville raid intensified these debates after it was discovered that

Agriprocessors' owners had violated both the ethical tenets on the humane treatment of animals and those addressing the exploitation of workers. In the months following the raid several Jewish denominations, American Jewish youth organizations, and youth camps, along with a wide range of Jewish social justice organizations, issued calls for a boycott of meat produced at the plant until the unethical practices had been corrected. The Jewish Council on Urban Affairs (JCUA) of Chicago launched a campaign to help provide food, housing, and legal assistance for some two hundred and fifty families, including five hundred children, affected by the raid in Postville. They also organized members of Chicago's Jewish community to travel to Postville, Iowa for a solidarity rally and march in support of workers at Agriprocessors.[79]

Mounting stories of abuses of the 287g program also activated a broader cross-section of religious people. Chris West, who works on building grassroots support for immigration reform among Catholics, says that many Catholics were outraged by stories of immigrant families being ripped apart.[80] Some of the most outrageous abuses of the 287g program occurred in Maricopa County, Arizona. Joe Arpaio, the local sheriff had signed a memorandum of understanding with ICE in 2007. As a result, there were numerous cases of his deputies using the pretense of minor traffic violations to arrest people on immigration violations. He also enlisted the aid of right-wing vigilantes to serve as volunteer deputies as his department conducted massive sweeps through entire neighborhoods. In February 2009 he made national news after forcing more than two hundred Latino immigrants, who had been chained and dressed in prison stripes, to march down a public street from a county jail to a detainment camp in a desert industrial zone outside Phoenix.[81]

According to Chris West, news of such "harsh abuses have proven to be good for organizing people of faith who are reacting by saying that these are not the kinds of people we want to see deported."[82] In Arizona, both Christian and Jewish religious leaders have publicly condemned Arpaio's tactics. In the spring of 2008, a group of eight prominent interreligious leaders, including the Arizona bishops of the Lutheran, Episcopal, Methodist, and Presbyterian denominations, held a press conference condemning the sheriff's divisive enforcement campaign. Speaking of Arpaio's vigilante style enforcement actions at a 2009 national faith leaders' press conference in Washington DC, Minerva Carcaño, the United Methodist bishop of Arizona, said, "What is clear is that his style of policing has created a climate of fear in our communities, unleashed a vicious wave of ethnic bashing, and shown a complete disregard for basic human rights. Arizona does not stand alone in this shameful scene, for what is happening in Arizona is happening all across this country."[83] Public anger against Sheriff Arpaio led people to turn out for several mass marches organized by a broad coalition of Latino/a civil rights, immigrant rights, and worker rights organizations, including the Phoenix chapter of NMD. An estimated four thousand people responded to a call initiated by the National Day Laborer Organizing Network for a peaceful six-mile march from Arpaio's headquarters to the "tent city" jail as a way of calling attention to the mounting human rights crisis in Phoenix. In late 2009, the U.S. Department of Homeland Security rescinded Arpaio's 287g contract. Arpaio responded by vowing to continue his raids.

Religious advocacy groups, including some of the mainline denominational legislative offices in Washington DC have gradually begun to see the results of their more concerted efforts to mobilize grassroots support. As we have seen, the effectiveness of these denominational legislative offices has been weakened by declines in their funding and by ongoing attacks from conservatives within their denominations. They recognized that in 2007, the opponents of immigrant rights had been far more successful in mobilizing emails, faxes, and phone calls to members of Congress. According to Bill Mefford, who works for the United Methodist General Board of Church and Society, "as a general rule the denominations don't do organizing."[84] In this case, the gap in grassroots organizing in favor of comprehensive immigration reform was initially filled by the national congregational-based community organizing networks, including IAF, PICO, and especially Gamaliel (see Chapter 3). Gamaliel has made immigration reform one of their leading national issues and has worked hard to build support for it among their African American clergy. Yet these groups are known for not working cooperatively and are not members of the Interreligious Immigration Coalition (IIC), the main national clearinghouse for religious legislative work in support of comprehensive reform. As the Obama administration took office in January 2009, the IIC finally launched its own efforts to do grassroots organizing by encouraging its members to hold prayer vigils in key legislative districts. The events were scheduled for the week of February 13–22, 2009, while members of Congress were to be in their home districts. By the week's end, 170 vigils had taken place, a powerful expression of the sentiments of a broad spectrum of the religious mainstream. It was estimated that the vigils mobilized five thousand people who were now poised for further action. As they visited key members of Congress in Washington, religious lobbyists were able to point to the turnout at these events as proof that there was visible grassroots support for comprehensive reform.

Bishop Carcaño believes these prayer vigils were tangible signs of the church's willingness to finally assert its moral voice: "I was befuddled by our unwillingness to use our voice. I think it was nationalism that prevented us from speaking. I believe prayer has had an impact. At first, Joe Biden had said that immigration reform wasn't part of the 2009 legislative agenda. The vigils brought together people from across a wide socio-economic spectrum to pray for God's justice and the administration then said it would move forward on immigration reform."[85] The successful prayer vigils were followed by efforts to organize visits to the district offices of key members of Congress.

Religious Lobbying for Immigration Reform

Because immigration is ultimately a national policy issue, many of the core issues, including the nature of the U.S. enforcement strategies and access to rights, including full citizenship, will be determined through the enactment of congressional legislation. As was the case in earlier social movements such as the civil rights movement, the legislative lobbying on immigration is not led by those organizations who are working on the ground. Instead, the religious voice is carried by a wide variety of denominational staff who as a rule are not directly involved in the grassroots work. Since immigration has now been a major policy issues for a number of years, many religious bodies, denominations, and social service networks have had an opportunity to either rework or adopt new official positions on immigration reform. The majority of religious bodies now have official positions in support of comprehensive immigration reforms. The IIC is currently the largest and most diverse coalition of religious organizations collaborating to secure national immigration reform. Its key members are Catholics, mainline Protestants, Unitarian Universalists, the Hebrew Immigrant Aid Society, the Religious Action Center of Reform Judaism, World Relief, American Friends Service Committee, Interfaith Worker Justice, and Sojourners. These organizations do not have unanimity on all aspects of immigration reform, yet they have been able to collaborate on broad initiatives, including the grassroots prayer vigils, national press conferences in DC, and joint visits to individual members of Congress.

At their press conference in February 2009 they unveiled the common interfaith platform on which they would lobby the Obama administration and the 111th Congress. The document itself lists the names of more than five hundred national, local, and individual endorsers. It begins by citing texts from the Hebrew Bible, the New Testament, and the Qur'an that affirm a responsibility to love and care for the stranger or the wayfarer. The common platform contains seven carefully crafted points to build common ground in the midst of divergent views. The coalition emphasizes making family unity the centerpiece of any immigration reform measure. They also agree that any legislation should create a pathway to citizenship for those who are now living in the United States without documents. Some individual groups place various caveats on exactly who ought to be eligible, such as excluding people with criminal backgrounds. The policy issue over which there is the greatest disagreement is enforcement and border control.

The IIC's joint platform criticizes the ineffectiveness of current enforcement policies, while calling for "improved access to the legal immigration system."[86] It also states that border policies must be consistent with humanitarian values and with the need to treat all individuals with respect. According to Allison Johnson, who works for Sojourners and oversees the Christian Coalition for Immigration Reform (CCIR), the IIC says it wants smarter enforcement that would listen to the concerns of border communities. "We're not advocating for enforcement, but if it is done then it must be done with dignity. That's the bottom line for us."[87] Yet, for many in the religious community, the issue of enforcement remains deeply problematic. According to Rev. Walter Coleman, who has close ties to the CHC, whatever new legislation emerges from the 111th Congress will contain border enforcement measures. "We have lost the border enforcement issue because of all the coverage on narcotics trafficking and shootings along the border."[88] The Mennonites, a historic peace church, and the Unitarian Universalists, both of whom are members of the IIC, are publicly committed to serving immigrants even if doing so results in disobeying the laws of the United States. The statement of the Mennonite Central Committee reads, "We are committed to obeying God rather than human authority, especially when laws call us to harm others and block us from efforts to protect life."[89] Similarly, the General Assembly of the Unitarian Universalists passed a resolution in 2006 that called on Unitarian Universalist congregations and individuals to "continue providing services and fellowship to undocumented individuals even if legislation is passed that criminalizes these humanitarian acts." A number of the mainline denominations such as the Evangelical Lutheran Church of America, Presbyterian Church USA, and the United Methodists are simply silent on the issue of enforcement.

The Catholic Church takes a more Kantian view of border enforcement. They initially entered the current immigration debate in 2001, in response to the growing number of deaths in the desert. In a joint statement issued by American and Mexican bishops, the Catholic Church outlined a set of principles that continue to inform their policy positions on immigration. They began by affirming people's right not to migrate, which is an acknowledgment that the root causes of migration must also be addressed. It signals their interest in creating the conditions needed for people to live safe and economically sustainable lives in their home countries. They also affirmed the right to migrate if one cannot lead a dignified life in one's home country. These first two points follow the language of the Universal Declaration of Human Rights quite closely. In their third principle the Church affirms the sovereign rights of nations to enforce their borders, yet for rich nations that right is bound together with the higher moral obligation to care for the poor.[90] Here the bishops are acknowledging what in Kant's view would be a moral obligation on the part of rich nations to in some way compensate those who have less. The bishops' positions are firmly grounded in Scripture, the long history of Catholic social thought, and jurisprudence.

Latino/a evangelicals, who are critical to the passage of immigration reform, all include support for enforcement in their reform platforms. They also tend to make the process of attaining citizenship more protracted. For these denominations, achieving immigration reform is an immediate concern, which has given them a strong sense of urgency. This contrasts with the denominations whose membership is overwhelmingly Anglo citizens. The Rev. Gabriel Salguero, executive director of the Hispanic Leadership Program at Princeton Theological Seminary, says that Latino evangelicals are being pragmatic when they include support for enforcement in their positions on immigration reform. "We understand the complexity of the situation and see it as the only way anything will get through Congress. After the first bill got defeated in 2006, people sought a middle ground going forward so they could talk to everyone."[91]

The strongest pro-enforcement statement among Latino evangelicals was issued by the National Hispanic Christian Leadership Conference (NHCLC) in 2006 during the Bush administration's first attempt to pass a comprehensive bill. In their opening statement on immigration the NHCLC affirms that "As Hispanic Evangelical leaders we are concerned with the security of our nation and the simultaneous well-being of our immigrant families of which the majority is of Latin American descent." The first item in their four-point platform addresses enforcement, calling for "Border enforcement and protection initiatives that include the application and enhancement of technological, military and law enforcement capabilities that will protect our borders while enabling and facilitating the implementation of our nation's immigration policy. Let us put an end to all illegal immigration."[92] This statement makes no mention of "humane" enforcement, which is the language used by the IIC and other progressive evangelicals, such as the platform of Christians for Comprehensive Immigration Reform (CCIR), which was convened by Sojourners. Samuel Rodriquez, the NHCLC's president, reiterated the organization's strong position on enforcement at a June 2009 press conference convened by CCIR to announce the relaunch of its campaign for comprehensive reform.[93]

Among Latino evangelicals, Esperanza USA, a community-based organization in Philadelphia, has developed the most extensive relationships among both Democrats and Republicans in Washington DC. Esperanza has been the convener of an annual Hispanic Prayer Breakfast through which it built ties with powerful members of Congress. In recent years, the organization and its leader, Rev. Luis Cortes, have leveraged their access into an extensive lobbying effort on behalf of its agenda for comprehensive immigration reform. The organization also begins its platform with a call for strengthened border enforcement by the federal government so as to end unauthorized entries. However, in an apparent criticism of the 287g program, it states, "There are serious unintended consequences of granting state and local law enforcement authority to enforce federal immigration laws. To do so would instantly transform the close, cooperative relationship community leaders—especially Hispanic clergy—have with local police, into an adversarial one." It goes on to call for an overhaul of the broken visa system that forces families to wait for decades and for the creation of a temporary worker visa. Their platform would create a two-stage process for undocumented immigrants to receive citizenship where they would first have to qualify for legal status. Only then would they go to the back of the line in applying for citizenship. Most of the groups in the IIC would require initial registration and then a process of paying any back taxes and learning English to achieve citizenship.[94]

While a broad spectrum of religious organizations have now endorsed some version of comprehensive immigration reform, not surprisingly there are also religious conservatives who have come out in support of the present set of laws and simply call for their full enforcement. This stance reflects their triumphalist understandings of the United States as a Christian nation whose laws are sacrosanct and must therefore be obeyed. The prime example of such a perspective is that held by the Southern Baptist Convention (SBC), the largest Protestant denomination in the United States. In 2006 it passed a resolution "On the Crisis of Illegal Immigration," whose title alone indicates the denomination's emphasis on enforcement. The scriptural grounding for their position is a passage in the New Testament book of Romans, which has historically been used to justify Christian obedience to the state. It reads "Let every person be subject to the governing authorities; for there is no authority except from God, and those authorities that exist have been instituted by God. Therefore, whoever resists authority resists what God has appointed and those who resist will incur judgment" (Rom. 13:1–2). Relying on the words of the apostle Paul, who was a Roman citizen, the SBC's resolution states that "As citizens of the nation, Christians are under biblical mandate to respect the divine institution of government and its just laws, but at the same time, Christians have a right to expect the government to fulfill its ordained mandate to enforce those laws." It goes on to say that the federal government's failure to enforce immigration laws "has caused severe consternation among a sizable constituency of Americans and has led to the crisis we now face . . . it urges the federal government to provide for the security of our nation by controlling and securing our borders" and that the federal government "enforce all immigration laws, including the laws directed at employers who knowingly hire illegal immigrants or who are unjustly paying these immigrants substandard wages or subjecting them to conditions that are contrary to the labor laws of our country." According to the SBC, existing laws are regarded as just and must be enforced. In a remaining passage of the statement, Southern Baptists are encouraged "to act redemptively and reach out to meet the physical, emotional, and spiritual needs of all immigrants."[95] There is no mention of immigrant rights or a just resolution to the presence of 12 million undocumented immigrants. Here the Southern Baptists' echo the enforcement-only positions of other right-wing conservatives, using certain Scriptural passages to justify their nationalistic expression of Christian triumphalism.

Concluding Remarks

In the spring of 2010, a renewed push to pass comprehensive immigration reform was under way. The deep economic recession, coupled with this country's history of xenophobia, will make the legislative battle for humane reform tough. The national debate over immigration was further polarized by the Arizona state legislature's April 2010 decision to enact a tough new anti-immigrant law (SB 1070) that would require non-citizens to carry their visa documents with them at all times and police departments to check the immigration status of every person they arrested. Yet, the rising anti-immigrant fervor has also mobilized increasing numbers of religious activists, including many who had not previously been focused on immigration issues. On July 29, the day on which SB 1070 took effect, busloads of religious, immigrant, and labor activists poured into Phoenix for day-long protests that included acts of civil disobedience. At the same time, Hispanic Christians continue to press for some legislative action toward comprehensive immigration reform with La Familias Unidas vowing to "never give up the struggle for their families."[96].

Religious activism on behalf of immigrant rights is primarily situated within the borderlands—either quite literally at the border, or in major immigrant receiving cities such as New York, Chicago, or Los Angeles. However, the presence of significant numbers of immigrants in small towns such as Postville is also extending the borderlands deeper into the American heartland. Among the activists who are deeply committed to living out a religious mandate to "care for the foreigner in our midst," we again encounter the use of contextualized forms of nonviolent resistance and popular education. In this case, nonviolent resistance is embodied in leaving water jugs along migrant trails, even where it is legally prohibited, and in sheltering families faced with pending deportation orders. In some cases, this work has become a form of civil disobedience as activists consciously choose to disobey laws that they believe are harmful to immigrants and their families. Popular education takes the form of trips into the desert. The humanitarian work along the border is also another manifestation of religious activists acting as bridges between those people who are at the very edges of American society and those who possess a privileged status. We have again encountered examples of religious cosmopolitans, who have undergone transformative experiences through which they have come to see themselves not only as American but as world citizens. Organizations such as No More Deaths have purposefully incorporated readings on white privilege into the required reading for all of their volunteers to make sure that encounters with migrants occur within an atmosphere of mutual respect. For the volunteers, the readings coupled with their time in the desert, where they occasionally find the bodies of dead migrants, are transformative experiences that will force them to rethink their own identities.

It is important to note that NMD conceives of the extensive militarization of the Sonoran desert as a low-grade war zone. This suggests a close connection between their humanitarian work in the desert and the solidarity work of organizations such as WFP and CPT, which we encounter in the following chapter. It is not at all surprising that CPT has lent volunteers to NMD since there are striking similarities in the character of the two organizations' work.

6

Peacemaking

In the aftermath of the attacks on September 11, 2001, a resurgent Christian triumphalism successfully reframed the U.S.' policy options in the context of a civilizational battle between good and evil. In its most polemical form, the situation was portrayed as a battle between morality and immorality; between the light of freedom and the darkness of dictatorship. President George W. Bush's speeches were sprinkled with biblical images depicting his perception of this cosmic struggle. These references served as coded messages to Bush's solid base of supporters among Christian conservatives who had come to embrace the Republican Party as though it were the party chosen by God. At its most extreme, triumphalist Christian rhetoric projected an image of the United States as a nation uniquely ordained by God to assume the mantle of the world's hegemonic superpower. It was simply the latest manifestation of what the theologian Walter Wink has termed "the myth of redemptive violence," which establishes a patriotic religion at the heart of the state while repeatedly giving divine sanction to the nation's imperialism. "The myth of redemptive violence thus serves as the spirituality of militarism."[1]

The Bush administration's initial decision following 9/11 to retaliate against al Qaeda by invading Afghanistan aroused little opposition. In sharp contrast, a little more than a year later, despite the administration's full-scale propaganda campaign, the looming invasion of Iraq triggered the "most intensive mobilization of antiwar sentiment in history. On February 15, 2003, in hundreds of cities across the globe an estimated 10 million people demonstrated against the war."[2] In the course of just a few months, the peace movement in the United States had reached levels of mobilization that had taken years to develop during the Vietnam War. Even more significantly, the anti-Iraq-war movement had a much more global character than any previous antiwar movements, as protests were coordinated throughout the world, and activists understood themselves to be part of a global opposition. The political scientists Michael Hardt and Antonio Negri interpret this massive global turnout in opposition to the U.S. invasion as the pinnacle of a longer cycle of antiglobalization struggles that began in Seattle in 1999. "The war represented the ultimate instance of the global power against which the cycle of struggles had formed; the organizational structures and communication that the struggles had established made possible a massive, coordinated mobilization of common expression against the war."[3]

The massive opposition to the invasion also manifested a growing consensus in opposition to war among many of the world's religious leaders. The decision to invade Iraq was condemned by religious leaders throughout the world. National conferences of Catholic bishops in Europe, Asia, and Africa joined the Vatican in issuing statements against the war. In the United States, nearly every mainline Christian denominational body opposed the war.[4] Religious opposition to the Iraq war was broader than any previous conflict in modern history, with religious activists serving as major players in the principal U.S. coalitions against the war. Traditional religious peace groups, including the Catholic pacifist organization Pax Christi and grassroots groups within the Quaker, Mennonite, and Brethren communities, played leadership roles in raising awareness and organizing opposition.

While this opposition did not stop the Iraq war, it did limit international support for it; including among countries such as Germany and France, otherwise considered to be among the U.S.' closest allies. The UN Security Council decisively rebuffed the U.S.' attempt to secure its authorization for war in February 2003. Not only did France, Germany, and Russia vote against the war, but six other nonpermanent member states did as well. The Security Council's rejection of the U.S. and Great Britain's attempt to gain its support for an invasion marked the first time since the UN's founding that the United States, on an issue that mattered to it, could not get a majority on the Security Council.[5]

The important role of religious activists in building opposition to the war in Iraq is emblematic of a widespread commitment to the practice of peacemaking among an increasingly broad spectrum of American religious believers. Religious and secular peacemakers are components of a broad peace movement in the United States. The huge religious coalition that was active at the beginning of the Iraq war has not been sustained, but that has also been equally true of secular antiwar activists.[6]

At its core, religious peacemaking is grounded in the belief that violence is antithetical to the search for justice—lasting justice cannot be attained through the use of violence. While the Christian pacifists of the early twentieth century were singularly focused on the abolition of war, religious pacifism has evolved into opposition to all forms of violence, arguing that the problem of the twentieth century was the problem of violence. "It was not, as such, Fascism, Communism, economic inequality, or the color line, though all of those were deeply implicated. It was, above all, the fact of human beings killing one another with extraordinary ferocity and effectiveness."[7] Contemporary religious pacifists fall along a continuum from absolute pacifists to pragmatic pacifists, who constitute the majority of those working for peace today. The latter prefer to avoid war but can accept some limited use of force for self-defense or to uphold justice and protect the innocent. The abdication of all or even most forms of war stands in opposition to the more dominant Christian conception of "just war" developed by Augustine in the fifth century. Just-war theories can also be placed on a continuum, as became evident during the 2003 Iraq invasion. Some theorists argued that the war did not meet the standards that justified war, while other argued that it did.[8]

Today, some form of pacifism is a widely accepted point of view among religious activists. This was certainly not the case at the outset of World War I. After the majority of the nation's religious leaders chose to support the war, the few remaining absolute pacifists quickly found themselves isolated and under siege. There proved to be limited public space for open dissent against Woodrow Wilson's Great War. Those pacifists who still sought to express their views were labeled as threats to national security, resulting in a number of antiwar clergy being forced to resign their pulpits and a small number of religious conscientious objectors being prosecuted for their refusal to fight. This led to a new focus on the protection of civil liberties, giving rise to the formation of the National Civil Liberties Bureau, which later became the American Civil Liberties Union. The widespread embrace of nonviolent forms of protest during the civil rights movement and subsequent anti–Vietnam War protests has embedded varying understandings of pacifism and practices of nonviolent resistance among a wide spectrum of contemporary religious and secular justice activists.

Contrasting Borderlands and Peace Activism

As we begin an examination of peace activism, the distinctions between activism that occurs in borderlands social locations and that done by cosmopolitans will become more apparent. More than any borderlands issues examined thus far, peacemaking seeks to transform politics at the national level, since the responsibility for the U.S.'s foreign affairs is exclusively lodged within the federal government. Foreign policymaking is one of the least transparent policy arenas within the federal government, much of which is cloaked in secrecy and enshrouded in an aura of nationalism. This is especially true of the nation state's war-making capacity. Many veteran peacemakers are critical of what they perceive as the fundamentally aggressive nature of American empire. Consequently, their organizing and advocacy work is aimed at engendering a radical rethinking of its foreign policy.

A concern for peace is fundamental to a much broader spectrum of religious traditions, and thus religious peace-organizing encompasses a number of Jewish, Muslim, and Buddhist organizations as well as several newly established evangelical ones. The Jewish Peace Fellowship was established in 1941 as an affiliate of the Fellowship of Reconciliation. At present, there are several other prominent Jewish peace organizations, a Buddhist Peace Fellowship founded in 1978, and several Islamic peace organizations, including American Muslim Voice, which was set up in 2006. While a number of the congregational community-organizing networks count Muslim and Jewish institutions among their members (there is also an interreligious thrust within Interfaith Worker Justice and CLUE), these peace organizations are independent institutions that contextualize peacemaking within the ethnic and religious concerns of their own communities. Indeed, it has been incumbent on each of these organizations to undertake the interpretative theological work necessary for the unearthing of activist forms of peacemaking within their religious tradition. For example, the Buddhist Peace Fellowship is rooted in the emerging conception of engaged Buddhism, which rests on elements of the Theravada, Tibetan, Zen, and Pure Land Buddhist traditions.[9] In a similar vein, several specifically evangelical peace voices have also emerged in recent years. Recognizing that traditional mainline Protestant or Catholic approaches often do not resonate within their churches, they are also recontextualizing their arguments against the use of torture and for nuclear disarmament to better reach their audiences.

While we earlier highlighted the presence of cosmopolitans as staff within community, worker justice, and immigrant rights organizations, their organizing methodologies in each case were aimed at empowering people at the margins of society. In contrast, religious peace activism takes advantage of the privileged status of many of its supporters. It is disproportionately located among and aimed at educating and engaging white middle-class cosmopolitans. Many of them have either had life experiences that have made them critical of American foreign policy or they identify with one of the religious peacemaking traditions. The sociologist Christian Smith provides evidence of this proclivity in his 1996 study of the United States–Central American peace movement. Smith found that 98 percent of all sanctuary activists were white; 96 percent of all Witness for Peace delegates were as well. Similarly, 91 percent of the sanctuary activists were college graduates; the same was true of 90 percent of Witness for Peace delegates.[10] Furthermore, Smith discovered that these activists were heavily recruited from human-service occupations such as religious workers, social workers, clergy, health-care workers, and teachers rather than more typically working-class occupations.[11] Opposition to the U.S.-sponsored counterinsurgency in Central America during the 1980s proved to be catalytic for many of the sanctuary and Witness for Peace activists, setting them upon long-term activist trajectories extending well past the original causes in which they became engaged.

Similarly, Peace Action, which was created out of a merger of the two most significant American antinuclear weapons organizations, SANE and the Nuclear Freeze campaign, has identified its average supporters as relatively well-educated, white women between the ages of thirty and sixty-five. For many, their involvement in Peace Action is rooted in the recognition that peace, war, and militarism are integrally connected to the possibilities of justice in other arenas such as labor rights or community and environment well-being.[12] The cosmopolitanism of their members shapes the character of work done by these organizations. A number of the older organizations are now facing a demographic challenge as their loyal longtime members are aging, while younger activists appear to be drawn to emerging causes that embody a stronger humanitarian dimension.

A further distinction between peacemaking activism and the earlier borderlands case studies is the remarkable extent to which Christian theologians and other seminary faculty are not only active in peacemaking but play high-profile roles in developing its theological foundations, as well as in establishing a number of existing organizations and initiatives. There are now several nationally recognized centers for religious peace studies, including the Kroc Institute for International Peace Building at the University of Notre Dame and Eastern Mennonite University's Center for Justice and Peacebuilding. Notre Dame offers both master's and doctorate degrees in peacemaking, and Eastern Mennonite offers a master's degree and a series of certificate programs to students from around the world. Responding to the destruction and loss of life caused by regional wars in Central America, Rwanda, Liberia, Zaire, the Sudan, Burma, Cambodia, Bosnia, Afghanistan, and Iraq, a group of Christian ethicists, theologians, international relations scholars, peace activists, and conflict-resolutions activists worked together for five years to identify a set of ten proven "just peacemaking" practices. Designed to exist alongside pacifism and just-war theories, these practices are intended to act as empirical guides in actual conflict situations. Glen Stassen, one of the project's initiators, asserts that these practices are indeed spreading peace. "They are engendering positive feedback loops, so they are growing in strength. They are pushing back the frontiers of war and spreading zones of peace."[13] More recently, the scholarly discussion of just peacemaking has been enlarged under the auspices of the United States Institute of Peace to include Jewish and Muslim scholars in an exploration of the "Abrahamic Alternatives to War."[14]

Contemporary peacemaking also rests on a far more extensive historical legacy of activism than is true of much of the borderlands work. Various strands of radical pietism had already been transplanted to North America during the colonial period with the arrival of Quakers, Mennonites, and a number of German peace sects such as the Dunkers and the Amish. While William Penn, a Quaker convert, established the state of Pennsylvania as a model Christian community, the German sects chose to withdraw into introverted rural communities. The first religiously grounded peace society in the United States was founded in 1815 by David Low Dodge, a wealthy Connecticut merchant who had concluded that "all kinds of carnal warfare were unlawful for the follower of Christ."[15] This group and a second one, formed shortly thereafter in Massachusetts, were dominated by businessmen, educators, and clergy, and embodied the spirit of New England humanitarian uplift.[16] Toward the end of the nineteenth century, the earlier pacifist demands for an end to war were increasingly superseded by more pragmatic proposals aimed at stemming the rising tide of European militarism even as the U.S. embarked on its imperial conquest of Cuba and the Philippines.[17]

The Fellowship of Reconciliation (FOR), the oldest of the contemporary peace organizations, was founded in December 1914 in Cambridge, England. A year later, a FOR group was formed in the United States. Dissatisfied with the pro-war stance taken by the mainline Protestant churches immediately preceding the outbreak of World War I, FOR was dedicated to absolute pacifism.[18] The organization was "'religious and liberal in the sense of being ecumenical, theologically modern, and socially concerned. Well over half of its members were ministers.'"[19] In the spirit of the Social Gospel movement, FOR held firmly to the ethic of love, calling for the nonviolent regeneration of society, which it believed was the ultimate goal of religion and religious people.[20] The Quakers founded the American Friends Service Committee (AFSC) in 1917 to provide young Quakers and other conscientious objectors an opportunity to serve those in need during World War I. In subsequent decades the organization expanded its humanitarian mission and increasingly focused on relieving the tensions that led to armed conflict. It has remained a mainstay of campaigns to oppose war and promote disarmament ever since. The War Resisters League, which also remains active today, was formed in 1924 as the U.S. branch of the War Resisters' International. It initially served as a registry for those who refused to participate in war, later evolving into an activist organization for nonviolent resistance.[21]

During the 1930s and 1940s, pacifist fellowships were formed within the major Protestant denominations, including the Methodists, Baptists, Episcopalians, Lutherans, Disciples of Christ, Unitarians, and Universalists. These fellowships remained quite small and were dominated by clergy rather than laity, yet they reached into denominations that had previously produced few pacifists.[22] Peacemaking expanded to American Catholics through the work of Dorothy Day and the Catholic Worker movement, which adhered to a Catholic form of pacifism beginning with the Spanish Civil War in 1936, when Day made pacifism one of the core beliefs of the Catholic Worker movement. As a result, she lost some of her supporters during World War II, but by the 1950s the Catholic Workers broadened their peace witness. During that decade, Robert Ludlow, a former conscientious objector and for a time the associate editor of the *Catholic Worker,* introduced Gandhian nonviolence to its readers "as a potential substitute for war and as 'a new Christian way of social change.'"[23] Sojourners has represented a progressive evangelical presence within the peace movement ever since its founding in 1971 among a group of students attending Trinity Evangelical Divinity School who began asking themselves why evangelicals were not saying more against the Vietnam War. Sojourners was later instrumental in launching several other well-known peace organizations, including the Nuclear Freeze campaign and Witness for Peace.[24]

The Fellowship of Reconciliation

The Fellowship of Reconciliation has played a catalytic role even though its actual membership remains quite small. The organization frequently criticized liberal Protestantism for its complacency, its socio-economic and racial exclusiveness, and its often uncritical embrace of secular values.[25] Yet, some of the twentieth century's most innovative liberal Protestant thinkers on peace and social justice have been associated with FOR, including A. J. Muste, John Nevin Sayre, Reinhold Niebuhr, Henry Sloane Coffin, Richard Gregg, Bayard Rustin, and Glenn Smiley. The organization was one of the main conduits through which Gandhian forms of nonviolent resistance entered the United States. In fact, several of the FOR's white and African American staff founded the Congress of Racial Equality (CORE), which pioneered the use of nonviolent resistance against institutionalized racial segregation. The organization has stood in the forefront of ecumenical and interreligious peace work, by first supporting the creation of the Jewish Peace Fellowship, followed by the Catholic Peace Fellowship in 1964 and later separate Buddhist and Muslim Peace Fellowships.[26] Finally, FOR pioneered the fusion of Christian narratives of suffering and redemption with mass media spectacles designed to excite "the sympathy of disinterested onlookers," which are now so effectively used in American peace and justice movements.[27]

Unlike the older Christian pacifist churches whose absolute commitments to peace led them to shun all forms of political engagement, choosing purity through disengagement from worldly affairs, FOR has consistently carried its pacifism into the political arena. It has long linked the violence inherent in war to that embedded in domestic forms of injustice. In the aftermath of World War I, FOR members recognized that there was a relationship between the nation's participation in war and an increase in violence and persecution against those at the margins at home. World War I had unleashed the official persecution of labor radicals and Communists along with increased violence against immigrants, the labor movement, and African Americans.[28] Some FOR members, including the pacifist leader A. J. Muste, sought to link pacifism to the emerging labor movement and the struggle for African American rights. Beginning in the 1920s FOR's condemnation of lynching, the resurgent Ku Klux Klan, and racial segregation led Howard Thurman, the pathbreaking African American pastor and educator, to join the organization even though he "had no particular interest in the peace movement per se." Already in the 1920s, as a result of their many personal ties to transnational Protestant missionary networks, some Christian pacifists had begun questioning their own Eurocentrism. Instead, they adopted increasingly global views, which led them to condemn the violence inherent in Western imperialism.[29] In 1927 FOR officially denounced the U.S. occupation of Nicaragua, sending out letters to thousands of ministers asking them to oppose military intervention in that country. The repercussions of this occupation would resurface in 1980s as the U.S. peace movement finally sought to bring an end to American support for right-wing dictatorships in Central America.

The Fellowship of Reconciliation had a strong interest in Gandhi, which was also decisive in nurturing an interreligious spirit within the organization. According to Mark Johnson, FOR's current executive director, "We try to have an intereligious component to everything we do."[30] Since its beginnings as a Protestant organization, its identity has broadened to include Catholic members as well as fifteen or sixteen affiliated peace fellowships, including a number of Jewish, Buddhist, and Muslim organizations. At present, FOR is in conversation about opening itself up to atheists and humanists as well.[31]

Much of FOR's current work is collaborative, often in conjunction with other organizations that do not necessarily fully share its commitment to nonviolence. As is the case with a number of the older organizations featured in this chapter, FOR's membership is aging and rather constant, which places a constraint on the scope of its work. At present, it is working to ensure the continuity of its principal publication, the *Fellowship* magazine. In an effort to reach a younger audience, FOR also sponsors a Peacemaker's Training Institute aimed at youth and young adults who are interested in peace and justice activism.

A great deal of what FOR does can be understood as efforts to affirm the humanity of the *other* who is a foreigner, by giving voice to their realities, which would otherwise remain hidden from American audiences. Since 2004, FOR has maintained a presence in Colombia in support of the agrarian pacifist community of San José de Apartadó. This community declared itself a peace community in 1997, asserting its neutrality in the midst of escalating violence between the FARC guerillas, the paramilitaries, and Colombian military. Since its founding, the community has suffered over 160 deaths, including the 2005 massacre of the community's founder and seven others, allegedly by army soldiers.[32] The organization understands its presence among the people of San José de Apartadó as an act of solidarity. It is a form of *acompañamiento*, which also inspires the work of U.S. religious immigrant rights activists, including involvement at the Arizona border and aspects of the New Sanctuary Movement. In addition, FOR has recruited volunteers who commit to accompanying agrarian leaders connected to three indigenous organizations in Colombia. The volunteers agree to work on site for at least a year. Prior to going, each receives extensive training, which also serves as a time of mutual discernment, making certain that the volunteer is fully prepared for the experience. Volunteers are expected to speak and write about what they witnessed upon their return to the United States.[33]

Sarah Weintraub, a second-generation American Buddhist who recently became the executive director of the Buddhist Peace Fellowship (BPF), spent five years working as a FOR volunteer in Colombia. Having attended a college where she learned about the strategy of *acompañamiento*, she was drawn to FOR's Colombia work "as a way to use my privilege as a white middle-class American." Sarah cites anecdotal evidence that *acompañamiento* does have an impact in protecting these peace villages. "Soldiers have been heard saying, 'we have to watch out because the foreigners are here.'"[34] As *acompañamiento* is one of San José de Apartadó's main strategies for survival, Sarah states that "so many other communities in Colombia would also like to have it, but there are not enough people to do it."[35] In response to the 2005 massacre, a high-level delegation, including a congressional representative, was brought to visit the community. The U.S. Congress withheld a portion of Colombia's military aid allocation, which is contingent on the country meeting certain human rights targets. There were also vigils and increased accompaniment in the community. An initial trial of some of the perpetrators of the massacre began in Colombia in 2009. This alone was remarkable, but even more so was the fact that the trial included some who were higher up in the chain of command. Without the international attention brought to the killings, it is unlikely that this would have occurred.[36]

Since 2005, FOR has taken eight delegations to Iran as part of what the organization calls civilian diplomacy or friendship trips. This is an extension of its long history of sponsoring civilian delegations to countries that are in the midst of conflict, often with the United States, including the USSR during the Cold War, Vietnam during the 1960s, Central America in the 1980s, and Palestine/Israel and Colombia in recent years. The delegations enable American peace activists to witness conditions in these countries firsthand and then write and talk about what they experienced upon their return. The trips create opportunities for bonds to be established between civil society activists in both countries despite the presence of conflict between their governments. In a country such as Iran, delegations are also exposed to the country's rich history, art, religious, and cultural traditions. For Americans, such trips provide alternate sources of information about the realities in countries that are often misrepresented by the American press and national politicians. According to the FOR's Web page, the trips to Iran offer "all of us an opportunity to come up with ways to de-escalate larger-scale tensions. Participants reach out to fellow human beings from the 'other side' and find techniques to build trust between their two nations."[37]

In mid-December 2009, an interfaith American delegation of forty people traveled to the Middle East. The group had intended to join an international group of peace activists who were assembling in Cairo with the intention of crossing into Gaza to participate in a Gaza Freedom March. Code Pink, a leading women's peace organization, had issued the call for the march to mark the first anniversary of the Israeli massacre of 1,400 Palestinians in

Gaza in December 2008.[38] The 1,362 marchers from forty-two countries who had assembled in Cairo were prevented from entering Gaza by the Egyptian police. In response, they began staging daily rallies in various parts of Cairo. A few hundred French delegates held a "vigil" outside of the French embassy for five days demanding that their government work to open the Raffah Gate into Gaza. In Gaza, another one hundred delegates were able to join a Palestinian community of five hundred people and together walk to the Erez crossing as was originally planned. The larger Cairo-based delegation staged actions in front of the United Nations Development offices, which have responsibility for Gaza, as well as at the American and Israeli embassies (spearheaded by dozens of Jewish delegates from around the world) and, for six hours on New Year's Eve, on a sidewalk opposite the Egyptian Museum in downtown Cairo. After a number of brutal encounters with the Egyptian police, Mark Johnson, the co-leader of the American delegation, wrote in his blog that "the Egyptians were beginning to appreciate active nonviolence and passive resistance," finally allowing "the New Year's Eve vigil to proceed in peace, despite Egyptian law prohibiting the gathering of more than five people in a public space."[39] While the delegation was unable to enter Gaza, its use of peaceful protest in Cairo brought considerable international press attention not only to the captivity of Gaza's residents due to Israel's blockade in response to terrorist attacks, but also to the complicity of the Egyptian government. The attacks on peaceful protesters in Cairo gave the global peace community new images of the Egyptian government's willingness to use violence to repress all dissent. The participation in this event by FOR was in keeping with its long-held belief that nonviolent resistance will have a psychological impact on opponents as well as bystanders, opening them up to the truth of the nonviolent resisters' cause.

Disarmament

Calls for disarmament had long been a component of the pacifist political agenda, yet the accelerating nuclear weapons build -up by the United States and the Soviet Union in the late 1970s catalyzed a massive antinuclear weapons movement in the States. It was triggered by the Soviet Union's deployment of new intermediate-range nuclear missiles in Eastern Europe and the corresponding deployment by the United States of cruise and Pershing missiles in Western Europe. The Soviet invasion of Afghanistan added to increasing tensions between the two superpowers, which ultimately contributed to the election of Ronald Reagan as president in 1980. The peace activist and scholar David Cortright asserts that by the early 1980s, nuclear fears had reached unprecedented levels. In September 1981, the Gallup Poll announced that 70 percent of those surveyed felt that nuclear war was a real possibility. There was now widespread doubt about the possibilities of humankind surviving a nuclear war.[40] In addition, there was growing frustration with what appeared to be counterproductive arms-control agreements, which in fact allowed for a continued escalation on both sides. These circumstances gave rise to calls for a halt to the arms race, which became the basis of the Nuclear Freeze campaign. According to Cortright, a leading activist in that campaign, the enormous popularity of nuclear disarmament in the 1980s transformed the politics of the nuclear debate. What had been an obscure and highly technical field reserved for experts now became the foundation of a popular citizens' campaign. Furthermore, the call on both the Soviet Union and the United States to disarm dispelled any earlier doubts about whether the peace movement was sympathetic to Communism and therefore unpatriotic.

The core constituencies of the 1980s Nuclear Freeze campaign were religious people, although nonreligious people were also involved.[41] The extensive involvement of the religious community gave the campaign greater credibility, helping it to generate the political pressure that ultimately led to changes in nuclear policy.[42] William Sloane Coffin, the senior minister at the prestigious Riverside Church in New York City, and Jim Wallis, who headed Sojourners, were instrumental in launching what became known as the Nuclear Freeze campaign.[43] As we have seen, opposition to the Vietnam War had contributed to the creation of Sojourners in the early 1970s, and it continued to be at the center of the organization's work in the early 1980s.[44] According to Wallis, "the Freeze idea started in our office with a lot of our language in the Freeze document."[45] Many other religious bodies and denominations took positions in opposition to nuclear weapons. One of the most significant was a statement by the U.S. Conference of Catholic Bishops titled *The Challenge of Peace: God's Promise and Our Response*, which denounced many of the foundations of U.S. nuclear policy. Some Protestant denominations went even farther in condemning the very existence of nuclear weapons. The United Methodist Church issued a particularly radical statement, which not only rejected the arms race and the entire concept of deterrence, but was also one of the first religious documents to critique the arms race as a massive squandering of wealth, which could be redirected toward stemming the growing impoverishment of the world's poorest people.[46]

The collapse of the Soviet Union and the fall of the Berlin Wall in 1989 left the United States as the singular hegemonic power, which necessitated a refocusing of the movement. The result was the eventual restructuring of SANE/Freeze, the organization that had led the 1980s Nuclear Freeze campaign (SANE had been formed in 1957 in opposition to nuclear weapons testing). As a result, the organization was renamed Peace Action, which is now the largest single peace organization in the United States. Peace Action has roughly one hundred thousand grassroots members.[47] While some of its older members were first recruited during the Vietnam War, people now in their mid-forties were mobilized by the 1980s Freeze campaign and have remained with the organization ever since. Peace Action's current executive director, Kevin Martin, who comes from a Mennonite family and is in his mid-forties, says, "For people my age, it was Reagan who scared the shit out of us."[48] Many others were activated out of their religious convictions even though Peace Action is formally secular. The organization's members tend to connect peacemaking to a wide range of local justice issues. As Martin explained, "For them, both parts of our name are important—they want to be active to counter so many forces in our society that are atomizing."[49]

Peace Action's overall mission is to create a safer world. Central to that goal is eliminating war as a resolution of conflict, eradicating nuclear weapons, and instead, building a national budget that reflects human needs.[50] These multiple priorities situate the organization within two distinct activist communities: the nuclear disarmament movement, and the antiwar movement. Since defense policy is highly expert and industry driven, it receives little public scrutiny. As a result, the public has largely ceded its role in nuclear policy decisions. Peace Action targets national policymakers, especially members of Congress, but recognizing the need for a grassroots base of supporters, it has intentionally cultivated networks of local supporters. This is done with a very small national staff. The majority of its work takes place through its roughly eighty to ninety chapters, some of which are set up on a regional basis, others as state, city, or congressional district chapters. These chapters have a great deal of autonomy in how they choose to carry out their activism. For example, Peace Action West, which is one of the largest regional chapters covering the western states, is almost exclusively focused on legislative lobbying work.[51]

According to Kevin Martin, "We're pretty ecumenical in who we work with and which tactics we use."[52] This means that Peace Action is comfortable doing both lobbying work on Capitol Hill as well as getting involved in protest demonstrations that include acts of civil disobedience. While members generally embrace nonviolence as a guiding vision of life, Martin believes that there is gradual growth in embracing it as an operational model. He recognizes that being able to afford getting arrested is itself somewhat of a privilege—you have to be able to take the time off from work, or you have to be a citizen. Furthermore, many people of color are reluctant to place themselves in the hands of the police.[53] Much of the organization's efforts are directed at influencing members of Congress, not only to get their votes but also to get individual members to speak out on these issues. Yet, the politics of building support against war are difficult even when the Democrats have majorities in both the House and the Senate. There are only a few strong allies, with many Democratic senators reluctant to appear weak on militarism. It is the local affiliates that have often built long-standing relationships with key members of Congress; for example, the Peace Action affiliate in Massachusetts can talk to Senator John Kerry. Similarly, members of Peace Action West have targeted Congressman Howard Berman, who represents California's 29th congressional district and is the chair of the House Foreign Affairs Committee.[54] Beyond interacting with members of Congress, Peace Action also does national education and mobilizing campaigns, which include such disparate tactics as door to door canvassing, public speaking engagements, book tours, and even house parties.

Peace Action and others active in the antinuclear weapons movement faced one of the most significant windows of opportunity in their long-standing campaign for a nuclear free world during the fall of 2010. Upon entering the White House, President Obama made the elimination of nuclear weapons one of his key foreign policy goals, a commitment cited by the Nobel Committee in awarding him the 2009 Peace Prize. At the first meeting between President Obama and Russian President Medvedev in April 2009, both declared their commitment to "achieving a nuclear free world." Since then, their negotiating teams have achieved important progress in that direction. Since the United States and Russia possess 95 percent of the world's nuclear weapons, having these two countries reduce their nuclear stockpile would send a message to other countries and help close the U.S.' credibility gap.[55] Once the two countries complete their negotiations, the treaty must be ratified by a two-thirds vote of the U.S. Senate. Peace Action was also active in renewed efforts to pass the Comprehensive Test Ban Treaty, which President Clinton signed in 1996 but which the Senate failed to ratify in 1999. Even though the United States has had a moratorium on testing since 1992, Obama committed to again seek Senate ratification. Peace Action's chapters have been very active in mobilizing community leaders around the country, encouraging them to contact their senators. Peace Action West had earlier done an extensive email campaign asking their supporters to sign a petition to Obama asking him to take specific steps to implement the vision he laid out for a nuclear-free world. They eventually collected seventy thousand signatures.[56]

Peace Action's emphasis on email and Web-based networking is a common style of organizing among cosmopolitans, who are more likely to be computer savvy and email proficient. It is also seeking to attract younger adults and has recently established a presence on various social networking sites such as Facebook or Twitter. Both FOR and Peace Action have blogs connected to their Web sites, but they do not always have up-to-date entries. "Younger activists have skills in media technology, but won't pick up the phone—they think sending emails is organizing," says Martin.[57] Yet, the organization also finds itself adjusting to their aging, longtime members' life situations. These older members continue to prefer receiving information through the mail and are not accustomed to making donations online. In the midst of a generational transition, the organization is wrestling with how to remain participatory through email instead of through annual chapter meetings. The organization's issue priorities are now set two years at a time rather than every year to reduce the frequency of physical gatherings of the membership.

The current campaign to abolish nuclear weapons has broad religious support, both in the United States and internationally. Pax Christi International is among the organizations best positioned to work on this issue on both fronts. This sixty-five-year-old Catholic peace organization, which currently exists in sixty countries around the world, has also mobilized its global network to work for nuclear disarmament. The U.S. branch of Pax Christi is collaborating closely with several European Pax Christi sections to move the antinuclear campaign forward. According to Marie Dennis, president of Pax Christi International, "The Europeans are actively working to get American nukes out of their countries, the United States is working on the Obama administration, and all of us go to the United Nations to work together. We are trying to respond in as agile a way as possible by using our international components."[58]

In the past three years the Two Futures Project, an evangelical organization singularly focused on nuclear disarmament, has also emerged. This organization was created out of the recognition that the approach to nuclear disarmament developed by the 1980s Freeze campaign did not appeal to evangelicals. Instead, according to its founder, Tyler Wigg-Stevenson, the Two Futures Project has sought to reframe the issue of nuclear disarmament for a post Cold War, post 9/11 context, making the argument that maintaining the nuclear status quo at present will lead to a crisis. "Lots of people who supported a robust nuclear deterrence in the Cold War can support us now, because a prudential analysis shows that the odds of a nuclear disaster have increased." Also recognizing that the vast majority of nuclear weapons are in the hands of the United States and Russia, the Two Futures Project believes that the United States must take the lead, but it cannot do it alone. Wigg-Stevenson stated that "the nuclearization of Iran is flatly unacceptable, but they have little incentive to de-escalate if nuclear weapons remain the world's final arbitrator."[59] He sees Two Futures as a confessional movement led by young evangelicals. He has found the strongest support for his arguments among those born after 1968, who started college at the end of the Cold War.

To get the organization off the ground, Wigg-Stevenson first sought support from a broad spectrum of older validators within evangelical circles who would give the project legitimacy. These included Tony Campolo, Ron Sider, and Jim Wallis, all well-known progressive evangelical voices, as well as Chuck Colson, Leith Anderson, president of the National Association of Evangelicals, and Rob Bell, the founding pastor of Mars Hill Bible Church.[60] Wigg-Stevenson then chose to go public at the 2009 Q conference, an event that draws pastors and graphic designers who are interested in "the cutting edge of what Christians are thinking about."[61] The annual event attracts the same target demographic of younger evangelicals that the Two Futures Project is also seeking to reach. Wigg-Stevenson is now focused on educating evangelicals on the issues by following up on speaking engagements that he received as a result of his appearance at the event. The project is also seeking evangelical support for ratification of both the START and the test-ban treaties.[62]

Solidarity Work

Witness for Peace emerged out of religious activists' efforts to raise American awareness concerning the activities of the U.S.–financed Contras during the Reagan administration. In 1983, Gail Phares, a former Maryknoll nun who had returned to the United States after spending a decade working among the poor in Nicaragua, organized the first group of church people to witness what the Contras were doing in that country. The initial group of thirty consisted of middle-aged, middle-class, religious leaders, pastors, college teachers, housewives, and retirees.[63] Following their return, they organized a much larger intereligious delegation of 153 people from forty states. This group was so deeply moved by the stories they heard from survivors of Contra massacres that they organized a permanent vigil in Nicaragua. What came to be called Witness for Peace received both organizational and financial support from a host of existing religious denominations and organizations, including Clergy and Laity Concerned, the American Friends Service Committee, the Fellowship of Reconciliation, the InterReligious Task Force, the Quakers, the Presbyterian Church USA, the United Methodists, the *Catholic Worker* and *Sojourners* magazines, Washington DC's Religious Task Force on Central America, and many others.[64]

Witness for Peace became the vehicle through which a host of religious organizations channeled their supporters into the Central American peace movement. According to one WFP estimate, by 1990, the organization had sent five thousand delegations to Nicaragua.[65] Throughout its twenty-five-year existence, WFP has sent "more than thirteen thousand U.S. citizens on transformational travel delegations to Latin America, infusing the global justice movement with the critical analysis, grassroots activism, and the passionate energy of our returning delegates."[66] Central to WFP's self-identity is its commitment to using the privileges of U.S. citizenship to "claim the moral right and responsibility to challenge U.S. foreign policy."[67] Largely made up of middle-class whites, its members make use of their social locations to gain access to political leaders, while claiming the authority to challenge U.S. government policies toward Central America.

In the 1980s, delegations were sent to Nicaragua as a form of nonviolent action so they could witness U.S.–sponsored violence firsthand in that country. Upon their return, they were asked to speak about their experiences as a means of mobilizing a still wider movement calling for a halt to U.S. intervention in Central America. Witness for Peace worked closely with a number of Nicaraguan organizations and has maintained a consistent commitment to taking its direction from its Central American partners. In addition to short-term delegations, the organization also recruited long-term volunteers to provide accompaniment to Nicaraguan local activists who were in danger of being kidnapped or killed.

Just as was the case with the sanctuary movement, WFP is also grounded in the decades-long presence of both Catholic and Protestant missionaries in Central America. Much of the Catholic presence dates back to the 1960s, when Pope John XXIII called for religious people to go to Latin America. Those priests and nuns who responded lived among the countries' poor, with little interaction with the elite.[68] As a result, they developed cosmopolitan worldviews characterized by strong personal affinities to the suffering of the poor with whom they had built close associations. Gail Phares, recounts her personal transformation, "I am who I am from living in Central America. I came from a Republican family; my whole intellectual formation came from living in the United States. Yet, I know people who were killed in Central America. If you believe in God then we are all brothers and sisters. We're called to build the kingdom of God on earth, which means building peace and justice."[69] These sorts of profoundly transformative experiences under-girded WFP's 1980s work and remain the foundation for contemporary religious solidarity work.

Ultimately, the Central American peace movement could not pressure the Reagan administration to terminate its support of the counterinsurgency in Central America. Yet, it did force the administration to expend considerable political capital in defending its policies, making them much more difficult to implement, and thus limiting the severity of the destruction. The 1980s movement also nurtured numerous new activists as well as new methodologies that continue to be used today.

Although it has historically been focused on nuclear weapons and disarmament, Pax Christi USA, an affiliate of Pax Christi International, also began making deeper linkages between those issues and the growing violence in Latin America in the late 1980s, just prior to the five-hundredth anniversary of Columbus's arrival in the Americas. Judy Coode, Pax Christi USA's former board president, remembers that Pax Christi's members came to realize that the Spanish conquest had resulted in much violence in the Americas. This realization opened up the linkages between the organization's focus on weapons and nuclear disarmament and engagement in Latin America. As an organization it too began sponsoring delegations to give "voice to those who are experiencing oppression since it is most appropriate for those experiencing the events to tell the story."[70]

Both Gail Phares and Judy Coode are articulating forms of liberative praxis that are very similar to those used within congregation-based community organizing and worker-justice organizing. In both cases, the organizations understand storytelling by those who are marginalized as transformative experiences for privileged North Americans. Effectively, both sets of organizations are seeking to nurture cosmopolitan worldviews among their American audiences. Participants in the delegations to Latin America are themselves transformed into storytellers. Rose Berger, an associate editor at *Sojourners,* has used the magazine as a forum for telling the story of her experiences as a member of a 2001 WFP delegation to Colombia. Rose comes from a progressive Catholic family in Sacramento, California. Her parents were supporters of the Catholic Worker movement and Rose, as a three-year-old, joined her family on César Chávez's pilgrimage to Sacramento. Rose's decision to go to Colombia grew out of her vocation as a writer, which is "the peculiar vocation of a person who is the bearer of stories. I am challenged by how to allow people to tell their stories in ways that it becomes a healing process. And then to carry their story with me and retell it respectfully."[71]

As is the case with WFP, sending delegations to conflict regions—in recent years they have gone to Iraq and Pakistan—gives Pax Christi USA a sense of these same contexts, thereby "providing authenticity to what we are trying to do in our advocacy work."[72] The Maryknoll Office of Global Concerns, for which Judy Coode now works, focuses on U.S. policy toward those countries where the Maryknolls are working. They then collaborate with the mainline Protestant advocacy offices to form a cohesive common message to Congress. "We always try to make the connections to poverty in a given nation and the fear of its falling into violence. The danger facing most nations is that they choose to build weapons rather than respond to human needs. We emphasize a reliance on providing health care, food, and shelter as a sustainable pathway to peace."[73]

The Christian Peacemaker Teams are yet another very important example of religious solidarity work. It too was founded in the 1980s as people within the "peace church" tradition sought new ways of addressing the issues of social violence. It gained further impetus following a speech given by the Brethren theologian Ron Sider at the 1984 Mennonite World Conference. Sider challenged those from the peace tradition to risk their lives in the same way as those who go into the military are willing to risk theirs.[74] After a formal study process within the Mennonite Church, CPT was founded in 1986 to act "as a witness to Jesus Christ by identifying with suffering people, reducing violence, mediating conflicts, and fostering justice through peaceful, caring, direct challenge of evil."[75] These peacemaker teams accomplish these goals through the accompaniment of those threatened by violence, the monitoring of events in tense settings, and by providing a "ministry of presence" through living in the midst of conflict. Sometimes, they literally "get in the way" of violence by standing between violent aggressors and unarmed groups or individuals. The teams also advocate for those who have little voice in a given conflict, both by talking to police and the government in the countries where they live and by relaying their stories back to communities and officials in the United States. Finally, they are able to impact the church by raising the call to peacemaking to a greater level of consciousness. Thus, Getting in the Way became CPT's motto.[76]

Today, CPT works with an indigenous partner that is also committed to nonviolence in each of the places to which it sends a team. The Colombian

Mennonite Church knew of CPT and asked for a partnership. In addition to their work in Colombia, CPT currently has ongoing projects in Iraq, among Aboriginal people in Ontario, Canada, and in the African Great Lakes region that includes the Congo, Rwanda, and Uganda. They also have teams in the Palestinian city of Hebron/al-Khalil and the village of at-Tuwani, and they are loaning people to work with NMD at the U.S.–Mexico border. In 2008 they had a team along the Arizona border reporting on immigration issues, after which they did advocacy work in Washington DC. According to Carol Rose, CPT's co-director, "it was fascinating to be at the U.S.–Mexico border with someone who had been in Palestine and could compare the two walls."[77]

The organization sends out very regular email bulletins to its supporters with first-person accounts from their teams on the ground in these various locations. The emails are narratives of events that transpire between, for example, Palestinian villagers and Israeli settlers and the military. They give the readers a real feel for the grinding low-intensity confrontations that take place daily between Palestinians and Israeli settlers on the West Bank. Occasionally, there is also video footage posted on their Web site, which gives viewers an intimate look at events as they are unfolding half a world away.

In each of these places, CPT sees its mission to act as witnesses, hoping that their presence will deter violence, although that is not always the case. In 2006 four Christian Peacemakers were kidnapped in Iraq during some of the worst sectarian fighting. The kidnappings elicited a global outpouring of prayers and support, including from Muslims in the Middle East, Europe, and North America. Nonetheless, after three months, the body of one of the team members, Tom Fox, was found on the road to the Baghdad airport.[78] A month later, the three remaining men were rescued by a military team that respected CPT's commitment to nonviolence by not firing a single shot or injuring any of the parties involved.[79] More recently, two CPT members, along with a Palestinian shepherd and his family, were accosted by Israeli settlers. After the shepherd took off, the two CPT members were beaten, proving once again that the CPT presence is a deterrent to violence but not a guarantee against it.[80]

Anyone who becomes a member of a long-term team must first participate in a one-week or two-week-long delegation where they spend a great deal of time listening to local people who have varying perspectives on the conflict. For example, in Palestine, the delegation would listen to Israeli settlers, the Palestinian Authority, village and city people. They spend time with a Palestinian family, participate in nonviolent action, and spend a couple days dipping into the work.[81] According to Carol Rose, "Lots of the time people come to the delegation with the attitude, 'I just want to help.' We've all made deals with the system. These partnerships and relationships are where those deals become clear. People say, 'I need to stop collaborating with the system. The delegations are a great school of conversion.'"[82] Those who decide to join a longer-term team must still go through another month-long intensive training where they study biblical nonviolence and do further self-reflection about their own identities. Christian Peacemakers are currently in the midst of further indigenizing their work by recruiting local people to join teams from within some of the countries in which they are currently working.

There are clear connections between the work of presence outside the United States done by CPT and others, and the work being done by religious justice organizations within the U.S. borderlands. The theological understanding of CPTs work is similarly rooted in truth-telling and giving voice to those whose cries are not being heard. The presence of a team in the midst of conflict is first an act of documentation, followed by the act of truth-telling. Those Americans who join a Christian Peacemaker Team are asked to come to terms with the complicity of their own government within the conflicts they are witnessing. This can be difficult to discern in places such as the Middle East where militant Palestinian organizations remain committed to the destruction of Israel and to supporting continuing terrorist attacks, and where the U.S. government has at times given uncritical support to Israel, despite its continued construction of settlements on the West Bank and in East Jerusalem. Carol Rose explains, "My government is part of what makes the occupation possible. I am connected to it and I can be connected to undoing it. I can be in right relationship and not be a puppet in the region, by not making it possible for Israel to hurt Palestinians. The Palestinians are not heard, they're invisible. We are the megaphone."[83]

Anti-Torture

Not only did the impending U.S. invasion of Iraq in 2003 give rise to a massive global antiwar movement, but the subsequent shocking abuses of Iraqi prisoners led to new campaigns against torture. The most significant religious anti-torture organization is the National Religious Campaign Against Torture (NRCAT), with a staff of fifteen and an annual budget of $850,000.[84] This group was launched at a conference on human rights and religious commitment held at Princeton Theological Seminary in January 2006. Dr. George Hunsinger, a professor of theology at the seminary, began mobilizing religious people against torture shortly after the revelations of systematic torture at the Abu Ghraib prison first emerged. Since its founding, NRCAT's work has been centered on efforts to encourage religious people to sign their online "Statement of Conscience" condemning the use of torture. According to NRCAT's Web page, fifty-two thousand people have done so thus far.[85] The organization functions as a broad coalition consisting of more than 270 religious organizations including evangelicals, Catholics, Orthodox Christians, mainline Protestants, Muslims, Jews, Sikhs, Hindus, Bahá'ís, and Buddhists. Some of its members are national denominational and faith group bodies; others are regional entities such as state ecumenical councils, as well as congregations and other local religious organizations.[86]

The organization also does extensive grassroots work with as many as thirty recruiters from various partner state-level organizations reaching out to local congregations and places of worship. This grassroots work undergirds a strong congressional lobbying presence, and NRCAT currently employs two lobbyists working on Capitol Hill.[87] According to Bill Mefford, the General Board of Church and Society staff person who oversees the United Methodists' involvement with NRCAT, this group is the lead religious organization in the legislative fight against torture. Says Mefford, "I lean on NRCAT, when I go to the Hill with them, they take the lead; I show up and they tell me what to do."[88] As is true of other peacemaking organizations, accomplishing its goal of ending torture requires that it secure changes in national policy. To that end, NRCAT asked each of the 2008 presidential candidates to make a pledge that they would ban torture. Having agreed to do so as a candidate, President Obama signed an Executive Order on January 22, 2009, halting all use of torture; just one day after taking office. Now NRCAT is pushing for the establishment of a commission of inquiry to fully examine the Bush administration's use of torture and interrogation. They are also working to codify Obama's Executive Order into legislation, which would prohibit any future use of torture.

In 2006 Richard Killmer, NRCAT's executive director, approached a small group of evangelical peace activists, including Ron Sider, Glen Stassen, and Richard Cizik (then the policy director of the National Association of Evangelicals [NAE]), about the need for an evangelical partner. They in turn founded Evangelicals for Human Rights (EHR) in the summer of 2006. The new organization issued a public statement signed by a still larger group of evangelicals who were opposed to torture. The statement includes an extensive analysis of the biblical and theological grounding for a Christian stance against torture rooted in the dignity of all human life.[89] Following the issuance of the statement, the group worked to mobilize individual evangelicals to publicly oppose the use of torture. According to David Gushee, Distinguished University Professor of Christian Ethics at Mercer University, one of EHR's founders and its current executive director, the declaration "sought to witness that this group of evangelicals were not OK with what the Bush administration was doing." While they were able to get some prominent, more progressive evangelicals such as Rick Warren, the pastor of Saddleback Church in California and author of the best-selling book *The Purpose Driven Life*, to sign the statement, the Christian Right flatly rejected participation. Reflecting back on the effort, Gushee has come to recognize that "the white evangelical community is susceptible to seduction on partisan grounds, especially when it comes from the Republicans. Our theology of the state is dominated by a kind of authoritarian interpretation based on Romans 13 and refracted through Luther. As a result, evangelicals have very little respect for international law and don't see the need to be governed by the same rules as other people because we are a good people."[90] Gushee's sense of discouragement stemmed from the fact that after three years of EHR's advocacy work, white evangelicals were found to have the worst record on torture of any religious grouping in the United States. The results of an opinion poll conducted by the Pew Charitable Trust found that 62 percent of white evangelicals were willing to support torture under some circumstances.[91]

The abuses of detainees at Abu Ghraib, Guantánamo, and secret detention centers are also one of the foci of Rabbis for Human Rights-North America (RHR-NA), which was officially formed in 2001 "to support for the mission and work of RHR in Israel, and to conduct education and advocacy on human rights issues in North America."[92]

Interreligious Peacemaking

There is now a significant presence of Jewish, Muslim, and Buddhist peace organizations in the United States. These organizations have been founded over the last seventy years as their practitioners either settled or converted in the United States. Set against the backdrop of American Christian dominance, each of these religious traditions has undertaken the task of explicating peacemaking from within their own religious traditions. While this remains an ongoing process, there are also clear overlaps among the religious traditions, such as the affirmation of the dignity of all human life, common to all three Abrahamic faiths. Similarly, the Buddhist Peace Fellowship's understanding that at times systems can take on a life of their own is quite similar to the writings of William Stringfellow (see page 3) as well as the work of the Christian theologian Walter Wink.[93]

There are now a number of Jewish peace organizations who have a range of views on peacemaking as well as on the Israeli-Palestinian conflict. The Jewish Peace Fellowship is the oldest, having been founded several decades after the large influx of late nineteenth- and early twentieth-century Jewish immigrants. Initially set up to assist Jewish conscientious objectors just prior to U.S. entry into World War II, JPF sought to educate local draft boards—accustomed only to the Christian roots of conscientious objection—to the theological basis of a Jewish position on conscientious objection, grounded in the Torah, Talmud, and other sacred and religious texts.[94] The JPF has consistently staked out an absolute pacifist position within American Judaism. It supports a two-state solution and has worked with Israeli peace groups, yet their commitment to pacifism places them on the margins of the Jewish community. According to Rabbi Gerald Serotta, most Jews support some form of just-war theory, especially as it pertains to the integrity of the state of Israel, "We will fight tooth and nail against any potential Holocaust."[95]

Since peace activists are a minority view within American Judaism, the Jewish Peace Fellowship has worked to place their arguments for nonviolence within a Jewish historical context. Members of the organization have disseminated their views through several edited books, including *Roots of Jewish Nonviolence* (Allan Solomonow, ed., 1981), *The Challenge of Shalom* (Murray Polner and Naomi Goodman, 1994), and *Peace, Justice, and Jews: Reclaiming our Tradition* (Stephen Schwartzschild, 2007) in which various authors seek to develop a uniquely Jewish perspective on pacifism. For example, in unpacking the impact of the Holocaust on Jewish self-understanding, Evelyn Wilcock writes,

> Ever since biblical times, Jews have regarded defeat and natural disaster as God's punishment for their sins. It provided an explanation for suffering, and furnished hope that they could avert future catastrophe by mending their ways. We, too, want to feel we are in control and that it won't happen again. One is struck by the way the Holocaust literature—whether personal memoirs or academic analysis—is characterized by Jewish accusation and self-reproach.[96]

Wilcock asserts that too often Jewish self-reproach resulted in criticizing those who were killed for being too passive and not resisting Nazi genocide. She writes, "The view among many Israelis that Jews died without resistance during the Holocaust and that if we do something different next time around—fight, for instance—the outcome will be different, is widely prevalent." As a counternarrative, Jewish pacifists tell the stories of innumerable Jewish acts of nonviolent resistance against the Nazis as well as remarkable individual acts of heroism. Responding to the Jewish criticism that they have been repeatedly betrayed by Gentiles and by other Jews, JPF activists recount the stories of Jewish and non-Jewish groups who worked to rescue Jews in many parts of occupied Europe. Helen Fein links the argument that Jews can depend only on their own strength because of their past betrayal to justifications of "Zionist maximalism," which defines the troubles and isolation of Israel "as a continuation of historical Jewish isolation, a product of international anti-Semitism wearing new masks." Fein is critical of what she calls "messianic Zionism," arguing that their rhetoric can lead to Israel's isolation and risks estranging important constituencies and friendly states at a time when Israel needs allies.[97] She acknowledges the reality of Palestinian terrorism but places the emphasis on Zionist provocations and Israel's reluctance to prosecute violations of human rights in Israel.[98]

The Jewish Peace Fellowship's original membership consisted of a mixture of rabbis and rabbinical students from both Orthodox and Reform traditions. Murray Polner, a longtime member of JPF and former editor of the journal *Shalom*, joined the organization during the Vietnam War when JPF reached its peak strength. During those years, it spearheaded draft counseling for Jewish conscientious objectors.[99] Today, JPF opposes the use of capital punishment and has maintained a prison visitation service, especially for federal prisoners, Jewish and non-Jewish, who lack families. Like several other older peace organizations, JFP appears to be in a period of uncertainty. Unable to keep up with the costs of publishing hard copy versions of its monthly newsletter, it moved to an online format in early 2010. In its March 2010 edition, Stefan Merken, the organization's chair, appeals for donations so JPF can "continue to be a voice in the Jewish community and the peace communities."[100]

Several other activist Jewish peace organizations have emerged in more recent decades. In 1982 Rabbi Arthur Waskow, already a well-known figure within the Jewish renewal movement, founded the Shalom Center to articulate a Jewish perspective on the escalating nuclear arms race. Waskow believed that the nuclear arms race threatened a worldwide nuclear holocaust. He has consistently been a prophetic voice within American Judaism, always seeking to tie his views on various issues to a deeply held Jewish spirituality. During the late 1960s Waskow had been a leader of Jews for Urban Justice (JUJ), founded by young Jews who were active in various civil rights organizations, including CORE, the Student Nonviolent Coordinating Committee (SNCC), and Students for a Democratic Society (SDS). As a group they were critical of organized Judaism for its failure to be more active on matters of social injustice.[101] Waskow gained particular renown as the author of the Freedom Seder, which was initially held to mark the first anniversary of Martin Luther King Jr.'s assassination. According to Michael E. Staub, a professor of English at Baruch College, the Freedom Seder sought to renew the relevance of the traditional Passover message by consciously universalizing its twin themes of liberation from oppression and "'the issue of violence in the struggle for freedom' for the contemporary historical moment."[102] The act drew both immediate praise and condemnation from within various sectors of the Jewish establishment.

By the 1990s, Waskow shifted his focus onto the conflict between Israel and Palestine.[103] The Shalom Center was one of the earliest voices to oppose the invasion of Iraq; it spent "five years working with grassroots rabbis and activists within Reform Judaism toward moving the Union for Reform Judaism to decide to call for an end to the U.S. military presence in Iraq—which it ultimately did."[104]. Aside from its emphasis on peacemaking, it has developed a second focus on climate change. Waskow connects the two by saying that while "war is one of the most intense forms of destroying the planet, heat scorching is even worse."[105] For him, the great choice of the twenty-first century is between either domination or community: "The legend of Pharaoh is the story of over control which turns into domination. Imperial states never allow communities to control themselves and this eventually leads to their destruction."[106]

According to its Web site, the Shalom Center's mission is "to awaken conscience and activism within the larger Jewish community; to influence Jewish communal organizations and structures to take up questions of peace and justice; and to inspire individuals with public visibility to speak out and take needed action."[107] To that end, the Shalom Center emphasizes educational work, with Waskow offering week-long seminars as well as short telephone discussions in which he regularly explicates his prophetic understanding of a variety of current topics. Waskow believes that the Shalom Center's educational work has played a role in creating change within the Jewish community on the question of Israel and Palestine: he believes that "there is now an independent-minded chunk of the Jewish community that didn't exist ten years ago."[108] The Shalom Center also sends out periodic emails to its supporters asking them to sign letters on specific environmental or peace related issues. Prior to a 2009 leg injury, Waskow was a frequent participant in public acts of civil disobedience.

Rabbis for Human Rights-North America (RHR-NA) was partly founded as a consequence of the Shalom Center raising the issue of torture as one with specifically Jewish religious implications.[109] Initially set up in 2001 to support its partner organization, Rabbis for Human Rights, Israel, RHR now advocates for human rights from a Jewish religious perspective, in the Israeli and American contexts. According to Rabbi Gerald Serotta, almost all non-Orthodox rabbis in Israel are members of RHR-Israel, which has worked on Palestinian issues such as preventing home demolitions on the West Bank along with issues such as trafficking and foreign labor rights. The organization then moved into U.S. human rights issues with the launching of *Honor the Image of God: Stop Torture Now*, a specifically Jewish campaign to end U.S.–sponsored torture. The campaign includes developing educational resources and programming for rabbis and Jewish communities nationwide, and for organizing Jews in local communities to participate in Jewish and interfaith efforts to end torture.[110] The organization recruits rabbis across Judaism's denominations, as well as other interreligious supporters of RHR-NA.

The organization was a major impetus behind the founding of NRCAT, with the Jewish religious community strongly voicing its opposition to torture. They have done extensive lobbying on the issue in Washington, including a very positive meeting with Sen. John McCain prior to his becoming the 2008 presidential nominee. Even the Israeli Supreme Court has issued a "wonderful decision against torture even though torture still exists."[111] The organization has also invested serious efforts into disseminating educational material on human rights within the Jewish context. For example, among their numerous online resources is a lengthy article by Rabbi Melissa Weintraub, "*Kvod Ha-Briot*: Human Dignity in Jewish Sources, Human Degradation in American Military Custody." The article begins with detailed documentation of the extensive use of sexually explicit acts as a means of degrading Muslim captives in U.S. detention centers. This is followed by an equally detailed explication of the meaning of *Kvod Ha-Briot* or "the dignity of all created beings." *Kvod Ha-Briot* is grounded in the recognition that the Creator is the source of human dignity, which must be protected at all times given each human being's divine origins.[112] Another online article by Weintraub provides a thorough analysis of the Jewish prohibition against self-incrimination, a concept that remains underdeveloped within Christian thought.[113]

J Street is the newest Jewish peace organization. Established in 2008, it has quickly become the most visible Jewish peacemaking organization in the United States, with between forty thousand to fifty thousand members. The organization identifies itself as "the political arm of the pro-Israel, pro-peace movement."[114] Its founders, who brought extensive Washington DC experience to J Street, are seeking to create an alternative to the increasingly conservative voices among both Jews and Christians, such as the American Israel Public Affairs Committee (AIPAC) and Christians United For Israel, a Christian Zionist group founded by Rev. John Hagee, who dominated national advocacy concerning U.S. policy toward Israel during the Bush years. According to Rabbi Gerald Serotta, "it became obvious that whenever Israel wanted to negotiate with the Palestinians, the right wing in the U.S. became vitriolic. They screamed so much that their arguments are now less persuasive."[115] Despite the presence of these conservative lobbying organizations, polling done within American Jewish communities showed continued strong support for a two-state solution. This viewpoint is rooted in the core Jewish value of justice that demands a homeland for both Jews and Palestinians.[116] J Street is seeking to serve as the voice for that constituency.

According to Amy Spitalnick, the spokesperson for J Street, "Many of the organization's founders have lived in Israel and have been committed to this issue for years, yet felt there was no organization saying what needed to be said."[117] J Street believes that being a friend of Israel means speaking up when Israel does something against its core values. The future of Jewish democracy is at stake. Given the demographic trends, in the near future Israel, including the occupied territories, will have to choose between being either a Jewish state or being a democracy. J Street supports a freeze on further settlement construction because their expansion endangers the viability of a future Palestinian state. J Street has also criticized the arrests of Israeli pro-peace activists who were demonstrating against the takeover of Palestinian homes in East Jerusalem.[118]

J Street is set up specifically to speak for American Jews and to impact U.S. policy toward Israel, which during the Bush administration had often given the Israeli government unequivocal support while taking little initiative to restart peace talks. Spitalnick says that unlike in the United States, there is a much more vibrant debate over these issues in Israel where some political parties also take a two-state position.[119] Although the two-state solution is gaining more public support in the United States, J Street has nonetheless encountered some harsh criticisms for its public stance. For example, in late December 2009, the Israeli ambassador to the United States, Michael Oren, referred to J Street as a "unique problem" that "opposes all policies of all Israeli governments."[120] This is an exaggerated reaction to J Street's growing success in gaining political momentum for its peace positions. In February 2010, the organization sent its first congressional mission to Israel. According to a February 10, 2010, J Street press release, the trip consisted of five members of the U.S. House of Representatives who met "with Israeli, Palestinian, and Jordanian government officials as well as civil society leaders to get an in-depth, on-the-ground look at the state of the peace process, and to explore the American role in bringing about regional, comprehensive peace."

J Street is very savvy in its use of new media, which is partly attributable to the skills of its executive director, Jeremy Ben-Ami, who had previously been a senior vice president at Fenton Communications, a media group for progressives in DC. They are quick in providing a public responses to emerging developments in the Middle East peace process. Among the peace organizations discussed in this chapter, it alone has set up three separate corporate entities: a 501(c)4, which allows it to do lobbying; a political action committee (PAC), enabling it to endorse and raise money for political candidates who endorse its two-state position; and a 501(c)3 not-for-profit, through which it does its educational work. Shortly after its founding in 2008, the organization's PAC chose to endorse forty-three congressional candidates after interviewing candidates on where they stood in relationship to J Street's principles. The PAC raised $600,000 to support the endorsed candidates, of whom thirty-three won. Their lobbying entity employs six lobbyists who have built relationships with more than 350 offices on Capitol Hill. J Street was supportive of the Obama administration's pledge to make the Israel/Palestinian conflict a priority.

American Muslim Voice (AMV) is a unique peace organization, which focuses on building personal relationships across cultural and religious boundaries rather than policymaking. This organization is largely the vision of one woman, Samina Sunda, who announced its formation on July 4, 2003, and is very much a grassroots Islamic peace organization, which Samina sees as being modeled on the work of Martin Luther King Jr. Samina sees AMV as an expression of Dr. King's vision of the beloved community, yet as a Pakistani immigrant, she also understands its role from within her own cultural context. Thus, she compares it to communities in Pakistan where "everyone helped each other raise their children." [121] Having originally come to the United States as part of an arranged marriage, she raised her two children alone after the marriage ended. Following the post-9/11 escalation of hostilities toward Muslims, Samina decided to create an organization whose primary intention was "bridging the gaps between all communities." Her message to Americans is, "rather than listening to what the media says about Muslims, call us. We will talk!" Samina conceives of her work as movement building, which she recognizes will take years. In our conversation, she compared her work to planting a mango tree, "you know when you plant it that you will not eat the fruit, but you do it for the next generation."[122]

Based in the San Francisco area, AMV purposefully creates venues to bring people from various ethnic and religious backgrounds together, including African Americans, Chinese, Japanese Americans, Caucasians, LGBTQ, and Latinos. According to Samina, "We acknowledge that other people have suffered in the United States before us. Now we are suffering." The organization has done teach-ins, workshops, and open houses in Samina's own home that were attended by more than two hundred people. The only rule at her open houses is that people cannot talk to anyone they already know. Interestingly, Samina asserts, "You cannot build peace through email."[123] Thus far, she has been unable to secure any foundation grants for her work because it is perceived as being too dispersed among multiple agendas. Undaunted, Samina has instead taken out loans on her business and her home.

The Buddhist Peace Fellowship (BPF), which also formed under the auspices of the FOR, was started in 1978 in Hawaii as a gathering of Buddhist practitioners who were appalled by American proxy wars in Central America and by the flourishing of the Cold War arms race. Within three years the loose network, linked by friendships and a common purpose, had grown to several hundred members, with an office in Berkeley and a part-time coordinator. The organization draws its strength from the history of modern engaged Buddhist communities led by Buddhist activists such as Dr. Bhhimrao Ambedkar in India, Dr A. T. Ariyaratne from Sri Lanka, and the Vietnamese monk, Thich Nhat Hanh.[124] According to Allen Senauke, a former executive director and currently a senior advisor to BPF, at the time of its founding peacemaking was not widely understood as being part of Buddhism within the United States.[125] Like so many other activists, Senauke's views on activism were shaped by Martin Luther King, whose views were unique and truly inclusive. He now offers a workshop "The Darma of Martin Luther King" at various interested dharma centers.

Over the past thirty years, BPF and others have evolved an understanding of peacemaking based on the Buddhist concept of interdependency that includes both harmony and nonharmony. Senauke believes that "this has led to an understanding that there is a social dimension to suffering; it is not just a product of our minds, but is caused by the collective causes and conditions of society. There are systems, including nations, races, and genders that are composed of sentient beings, yet the systems function as though they are independent, as if they are human beings. Thus, one has to function at both levels and be able to say, this is not OK with me."[126] Yet, in their actions, Buddhists are mindful to adopt a nondual approach; to respect others even when they disagree with them to avoid an "us-versus-them" approach to social change. This perspective is embodied in an article in the *Turning Wheel,* BPF's magazine, written by a Buddhist monk, Claude AnShin Thomas, describing the meditation retreats he has conducted at Wewelsburg Castle in Germany. Wewelsburg served as an SS training-and-education center during the Nazi era. Thomas writes of how he comes to such places as Wewelsburg to learn more intimately about them by imagining himself as one of the suffering prisoners, or as a young SS soldier, or as the pastor of the local village, or even as the young girls from the village who might have been impressed by the SS uniforms.[127]

At present, BPF is also in a period of transition. Sarah Weintraub is a second-generation American Buddhist, and became the BPF's new executive director in late 2009. She is facing a paradoxical situation where the organization would like to maintain the work they have been known for, but at the same time, there is a desire to pass the organization on to a new generation.[128] Today, there are thirty-five local chapters around the country that use the name "Buddhist Peace Fellowship." The BPF works on peace issues in the United States, does work in American prisons, while also maintaining a particular interest in peacemaking in Asia. Allen Senauke is currently doing conflict-resolution work among the Burmese as well as providing aid to imprisoned Buddhist nuns and monks who were leaders in that country's 2007 Saffron Revolution, during which thousands of Buddhist monks led street protests against the country's military junta.

Concluding Remarks

While peacemaking is a significant expression of religious activism, it has rarely achieved the power needed to dramatically alter the trajectory of U.S. foreign policy. It has at times played a moderating role, however, by preventing presidents from achieving full support for certain military actions overseas. It is clear that support for absolute pacifism has always been quite small, even among peacemakers. Like other forms of activism, peacemaking activism is often reactive. It thrives during those periods when the dangers of U.S. military interventions are high as was true during and after World War I, which led to the founding of Fellowship for Reconciliation, and the ACLU's predecessor organization, and during the Vietnam War. Similarly, the escalation of U.S. military operations in Central America and of U.S. and Soviet nuclear weapons in the 1980s led to the creation of Witness for Peace as well as the Nuclear Freeze campaign and the Shalom Center. The 2003 invasion of Iraq and subsequent revelations of torture not only gave rise to a massive peace movement, it also led to creation of several new anti-torture and human rights organizations. In some cases, having started in response to one issue, organizations have are sought to continue their work by shifting their focus onto new issues. However, it is unclear whether in doing so they are able to retain their earlier momentum and visibility. Instead, many activists move on to still other more pressing issues. A number of peacemaking organizations are now facing the challenge of either transitioning their leadership to emerging younger activists as the Buddhist Peace Fellowship has recently done or to continue to decline as their older, long-term members slow down.

The methodologies of those organizations doing solidarity work, including FOR's work in Colombia, WFP, Pax Christi, and CPT overlap with ones being used by borderlands organizations. These organizations also emphasize the use of narrative and giving voice to people living in conflict zones. They too understand their work as a form of accompaniment in which people of privilege intentionally place themselves into conflict zones so to protect local peacemakers whose lives are in danger. Here, we again encounter the conscious use of privilege to advocate for people on the margins.

This chapter has also highlighted the recent efforts of two evangelical organizations to address peace-related issues. As is the case with Jewish, Islamic, and Buddhist peace organizations, evangelicals are working to reframe their theological and practical arguments so they will be more acceptable to evangelical audiences. To a large extent, it appears as though mainline Protestantism has served as the normative perspective on a variety of peacemaking issues, so that activists from every other religious perspective, including Catholicism, evangelicalism, Judaism, Islam, and Buddhism, have had to rework the religious understanding of peace for their own contexts.

A number of the cosmopolitan peacemaking groups make extensive use of email as an organizing tool. Some, like CPT, send their supporters a continuous stream of stories from the field; others use it to urge their supporters to act on behalf of their issues by sending letters to their legislators, signing petitions, or donating money. However, the political impact of such outreach is unclear when done without an accompanying grassroots presence. Yet, many of the peace groups have very small staffs and lack the funding needed to maintain extensive local organizing work.

7

Global Justice Organizing

On January 12, 2010, a powerful 7.0 magnitude earthquake struck Haiti, leveling the metropolitan capital city of Port-au-Prince and burying an estimated 250,000 people under the rubble. In the days and weeks afterwards, all the issues related to globalization, foreign debt, and free trade were laid bare for those who had eyes to see it. The American news media repeatedly reminded its viewers that Haiti was the poorest country in the Western Hemisphere, yet it rarely delved into the complex causes of that poverty. The day immediately after the earthquake, the conservative Christian TV talk show host Pat Robertson publicly blamed Haiti's woes on a supposed "pact made with the devil" by slaves seeking to rid their nation of French colonialism.[1] The comments drew immediate outrage from around the world, including from other religious leaders in the United States, but their utterance once again displayed a deep-seated contempt for the poor, which is embedded within much of conservative Christianity. Rather than probing the legacy of colonialism, capitalism, and the effects of contemporary globalization, the resultant poverty was once again blamed on the iniquities of the poor themselves.

Comments such as Robertson's effectively obfuscate the structural causes of Haiti's poverty, which began with the importation of African slaves; after liberating themselves they were forced to pay the French monarchy a sum of 90 million francs as restitution for its loss of the colony.[2] To pay off that debt, which finally occurred in the mid-1940s, the new nation borrowed heavily from banks in the United States, France, and other capitalist countries, putting it still further into debt.[3] Subsequently, Haiti was saddled with a series of corrupt dictators, bloody coup d'états, and U.S. military occupations. During the 1970s, wealthy nations, the World Bank, and the IMF imposed a series of structural adjustment policies (SAPs) that required Haiti to remove all tariffs on food and other imports, privatize its public enterprises, exempt foreign investors from paying taxes on their profits, and curb social spending. In the face of the almost complete privatization of all basic services, the majority of ordinary Haitians had become highly dependent on the services of foreign nongovernmental organizations (NGOs), which were providing 70 percent of rural healthcare and 80 percent of public services even prior the earthquake. In fact, before January 12, 2010, there were already more foreign NGOs per capita in Haiti than in any other country in the world.[4]

The disaster opened up a renewed discussion among wealthy, lender nations over how best to rebuild the island nation. According to a report in the New York Times on January 31, 2010, there was a contentious debate emerging among international funders on whether it would be best to temporarily place Haiti under the control of an international organization, "which would govern it and oversee its rebuilding." Others argued that Haitians should develop and implement their own plans since Haiti had been showing signs of improvement in recent years, despite years of failed international aid projects. In between those two poles, was a call for the creation of a joint Haitian-international reconstruction agency to administer some version of a Marshall Plan.[5] The UN General-Secretary Ban Ki-moon spoke of appointing former president Clinton to take on a more expanded role in Haiti. However, Clinton's growing role in Haiti's reconstruction was seen by some as problematic given that as president he had been a fervent proponent of free-trade policies. It was during his presidency that NAFTA was negotiated and signed by Mexico, the United States, and Canada. That agreement has been directly linked to the loss of thousands of agricultural jobs in Mexico, triggering the increased immigrant flow to the United States that we examined earlier (see chap. 5).[6]

Almost immediately, pressure mounted on bilateral and multilateral aid donors to cancel Haiti's remaining $1.15 billion debt, leading to an announcement on February 5, 2010, by the U.S. Treasury Department that it would support the complete cancellation of all remaining Haitian debt. Nicolas Sarkozy, the French president, also called for speeding up Haitian debt cancellation, including the 54 million euros owed to the French government. He went on to call for the convening of a "reconstruction and development" conference with other international donors to discuss ways to help Haiti recover.[7] Just one day after the earthquake, the ONE organization sent out its first email analysis, written by a Haitian staff member who clearly had direct knowledge of the full implications of the disaster. Three days after the quake, ONE began organizing its email supporters to sign a petition to the U.S. Treasury Secretary Timothy Geithner asking that he assist in securing the cancellation of Haiti's remaining debt. On the day the Treasury Department finally announced its support for Haitian debt cancellation, ONE broadcast a recorded message of thanks from the Haitian ambassador to the United States, thanking ONE for its lobbying efforts.[8]

Global Anti-Poverty Advocacy Gains Momentum

The quick response to ONE's call for debt relief is indicative of the considerable power that global anti-poverty advocates have achieved over the past decade. For David Beckman, the executive director for Bread for the World, the unprecedented progress being made against hunger, poverty, and disease represents "God moving in history."[9] Others would no doubt attribute it to the emergence of a global movement against debt along with the infusion of large sums of money, which has funded the highly skilled political organizing needed to pass critical legislation. During the 1970s and 1980s, Bread for the World was the lone religious voice in Washington on issues of global and U.S. hunger. In the last decade, a much broader movement has emerged. Beckman believes that a shift was already underway in the late 1990s but attributes its acceleration to the events of 9/11. "People realized that it is not smart to neglect the poor." Several organizations have been founded since 9/11 that are building sizeable constituencies, in part by effectively using popular culture in their appeals to an emerging youthful generation of activists. They recruit musicians to join their causes, thereby mixing popular music into their advocacy and mobilizations. They produce high-quality videos, which are downloadable from YouTube, and they connect to their supporters via social networking sites, including Facebook and Twitter. Several rock musicians, including Bono and Bob Geldof, have played leading roles in achieving tangible legislative successes. In the case of the U.S. campaign for debt relief, it was Bono and Bobby Shriver, the eldest child of Robert Sargent Shriver and Eunice Shriver, who revived the faltering debt relief campaign. They helped mount a successful lobbying campaign that reached down into key congressional districts to build bipartisan support for the approval of a $435 million U.S. contribution toward debt relief in 1999.

Support for aid to Africa has also grown enormously in recent years as a result of a very broad-based effort of which religious advocacy organizations constitute one element. Not only have well-known cultural figures played highly visible roles, there has also been an influx of large sums of money from high-tech entrepreneurs such as Bill Gates and the founders of Google, as well as George Soros and Warren Buffet. They have invested not only in the provision of humanitarian aid but also in the expansion of advocacy work. Both Beckman and Shriver also attribute the shift to the surprising support given to these issues by the former Bush administration, including his chief of staff Karl Rove, who doggedly pressured Republican members of Congress to enact the President's Emergency Plan for AIDS Relief (PEP-FAR), which committed $15 million to provide low-cost AIDS medications.[10]

As the world's largest economy, the United States plays a critical role in assisting development efforts among the world's poor countries. Historically, policymakers' choices in where to distribute aid given to the world's developing nations via the Office of Development Assistance (ODA) was primarily driven by what were viewed as the U.S.' own strategic interests, instead of targeting those countries where aid could have the greatest impact. Furthermore, between 1968 and 1998, the U.S.' share of official global development assistance had dropped from more than half of the total to less than a third. By 1998, the United States was contributing a smaller share of its total national income to ODA than any other wealthy nation. Japan had surpassed the United States as the largest donor in absolute dollars, even though Japan's economy was less than half the size.[11] As of 2001, roughly 10 percent of U.S. development assistance was disbursed through multilateral agencies including various UN groups and two international financial institutions, the World Bank and the IMF. The United States is the largest shareholder in both the World Bank and the IMF, which were established to rebuild Europe in the aftermath of World War II. Since countries are given a number of votes in both institutions proportionate to their contributions, the United States controls 16.5 percent of the votes at the World Bank and 17.6 percent at the IMF, about 10 percent more than the next largest shareholder, Japan, which gives the United States inordinate decision-making power in both organizations.[12] All of these factors, made the United States a key target, not only in the broader anti-globalization campaigns that emerged in the late 1990s, but in religious efforts to secure increased assistance to alleviate debt, poverty, and hunger among the world's poorest nations.

It is not unusual to see television ads by one or another Christian organization showing the faces of impoverished children as a means of raising humanitarian aid. A common tactic is to urge viewers to "adopt" a poor child somewhere in the developing world. While these programs may be well meaning, they often create dependency rather than addressing the systemic causes of poverty or increasing families' capabilities to sustain themselves. In contrast, we will see a number of organizations that prioritize organizing and advocacy for the creation of U.S. governmental policies, many of which contribute to increasing the capabilities of families in poor countries to improve their own well-being. Certain organizations are successful due their singular focus on a key issue such as hunger, displacement, or debt, building up strong grassroots networks and relationships with members of Congress.

Again, several have also benefited from the highly visible support of world-famous celebrities and major financial backing. Still, others have made use of innovative media strategies to mobilize youth and young adults, thereby contributing to the creation of a new generation of activists.

As is the case with the peacemaking organizations, these groups largely appeal to cosmopolitans; some of whom have witnessed global poverty or displacement firsthand, while others are being exposed to these realities through the use of film and YouTube. The easy distribution of new media is increasing the capacity of people to connect to issues in distant regions of the world. This work is closely intertwined with peacemaking: in many cases the presence of widespread hunger and poverty, along with the displacement of people, is the direct result of endemic violence. Several organizations overlap with those that focus on peacemaking, but they understand violence as a symptom of other deeper underlying structural problems that are linked to the effects of globalization.

While globalization has contributed to the destabilization of many of the world's poorest nations, it has simultaneously created new platforms for global organizing. As was true with regard to immigrant rights and peacemaking, the global nature of various religious institutions and missionary networks contributes to the growth of this work as well. Nonetheless, religious anti-globalization organizing is one component of much wider, and in many cases, much more radical anti-globalization movements. Rather than reject globalization entirely, religiously oriented organizations generally seek to mitigate the negative effects of globalization in ways that will benefit people at the margins. In some cases they are linked to global networks, through which activists elsewhere are able to provide critical leadership in shaping the policy proposals for which U.S. groups advocate. In that sense, these organizations are bridging a global divide between people living in rich *and* poor countries, which is similar to the religious activists within borderlands contexts who also serve as bridges between people on the margins and congregations consisting of more well-to-do American citizens.

The peacemaking organizations we have considered focused on particular regions of the world, prioritizing the Middle East, Central America, and Colombia. Religious organizing in response to global poverty and hunger is heavily centered on Africa, either in its entirety or on individual countries such as Sudan, Uganda, or the DRC. Only Witness for Peace's advocacy against the negative effects of free trade and structural adjustment policies continues to pay attention to Central America and Mexico. This organization chose to focus on those countries because of its long-standing relationships with local activists, thus acquiring a high degree of expertise on globalization's impact on those countries' citizens.

The focus on Africa, which has crystallized over this past decade, is undoubtedly in reaction to the continent's dire circumstances. According to the macroeconomist Jeffrey Sachs, by the start of the twenty-first-century Africa was poorer than during the late 1960s, with disease, population growth, and environmental degradation spiraling out of control. Three centuries of slave trade followed by a century of brutal colonial rule had left Africa bereft of educated citizens and leaders, basic infrastructure, and public health facilities. During the Cold War it had been a pawn of Western capitalist powers who opposed any African leader who demanded better terms on Western investments in mineral and energy resources. In the early 1960s, despite indicators that many of the newly independent African nations faced low economic growth prospects, the United States and its allies were unwilling to make investments at the level necessary to create sustained economic growth.[13] Beginning in the mid 1990s Sachs's own extensive research brought world attention to the negative impact of the twin diseases of malaria and AIDS. Writing of his own experiences, Sachs states, "Beyond anything I had experienced or could imagine, disease and death became the constant motif of my visits to Africa. Never, not even in the highlands of Bolivia, where illness is rife, had I confronted so much illness and death."[14] Indeed, by the year 2000, sub-Saharan African's life expectancy stood at forty-seven years, more than twenty years lower than in East Asia and more than thirty-one years lower than in economically developed countries.[15] Such dreadful human circumstances coupled with Africa's incredibly rich mineral resources have led to a series of human rights crises, including the 1994 Rwandan genocide in which more than 800,000 people were slaughtered.

Bread for the World

Arthur Simon, the younger brother of the late U.S. Senator Paul Simon (D-IL), was inspired to form what became Bread for the World (BFW) through his personal relationships with poor and hungry people. The son of a Missouri Synod Lutheran pastor, Simon pastored Trinity Lutheran Church on the Lower East Side in Manhattan, beginning in the early 1960s in what was then a largely poor African American and Puerto Rican community. He became involved in an early fight against New York City's attempts at "urban redevelopment" that threatened to displace a portion of the neighborhood's residents to make way for middle-class tenants. He was active in the local civil rights movement, attended the 1963 March on Washington, and marched with Dr. King in Selma, while also taking time out to assist in his brother's many electoral campaigns. Having a firsthand sense of urban poverty, in the summer of 1970 he spent five weeks driving through the rural South and Appalachia. The experience brought him to the conclusion that "Americans on the whole simply cannot believe or imagine the suffering because they seldom see it; when they do, it is a threat to their comfort, so they chose not to think about it. Blocking poor people from our minds, however, may be a passive way of wishing they did not exist, and it is a cause of many deaths."[16]

After writing several books on hunger, Simon concluded that there was a woeful lack of understanding concerning how government policies impact hungry people. Furthermore, he was struck by the ways that Christians were giving humanitarian aid both locally and internationally, yet they were not being challenged to weigh in as citizens to help shape the government's decisions regarding hungry people. The civil rights movement had taught him that extreme injustice could arouse people of faith to act, and the nonpartisan organization, Common Cause provided him with a model of a citizens' lobby. Drawing on these activist strands, he proposed the creation of a Christian citizen's movement that would build public support for more just policies toward hungry people.[17] Formalized in 1974, Bread for the World was established as an explicitly Christian, nonpartisan, and nonideological organization.[18] In its early days, BFW framed its understanding of hunger as a "right to food." This right was not just understood religiously but concretely as a right that is implicit in the Declaration of Independence and is stated in article 25 of the United Nation's Universal Declaration of Human Rights.[19]

According to David Beckman, BFW's current executive director, the organization is broadly interdenominational, seeking to appeal to evangelicals and liberals alike. Its singular focus on hunger, and its conscious efforts to build campaigns that can garner broad support has made it more effective than many of the denominational networks. In recent years, it has become a more multiracial organization with growing support from historic African American denominations. It also now translates much of its material, including YouTube videos, into Spanish.[20] A YouTube video posted online in both English and Spanish features Lee de Leon, the pastor of Templo Calvario in Santa Ana, California, the largest Hispanic congregation in the United States. De Leon speaks of his experiences with the "Offering of Letters" and visits to his congressional representative on behalf of BFW.[21] Bread for the World has further strengthened its ties among white evangelicals and Pentecostals as well, who are in agreement that more needs to be done on poverty in the United States. Beckman believes that "the old divide between evangelization and social justice is dead. Social justice must be rooted in the proclamation of the Word, and evangelization must lead to a concern for justice."[22]

At the heart of Bread's work for the past thirty-seven years is its annual "Offering of Letters" in which members of local congregations are asked to collect handwritten letters from their members to be sent to their congressional representatives. While each letter is designed to be personal, they are all written on a broad common theme that varies from year to year. It has been BFW's practice to alternate its lobbying focus from year to year, concentrating on domestic hunger one year and on international hunger the next. In 2001 it launched its "Africa: From Hunger to Harvest" campaign, committing itself to make Africa the main focus of its international advocacy until hunger actually begins to decline on that continent.[23] Bread collects the letters from individual supporters and through its network of "covenant churches," which have each agreed to integrate hunger issues into the life of the congregation. Every year during the fall, these covenant churches are asked to dedicate a specific Sunday worship service to hunger, during which the letters written by individual members are brought to the altar.

As part of launching their new focus on hunger in Africa, Bread held a four-day conference in Washington DC in June 2001, which culminated with a day of lobbying on Capitol Hill. The assembled audience of Bread activists heard speakers from a number of denominational relief agencies and Bread staffers. In addition, several African leaders spoke, including Bishop Ambrose Moyo from Zimbabwe and Ambassador Sheila Sisulu of South Africa. Sisulu gave the audience an African perspective that placed hunger reduction within a much broader agenda, including issues of peace, democracy, poverty eradication, and health care. She stated that African leaders expected that the developed world would support the economic development plans being set by African nations. According to Sisulu, the continent's leaders intended to seek African involvement in the internal deliberations of the IMF and World Bank to ensure increased accountability.[24] While Bread's intentional focus on hunger enables it to garner significant support within the U.S. Congress, Africans themselves see it as only one of the continent's most pressing problems. Thus, within global justice movements, one must be cognizant of variations in policy priorities between activists from Northern and Southern Hemispheres. Issues that are most politically feasible within developed nations are not necessarily uppermost on the agenda of activists in the global South.

Much like Interfaith Worker Justice, BFW's national office produces a booklet every year that contains suggested text for the letters, ideas for various awareness projects in which the congregation can engage, and references to additional resources on that particular year's focus. Just as IWJ does, Bread includes an outline of the biblical basis of the year's campaign along with a sample worship liturgy. The similarities between these two organizations are not accidental: IWJ's founder and executive director, Kim Bobo, was one of Bread's earliest members, joining in 1974 while she was still an undergraduate. Immediately after graduation, she joined the BFW's staff as an organizer, becoming its national director of organizing by the time she left in 1987.[25] Clearly, Bobo has transferred much of what she learned at BFW to the new organization she founded in 1995. This is a very concrete example of how models of organizing can be adopted and adapted from one context into another.

In addition to letter-writing campaigns, BFW also mobilizes its congregational members to make regular visits to their district congressional representatives. Bread has successfully built long-term relationships between members of Congress and local congregational-based activists who are well equipped to advocate for whatever legislative priority has been selected for that year. As of 2010, BFW had active volunteer leaders in all 435 congressional districts in the United States—an accomplishment unmatched by any other progressive religious organization. Recognizing that its grassroots networks are one of its strengths, Bread is investing still more resources into strengthening these local groups since they have the ability to drive change at the local level. They are intentionally using new technologies such as Facebook, Twitter, and YouTube to make their local volunteers more effective. Its YouTube videos are of professional quality, serving as an excellent format for explaining each year's new legislative focus to a wider audience. They can be easily adapted for use by the increasing numbers of congregations that have large-screen projection systems in their sanctuaries.

In recent years, BFW has also launched BFW's Student Coalition, which now has a presence on over three hundred campuses, enabling students to participate in many of the same activities that have traditionally been channeled through congregations.[26] Now, it appears that BFW has had far greater success in attracting young adults than the "older" activist peace organizations we examined earlier. One possible explanation is a greater attraction among young adults to issues that carry strong humanitarian overtones, which is certainly the case with hunger. Here again, the embrace of media such as Facebook, MySpace, Twitter, and YouTube help Bread connect to younger audiences who use these new social networking sites.

Bread chooses three or four specific legislative issues annually on which they intend to concentrate. One of those issues will receive half of all of BFW's resources and is the one that will be referenced in the "Offering of Letters." The organization chooses its key legislative issues based on those most likely to change the lives of hungry people, and, at the same time, win the support of the grassroots constituents in local congregations. The details of the actual legislation are then hammered out through lengthy negotiations among partner organizations and members of Congress who are willing to co-sponsor the bill and assist in moving it through the complexities of congressional approval. Located in Washington DC, Bread has enough of a pulse on the politics on Capitol Hill to know what legislation is likely to be possible within the political parameters of any given year.

In 2010, the "Offering" focused on strengthening the Earned Income Tax Credit (EITC) in the United States. Bread was calling for a strengthening of the EITC as the most effective means of putting more income into the pockets of low-income working families. Interestingly, EITC is not directly an anti-hunger program as is the Food Stamp program, which BFW has worked hard to protect and expand. Its YouTube video explaining the EITC campaign features a single, white mother of two who works as a preschool teacher and relies on Women, Infants, and Children (WIC), a federal food program, her church's food pantry, and her children's school lunch program to feed her family. Yet, she still does not always have sufficient income to pay all of her bills, including rent. A strengthened EITC would enable her to keep more of her earnings, thereby placing more cash at her disposal.[27]

Every year, the Bread for the World Institute, Bread's non-for-profit 501(c)3, produces a new thick, well-documented manual consisting of more than one hundred pages of research, policy analysis, and lessons from organizing campaigns interspersed with stories of the effects of hunger in particular corners of the globe. The articles break down the complexities of globalization, focusing on the growing income inequalities between rich and poor countries, and within poor countries between rural agriculturalists (who are mainly women) and the urban centers. They make frequent references to Amartya Sen's writings in arguing for the importance of poor countries investing in human capabilities such as public education, health care, and women's empowerment, alongside a strengthening of democratic governance. They discuss the role of various international bodies, especially the United Nations, the World Bank, and the IMF in supporting such efforts. The matter-of-fact tone of the manual's material is clearly intended to educate in such a way as to allow for the possibilities of collaboration with these various institutions. Bread's current executive director was previously employed by the World Bank for fifteen years, working on issues of slum improvement, low-cost housing, and microenterprise in East Africa and Latin America.[28]

Bread's emphasis on sound research is perhaps best suited to its primary commitment to lobbying for incremental, winnable improvements in anti-hunger policies. In contrast to the ongoing work of Witness for Peace, BFW does not understand itself as intentionally employing various liberative methodologies such as accompaniment or serving as a platform for those who otherwise have no voice by telling their stories.

Witness for Peace

Witness for Peace, whose 1980s peacemaking work we examined earlier, refocused its work onto the effects of globalization, taking a rather different approach to the issues than BFW. With the ending of the contra war in Nicaragua and the defeat of the Sandinistas in the 1990 national elections, many of WFP's supporters assumed that the organization had completed its task. It was unclear what role an American-based solidarity organization ought to have in light of the emerging realities of neo-liberal globalization. Challenged with finding a new message that would carry the same emotional resonance as the contra war, WFP hit a major fundraising crisis in the early 1990s with its revenues dropping from $1.2 million in 1990 to just $540,000 in 1998.[29]

At this same time, conditions in Nicaragua were shifting dramatically. The newly elected UNO government abandoned the Sandinistas goal of lifting all Nicaraguans out of poverty and instead embraced a set of neo-liberal economic policies favorable to international capitalist elites. Moreover, international monetary institutions such as the World Bank and the IMF imposed a set of structural adjustment policies (SAPs) on Nicaragua as conditions for the restructuring of the country's international debt. The SAPs were designed to reduce government intervention in the economy, privatize the economy, and open it up to foreign capital investments through the elimination or reduction of trade barriers. These policies undermined many of the social and economic gains made during the Sandinista era. According to Clare Weber, who had worked as a long-term WFP volunteer in Nicaragua, "they affected food security, increased unemployment, threatened land tenure for poor rural and urban Nicaraguans, limited access to credit for small producers, and cut state support for health care and education."[30]

Many Sandinista activists who had been part of the revolutionary government and mass organizations resisted the dismantling of the activist state and the rolling back of support for poor Nicaraguans. The ten years of Sandinista government had left a legacy of a politically mobilized population and an existing network of international solidarity organizations. As the full implications of neo-liberal structural adjustment policies became visible, Nicaraguan activists were forced to move beyond their earlier national struggle to build a new solidarity movement, based in their local conditions but connected to the larger processes of globalization.[31]

Once again responding to their Nicaraguan partners, WFP shifted its focus to the impact that structural adjustment policies were having on working people in Nicaragua. The organization drew on its expertise in documenting war by developing educational materials, which laid out the economic policies of the United States, and its attendant neo-liberal ideology, along with a critique of how these actually increased poverty in Nicaragua. Just as WFP had previously used the stories of the victims of the contra war, it now told the stories of workers whose lives were being disrupted by the implementation of neo-liberal SAPs. In its early 1990s publications, WFP directly implicated American consumers who were using a disproportionate share of the world's natural resources, thereby contributing to the depletion of those resources within the global South. In line with its earlier focus on human rights violations, it now began highlighting violations of labor rights committed by global firms that had relocated production in Nicaragua. By the end of the decade, WFP had refocused its message more directly upon the U.S.' policies, including the impact of NAFTA, which had led to a proliferation of American-owned, low-wage production sites located directly on the Mexican side of its border with the United States.[32]

Witness for Peace prioritized those countries in Latin America that were being most directly affected by U.S. policy. It now focuses its work on Mexico, Colombia, Honduras, Cuba, and Nicaragua—countries in which the consequences of U.S. economic policies are most prominently apparent. Following the 1994 passage of NAFTA between the United States and Mexico, WFP began work there, especially in the indigenous region of Chiapas. It took delegations to the Mexican state of Oaxaca to explore the roots of migration from that region to the United States. One of its Oaxacan delegations was specifically organized for African American and Latino leaders from North Carolina, which has recently become a major destination of migrants from that region. The organization also developed a new focus on worker justice in Latin America as a result of its delegations to Nicaragua. There they encountered the stories of sweatshop workers who were manufacturing clothing for sale at Kohl's and Target stores. The Nicara-guan workers asked delegates to picket the two stores, which led WFP to begin working with their managements to improve workers' wages. Unfor-tunately, these same sweatshops have now moved to China where workers have even fewer rights.[33] In both cases, WFP effectively links immigration and worker-rights issues globally to those same issues within U.S.–based borderlands communities.

At present WFP continues its solidarity work through well-established relationships with indigenous Latin American justice activists with whom it partners in sending American delegations. They still support a number of international volunteers who assist in coordinating the trips on the ground. The delegations to Mexico, Colombia, Honduras, Cuba, and Nicaragua bring back the stories of the people they meet, which are then passed on through WFP's network of supporters in the United States. Witness for Peace has a number of regional organizers here who keep those who have traveled on delegations connected and involved in the solidarity work after they return. It also organizes speaking tours for Latin American leaders that reach roughly five thousand supporters annually.[34] Witness for Peace currently maintains an annual budget of $900,000, most of which is raised from the various reli-gious orders to which it has historically been connected.[35]

The constant flow of stories out of the Latin American context continu-ously reshapes the organization's advocacy and legislative work. According to Gail Phares, the key to the organization's work is "that we stay with fami-lies and we learn from Latin Americans. We work at transforming Ameri-cans and then empowering them to work to change U.S. policy. Our mind-set is not to go to 'help.' We only go to countries where the United States is intervening. There are lots of hopeful things going on in Latin America right now. The only place where it is *not* happening is Colombia and that's the place where we are going."[36] According to Phares, many of those who were active in the 1980s remain involved in activism. As proof, she talked of having recently staffed WFP's table at the annual vigil outside of the School of the Americas, where the U.S. military has for years trained Latin Ameri-cans in counterinsurgency techniques. While there, a number of people stopped by and told her that they had traveled with her to Nicaragua during the 1980s. Like other older peace organizations, WFP is seeking to connect to a younger generation of emerging activists. To that end, they have begun organizing trips specifically for young adults, and these trips have resulted in college students making up more than half of the people who come to their organizers' trainings.[37]

The Jubilee 2000 Campaign

Bread for the World's and Witness for Peace's core commitments to halting the growing impoverishment of developing countries led both organizations to become early advocates of the Jubilee 2000 campaign. The concept of Jubilee is rooted in the book of Leviticus: "And you shall hallow the fiftieth year and you shall proclaim liberty throughout the land to all its inhabitants. It shall be a jubilee for you (Lev. 25:10)." A global movement arose around the goal of transforming the promise of this ancient text into a contemporary reality for the world's poorest nations. While debt relief campaigns had existed since the early 1990s, the idea of declaring a Jubilee at the time of the new millennium gave efforts a focal point that had not existed before.[38] The Jubilee proposals sought total debt forgiveness along with requirements that the World Bank and the IMF work together with each country's government to develop a national poverty-reduction strategy assuring that funds diverted from debt payments were invested in schools, health care, and poverty reduction.[39]

The Jubilee campaign is one of the most successful advocacy and lobbying campaigns ever led by the global religious community. The campaign, which began with the African Council of Churches' call for debt forgiveness to mark the millennial celebration, eventually grew into a worldwide movement of Catholics, Protestants, trade unionists, academics, social activists, and others in more than sixty countries.[40] The first organization was set up in the UK in 1994 to begin advocating for debt forgiveness. By the end of the twentieth century, a global ad hoc coalition had formed, making debt relief a simultaneous focal point of organizing and advocacy in both rich and poor nations. By the end of the year 2000, the campaign had gathered a record breaking 24 million signatures on petitions from around the globe.[41] For many, signing the petition became an educational experience because it required becoming informed about the debt issue. A journalist who questioned whether all of the 2 million people who had signed the petition in Peru really understood the issues decided to find out by visiting a remote village. To his great surprise, he was treated to a cogent explanation of global debt and its effects on the people of the local area.[42] Clearly, the debt campaign served as a vehicle for many participants' development of critical consciousness that could create a foundation for further empowerment. In Peru, the debt campaign coincided with the toppling of the authoritarian and corrupt Fujimori government in 2000, enabling the issue of the country's debt to move to the center of the nation's politics.[43]

Both Pope John Paul II and Archbishop Desmond Tutu gave the campaign their strong endorsement. In the United States, the United Methodist Church and the Evangelical Lutheran Church in America issued statements on behalf of debt relief in 1996 and 1997 after they heard of support for debt cancellation from their church leaders in the global South.[44] The Irish rocker Bono was a major organizer behind the campaign in the UK and later in the United States. According to Bobby Shriver, Bono's commitment to debt relief and subsequent campaigns against AIDS grows out of his Irish heritage—"'a folk memory of being starved to death.' They won't accept it happening to anyone else."[45] According to David Beckman, engaging in the Jubilee campaign "brought Bono back to church." Once he became committed he used his Rolodex to involve other celebrities, including stars such as Brad Pitt and Angeline Jolie.[46] By the year 2000, the *Guardian* reported, the Jubilee campaign had become "'one of the biggest global campaigns ever.'"[47]

The goal of the Jubilee campaign was to secure forgiveness of the international debt held by forty-one of the world's most highly indebted countries, those who owed so much money to the World Bank and the IMF that they had been forced to curtail government funding for such basic government services as public education and health care in order to pay just the interest on the debt. Speaking at a debt cancellation workshop in the UK, the Reverend Bernardino Mandiate from Mozambique explained that most of the poor Asian, African, and Latin American countries had been colonies whose resources were stolen by the European powers in order to develop their home country economies. After the colonies gained independence, their new governments borrowed money from the World Bank and the IMF in their efforts to spur economic development. Yet, in too many cases, the money was stolen by corrupt leaders or was used to invest in military hardware rather than schools and hospitals. "Now the debt is so huge even our great-grandchildren will not be able to pay it off. Our educational systems are not functioning; we lack clean water and basic medicines and are plagued by high unemployment."[48] That countries were quite literally sacrificing their futures to pay off increasingly exorbitant levels of debt formed the moral underpinning of the campaign. But it was also driven by the fact that much of the debt had simply become unpayable.

Given the U.S.' power within both the IMF and the World Bank, its support for the debt relief was crucial to its success. Thus, Jubilee 2000 USA was set up to organize within the United States and to lobby Congress for the necessary funds to write off debts owed directly to this country, while also allocating money to a larger debt relief initiative. The U.S. coalition consisted of a large number of denominations and the major religious relief agencies such a Catholic Relief Services, Church World Service, and Lutheran World Relief. According to Dan Driscoll-Shaw, who became the coalition's national coordinator, "for most of the church people, support for Jubilee grew out of having been in Latin America and in Africa. So, we were talking about the future of people we knew personally."[49] Driscoll-Shaw's own interest in Jubilee stemmed from his years as a Maryknoll priest in Latin America. Although he had studied Catholic social teaching in seminary, it remained theoretical until 1966 when he was assigned to work in a barrio in Caracas, Venezuela. It was there that he came face to face with injustice. "It didn't take long to see what was going on; to see the influence of the United States in Latin America and other parts of the world."[50] A little more than a year after his arrival, Latin American bishops met in Medellin, Colombia. Afterwards, Driscoll-Shaw and his fellow priests began implementing liberation theology along with the goal of empowering people in their parishes.

Analyzing the success of Jubilee 2000 in the United States, Joshua William Busby, an assistant professor of public affairs at the University of Texas, writes, "The religious symbolism, coupled with the timing of the new millennium, was such that the campaign was able to attract a wide swath of support from North and South, Left and Right. Whereas there was a tendency for radical elements to bash capitalism as in the 1999 WTO protests in Seattle, Jubilee 2000 brought on board influential supporters from the entire ideological spectrum as well as ordinary citizens."[51] Religious support for debt relief included the Christian conservative Pat Robertson, who publicly proclaimed his support of debt relief, saying, "It's the humane thing to do. These children are starving to death . . . it's the humanitarian thing and that's why I'm supporting it."[52] An April 2000 "Message to Congress" from Jubilee 2000 USA listed 115 mostly religious institutions as sponsors. The list included multiple Catholic missionary orders, all the mainline churches, the peace churches, the Mormon Church, the Reformed Church of America, Jesse Jackson's PUSH-Rainbow Coalition, the Women's Missionary Society of the African Methodist Episcopal Church, several Jewish institutions, the Muslim Public Affairs Council, the Fellowship of Reconciliation, World Vision, Pax Christi, Witness for Peace, and Bread for the World as well as nonreligious organizations such as the Embassy of Kenya and the U.S. Conference of Mayors.[53]

The prospects of substantial congressional support for debt relief had not been good at the beginning of 1999. David Beckman reflects, "At the beginning of 1999, we were nowhere—no one in Congress wanted to talk to us."[54]

According to Bobby Shriver, the debt relief campaign was based on an British strategy of collecting signatures on petitions, which worked in Europe but not in the United States. By 1999 Bono had collected 6 million signatures in Europe and only 10,000 in the United States. Looking for help, Bono first called Eunice, Bobby Shriver's mother, hoping she would put him in touch with her brother Senator Ted Kennedy. Instead, she connected Bono to Shriver directly. Together, they helped shape a broad legislative campaign that involved all the DC religious groups who were working on debt relief in reaching down to their supporters in key congressional districts. Hearing from their home-district constituents transformed key members of Congress into supporters of debt relief. Several key Republicans, including Rep. Spencer Bachus (R-AL), then chair of the House Banking Subcommittee on Domestic and International Monetary Policy, embraced the concept of Jubilee as a result of visits from groups of Bread supporters who lived in his home district. In the case of Congressman Bachus, who was known as a "conservative's conservative," BFW members had established a rapport with him through their annual visits. Bread supporters also generated roughly 250,000 letters to Congress in support of debt relief.[55] By mid-March 1999, a debt relief bill was introduced in the House with bipartisan support. In June, the G-7, comprised of finance ministers from the seven richest countries in the world, convened in Cologne, Germany, where the meeting was surrounded by 70,000 Jubilee 2000 protestors. The G-7 took the first concrete steps toward debt relief by agreeing to write off $90 billion in poor countries' debts.[56] By the end of 2000, further reductions led to a 33 percent drop in outstanding debt. Almost immediately, twenty-two of the Heavily Indebted Poor Countries (HIPC), most of which were in sub-Saharan Africa, began to shift their savings into programs aimed at poverty reduction.[57]

The global coalition that had formed around Jubilee 2000 was intentionally flexible, relatively informal, and temporary since the campaign was intended to terminate at the end of 2000. In assessing the overall campaign, Marjorie Mayo, a British scholar of community action, concludes that "While the campaign was certainly aiming to empower those who had been defined as 'victims' to redefine themselves as actors, speaking effectively with their own voices, the objectives were also very specific and intentionally achievable, or at least partially achievable, within the allotted time-span, in the run-up to the millennium."[58] Commenting on the coalition, David Beckman saw it as "an impossible coalition that was located all over the world. We were using new techniques of global organization to build a global movement to the surprise of the old powers. The Europeans thought that we were selling out, but the United States was much more difficult on providing aid to poor countries."[59] Beckman believed that missionary networks and the churches in the global South had been critical to the construction of an effective global campaign.

It is important to note that as with other campaigns against the negative impacts of globalization on developing countries, Jubilee was primarily designed to secure policy changes from wealthy nations and the international institutions that they fund. Although the campaign had successfully secured broad global backing, activists in poorer countries understood that debt relief alone would not address the complex problems hindering widespread economic development in their countries. For example, while Kenya has thus far not been eligible for debt relief, Kenyan leaders stressed the domestic impediments that inhibit growth of the Kenyan economy. Several church leaders emphasized the critical need for constitutional reforms that would democratize a political system that Kenyans had inherited from the British colonialists. Without a stronger democracy, there would be no checks on the ability of Kenyan politicians to borrow from overseas sources in furtherance of their own political careers rather than investing the money in enhancing the average Kenyan's quality of life. Many activists' understandings echoed Amartya Sen's assertions in *Development as Freedom* that democracy is a critical element in insuring that ordinary people have the power to hold their political leaders accountable for creating the conditions for broad economic well-being. According to one member of Parliament, the British had "turned over the government to a small group of Kenyans whom they had worked with during colonial times. Some of those same families are still in power today."[60] In an interview with the Reverend Ochola Chalton, who served as the program director of the National Council of Churches of Kenya (NCCK), he spoke of what he saw as the new forms of exploitation suffered by Kenya as a result of globalization. Yet the NCCK's own advocacy priorities were "working on AIDS, women and children in stress, constitutional reform, and election monitoring."[61] Thus, despite increasing transglobal organizing, activists in each country will still prioritize those issues that are most achievable within their local political context.

The debt relief achieved in 1999 and 2000 was seen as the first step. Religious organizing on global debt relief has extended into the new century as activists continue to press for still broader eligibility parameters with fewer conditions placed on those countries receiving relief. Further progress was made in 2005, when it was agreed that all countries that had reached the completion of the eligibility process would receive 100 percent relief. That same year, at the meeting in Gleneagles, Scotland, the G-8 countries agreed to increase their commitments to poverty relief efforts, especially in sub Saharan Africa. Despite such progress, however, too many countries that need relief, including Kenya and Lesotho, still remain ineligible because of the strict formulas used to determine eligibility. Additionally, the IMF and World Bank still impose onerous conditions on receiving countries, requiring them to emphasize export industries and privatize government services, thus limiting the effectiveness of debt relief in enhancing human development.[62]

The Jubilee USA Network, formed in 1999, is the principal American religious successor organization to the 2000 Jubilee campaign. This is a network of seventy-five constituent organizations, including many religious organizations we have already encountered elsewhere, such as the leading mainline denominations, the Mennonite and Brethren churches, the Unitarian Universalists, Pax Christi USA, Witness for Peace, Sojourners, and the American Jewish World Service, as well as the AFL-CIO, TransAfrica Forum, Africa Action, and the African Faith and Justice Network. Together, they comprise the network's governing body. Melinda St. Louis, the deputy director, emphasizes Jubilee's close collaboration with Bread for the World and ONE in supporting each other's legislative initiatives and signing each other's letters of support.[63] Interestingly, prior to coming to the Jubilee Network, Melinda had worked for Witness for Peace in Nicaragua for two years just as that country was receiving its first debt relief. According to Melinda, the WFP had focused on the negative impacts of U.S., World Bank, and IMF policies in Central America, but they lacked the capacity to do much advocacy in the United States, so they plugged their people into the Jubilee 2000 campaign.[64]

While Jubilee USA Network deliberately seeks to transcend partisanship, a characteristic that its predecessor organization also embodied, it remains dedicated to what it identifies as the "moral call" because it is determined to realize the full meaning of jubilee. According to its 2009–12 strategic plan, Jubilee USA is committed to "our original broader vision—the prophetic Jubilee vision of justice and right relationships among people and nations. The Jubilee text from Leviticus envisions a cyclical process of canceling debts, freeing people from slavery and letting the land lie fallow—this vision incorporates economic justice and stewardship of the land."[65] The network is also emblematic of other consciously cosmopolitan organizations in its acknowledgment of its own failures to become more racially diverse. In an online statement, it admits that

Jubilee USA Network also faces the issue of racism internally. . . . There-fore we call for both a moral and strategic imperative on race to be at the center of our outreach and activism, an imperative in which we seek to be more direct in our analysis of debt, deepening our criticisms and understandings of the debt problem to include issues of racism, and showing debt's place in the system of global apartheid that has existed for centuries.[66]

Unfortunately, a link on the organization's Web site to Spanish language resources remains undeveloped and simply refers viewers to the ONE campaign.

In addition to advocating for an expansion of eligibility to all countries that remain in need of debt relief, the network is also seeking limits on conditionalities that would, for example, require the imposition of school fees. To this end, it is organizing its grassroots supporters on behalf of a bill introduced by Rep. Maxine Waters (D-CA) in December 2009 that would require the U.S. Secretary of the Treasury to enter into negotiations with the global financial institutions to secure the cancellation of all remain-ing debt owed by eligible countries. The United States would also agree to cancel all debts still owed by eligible low income countries.[67] Reforming the governance structures of the IMF and World Bank to give the lowest income countries greater voice in the decision-making is still another of the network's priorities. Their partners in the global South are also advo-cating that all new loans require the approval of a country's parliament, not just the signature of the finance minister, which would ensure greater democratic control over a country's decision to borrow from these interna-tional institutions.[68]

Although the member institutions on its national council are committed to pushing Jubilee's messages out to their constituencies at key moments, the network's staff is working to build its own constituency of Jubilee activ-ists. To move its advocacy campaigns forward, the network now has a national field organizer who works with 120 Jubilee congregations as well as local chapters to cultivate good relationships with their local members of Congress. They also have an email network and send out a monthly paper newsletter. Like other organizations, they have created resources specifi-cally for use by congregations, including instructions on how to become a Jubilee congregation. The organization maintains a presence on Facebook as well as a blog that provides regular updates on various global debt relief efforts.

ONE Campaign

After working together on the debt relief campaign, Bono and Bobby Shriver decided to collaborate again in the formation of a new advocacy organization called DATA (Debt, AIDS, Trade, Africa). As the AIDS epidemic spread throughout Africa, they became concerned that countries' savings from reductions in their debt load would be spent on AIDS medications rather than improvements in education. Using relationships they had built with key Republican members of Congress during the debt relief campaign, including Sen. Jesse Helms (R-NC), they were eventually able to secure a meeting with President George W. Bush; he agreed to support legislation that would establish emergency funding for the distribution of inexpensive AIDS medications. Known as PEPFAR (U.S. President's Emergency Plan for AIDS Relief), it constitutes the U.S.' contribution to a larger Global Fund set up to combat global AIDS infections and deaths.[69] In addition, Shriver and Bono also set up a for-profit corporation that places the (RED) label on various popular consumer items such as Converse sneakers, Gap T-shirts or Dell computers. Each time a consumer purchases a (RED) product, the company places 50 percent of the profit from that sale into the Global Fund to invest in HIV/AIDS programs in Africa. (RED) also organizes rock concerts featuring RED artists. The concerts' proceeds are also contributed to the Global Fund, thereby creating a private sector funding stream for the purchase of HIV/AIDS medications.

In 2004, the Bread for the World Institute, along with nine other organizations, including Oxfam and World Vision, joined with DATA to launch the ONE coalition as a single unified campaign against global poverty. Beckman credits Bono with going "to Bill Gates to get the funding to create a big umbrella campaign. The idea flowed in part from the successes that MoveOn.org was having with its Web-based advocacy."[70] After the coalition proved to be unworkable, Bono and Shriver decided to formally merge DATA and the ONE coalition in 2008, forming a new organization while retaining ONE's name. The ONE organization, which is intentionally designed as a secular organization, brings together a collection of odd bedfellows, ranging from Pat Robertson to George Clooney.[71]

During its phase as a coalition, ONE's board had consisted of religious groups. Following the merger with DATA, its board of directors shifted to people who had access to a great deal of money and who were eager to be part of the organization.[72] The present board consists of people such as Bono and Joshua Bolton, who served first as the director of the Office of Management and Budget and then as chief of staff in the George W. Bush administration. Jeff Raikes and Joe Cerrell, respectively the CEO and the director of the European office of the Bill and Melinda Gates Foundation also sit on the board, which is just one manifestation of the strong ties between ONE and the Gates Foundation. In 2009, the Gates Foundation awarded ONE two grants totaling $27.8 million to be spent over four years on its advocacy and public policy work in global health and global development.[73] ONE has used the funding to establish a global presence, maintaining offices in Washington DC and several key European capitals including London, Berlin, and Brussels, as well as a monitoring office in Abuja, the capital of Nigeria.

Bread for the World has also received five grants from the Gates Foundation since 2003 totaling roughly $2.8 million for its advocacy and public policy work.[74] In addition, the Gates Foundation has invested in what it calls the "Living Proof Project," which consists of a series of reports as well as videos designed "to share good news" of the "successes of U.S.–funded global health initiatives." Through videos posted on its Web site, the project tells the stories of people, mostly in Africa, who are alive today because of U.S. investments in global health care.[75] The foundation's use of stories is effectively creating a counter-narrative to the all-too-frequent refrain that "nothing can be done" to solve these big global problems.

Shriver sees ONE's approach as distinct from other organizations because of its heavy use of pop culture in doing advocacy. Involving rock musicians and movie stars helps to illustrate these issues in nontraditional venues, such as articles in *People Magazine*. It lets politicians see that these are important issues within pop culture. Shriver has encouraged the religious community to also recognize its own pop culture role: "They are creating pop culture every week when they preach."[76]

`According to Adam Phillips, the faith relations manager for ONE, the singular focus on debt relief has now been superseded by a multipronged approach that emerged out of dialogues with African leaders. Phillips admitted that ONE's priority issues closely mirror the UN's Millennium Development Goals (MDGs) that were first articulated in a Millennium Declaration, which 189 countries endorsed in 2000. The MDGs focus on eight broad areas: (1) eradicating extreme poverty and hunger; (2) achieving universal primary education; (3) promoting gender equality and empowering women; (4) reducing child mortality; (5) improving maternal health; (6) combating HIV/AIDS, malaria and other diseases; (7) ensuring environmental sustainability; and (8) developing a global partnership for development.[77] Pledging to "spare no effort to free our fellow men, women and children from the abject and dehumanizing conditions of extreme poverty," the signatories set the target date of 2015 for accomplishing very specific benchmarks in meeting these goals.[78] The best known of these benchmarks is the goal of reducing by one-half the number of people living on less than one dollar a day. Essentially, ONE was established to advocate for the U.S.' commitment to the funding needed to meet these goals. Phillips agreed that the MDGs are the overarching rubric driving ONE's advocacy agenda. "ONE takes on the big issues, such as half of the world's people living on two dollars a day."[79]

ONE now has 2 million members, mostly online. It is also connected to global NGOs in Europe and Africa. To connect to its members, the organization has a presence on Facebook, MySpace, and Twitter, in addition to maintaining a blog on its own Web site. It has nearly half a million people following it on Twitter, which is used to ask its supporters to take action such as tweeting their senators to support a strengthened international relations budget. Working with religious communities is another area of emphasis. Adam Phillips explains that ONE has sought to give faith communities an "on ramp to its work" so that people will speak out for increased anti-poverty funding out of their own traditions. To that end, well-known religious leaders were enlisted to assist in developing resources that can be used by faith communities within four major religious traditions: Christian, Jewish, Muslim, and Hindu. For example, among the Islamic resources, there are materials that can be downloaded as a pdf file that provide

> guidance on how a masjid could dedicate its prayers, services, and activities to global poverty and disease. It offers sample jumah Khutbahs, Dua and other verses that could be incorporated into a ONE Sadaqa service. It also suggests creative ways that awareness-raising, education and advocacy about poverty could be incorporated into community gatherings, hunger banquets and small group discussions.[80]

ONE's efforts to engage religious communities are a component of its overarching commitment to building a genuinely broad coalition that includes both liberals and conservatives. To that end, the organization not only has good relations with progressive religious groups such as Bread for the World and Sojourners, but also with conservative evangelicals. For Phillips, who is ordained in the Evangelical Covenant Church, the moral dimensions are fundamental to the work he is doing: "My faith compels me to be involved in these issues because it embodies what it means to love my neighbor. We live in a globalized world so we have to recognize that people come at these moral issues from different perspectives, including different religious traditions."[81]

Save Darfur Coalition and Invisible Children

In 1885, Europe's colonial powers and the United States recognized the Congo Free State as King Leopold of Belgium's privately owned colony. Until his death in 1909, Leopold was responsible for the deaths of an estimated 10 million Congolese, half the colony's population at the time of Leopold's purchase.[82] As a testament to the historic lack of attention paid to events in Africa, this tragedy is rarely mentioned among the world's most horrendous genocides. Contemporary Africa has continued to be plagued by mass killings, including those in Rwanda in the 1990s and in the Darfur region of Sudan beginning in 2003. The conflict in Darfur began when two rebel groups launched attacks against the government's installations in protest against the region's ongoing neglect by the central government in Khartoum. In response, the central government mobilized armed militias known as the *janjaweed* to attack those Darfurian ethnic groups from which the rebels had received much of their support. As villages were attacked, those who could flee did so, women taking as many of their children with them as they could. At present many of the survivors are still living in refugee camps, where an estimated 4 million people are dependent on humanitarian aid. The continued fighting coupled with militia attacks on humanitarian aid workers has made the distribution of this single lifeline tenuous indeed. In February 2010, the French aid organization, Médecins du Monde, announced it had been forced to suspend aid distribution following attacks against a rebel stronghold in the Jebel Marra region of Darfur.[83] Five years ago, a Comprehensive Peace Agreement was signed that called for free and fair elections in Sudan in 2010. Yet after several major political parties withdrew their candidates, President Omar al-Beshir, who had been indicted for war crimes by the International Criminal Court (ICC), was declared the winner.

Will Fisher, a campaign field organizer for the Save Darfur Coalition, stated that "[Save Darfur] was started in 2004 by a group of folks concerned about the issue in the news."[84] This contrasts sharply to WFP's 1980s origins, which grew out of a delegation's visit to Nicaragua where it observed people's suffering firsthand. This has not been possible in the case of Darfur. Jerry Fowler, the president of the Save Darfur Coalition, traveled to the region for the first time in February, 2010, six years after the organization he leads was founded. He wrote from Khartoum, "I applied for a visa in 2004, but only recently did the Sudanese government give me permission to come. . . . The chance to meet with displaced Darfuris inside Darfur, and in general to see firsthand this country that I have read and thought so much about has been profoundly moving."[85] Fowler had brought a preexisting knowledge of genocide to his work with the Save Darfur Coalition, having served on the board of the U.S. Holocaust Museum in Washington DC. In neighboring Chad, only a few eyewitnesses have been allowed to enter the refugee camps, but here they have been able to film stories of survivors (see YouTube). Save Darfur activists' passion is quite remarkable given that so few foreigners have met the people for whom they are advocating. However, the ability to easily view video footage on the Internet transmits the realities of Darfur's genocide in ways that were unimaginable during the 1980s crisis in Nicaragua or the 1990s genocide in Rwanda.

Fowler describes Save Darfur as a mass movement, which he characterizes as "a politically salient constituency of conscience that cares about people under attack." His choice of words signals the global reach that this issue has achieved as well as the broad inclusivity of the U.S. coalition. The all-encompassing nature of the coalition is demonstrated by the lengthy listing of its member organizations, which are both secular and religious. It includes the American Humanist Association along with the National Association of Evangelicals, several Jewish and Muslim organizations such as the American Jewish Committee, B'nai B'rith International, the Hebrew Immigrant Aid Society, the American Islamic Congress, the Muslim Public Affairs Council, and the Arab American Institute. Many familiar denominations such as the Evangelical Lutheran Church of American, the Episcopal Church in the United States (ECUSA), the U.S. Conference of Catholic Bishops, and the Mennonite Central Committee are also present as are several other organizations: Bread for the World, the Jubilee Campaign, Sojourners, the Maryknoll Office of Global Concerns, and Pax Christi. Finally, there are a number of organizations that have long track records of advocacy on Africa, including the TransAfrica Forum, the African Faith and Justice Coalition, and the NAACP. Interestingly, the Armenian Church of America rarely shows up on lists of activist denominations, but because of Armenians' own legacy of genocide, their church's leaders have served as key spokespersons for Darfur.[86]

Since its inception, students have been in the vanguard of this movement. For many of them, this is their first exposure to a case of genocide as it is unfolding. Given its young adult constituency and its relative newness, the Save Darfur Coalition has built its organizing strategy around the use of social networking. Roughly fifty thousand people are connected to the coalition on Facebook, making it a remarkably grassroots-oriented organization that clearly thrives on unleashing the initiative of its youthful supporters. Save Darfur's blog has a category for activist stories, which features news about local activities initiated by its grassroots supporters. A February 2010 posting features A. J Fay, who first became interested in Darfur in high school and has now helped co-found the Idaho Darfur Coalition. Interestingly, A. J. attributes his ongoing passion to work on Darfur to "the personal and working relationships I enjoy with the Darfuri and Sudanese refugees in my community" of Boise, Idaho.[87] Once again, stories brought by refugees fleeing a conflict are triggering American humanitarian activism.

Will Fisher describes the coalition's organizing strategy as multifaceted. They have staged large public events, including bringing more than fifty thousand supporters to the Mall in Washington in 2006 and letter-writing campaigns that have mobilized thousands more. They have built international support through partner organizations in Europe, Africa, and the Middle East, which have resulted in a Global Days for Darfur. Recently, they pressed American corporations to divest from businesses that are supporting the current regime in Sudan. This includes five major mutual funds, all invested in PetroChina (PTR), whose parent company CNPC appears to be the worst of the "highest offending" companies helping to fund the genocide in Darfur, according to the Save Darfur's Divestment Campaign.[88] The coalition has also taken advantage of its highly visible supporters, including George Clooney, who has mentioned Darfur in interviews in *People Magazine* and at the Academy Awards. According to Fisher, Clooney's endorsement has "acted as a spark. People say, 'I've never heard of this—let me take a look.'"[89] Still others have gotten involved after going to the movies and seeing a documentary on genocide in Darfur as part of the previews.

To reach religious audiences the coalition has produced a DVD titled "Darfur: A Call to Action, Lessons from Faith Leaders," which it distributes for free. The DVD is part of an organizing kit for faith leaders that also includes discussion questions for interfaith, Christian, Jewish, or Muslim discussion groups, sample prayers, bulletin inserts, guides for event organizers, and an action guide. The materials are designed to enable religious communities to be self-generative, initiating independent forms of activism that are not necessarily linked to specific national campaigns. The DVD opens with a quote from Martin Luther King Jr. and expresses the fundamental religious premise of any campaign against genocide. The opening narration states, "We all share the same humanity, we are all flesh, blood, and spirit. We're all connected." The DVD is designed to appeal to the three Abrahamic faiths and features Bishop John H. Ricard SSJ, from the Diocese of Pensacola, Florida; Rev. Gloria White-Hammond, co-pastor of Bethel AME Church; Ingrid

Mattson, the president of the Islamic Society of North America; and Sir Jonathan Sacks, the Chief Rabbi, United Hebrew Congregations. Commentary by these four prominent religious leaders is interspersed with short interviews with Darfuri survivors, photos of earlier genocides, as well as footage of Gandhi, Desmond Tutu, Nelson Mandela, anti-apartheid rallies in South Africa, the 1963 March on Washington, and the fall of the Berlin Wall. These are presented as symbols of earlier successful efforts to throw off oppressive regimes and transform societies through nonviolent resistance. The DVD's message is that the situation in Darfur is unacceptable and immoral.

The Jewish World Watch (JWW) is the strongest member organization of the Save Darfur Coalition on the West Coast. Within one year of its founding in September of 2004, thirty synagogues had joined as members of JWW.[90] At present JWW has sixty-four member synagogues, giving the organization a constituency of at least 350,000 people.[91] The organization owes its founding to the inspiration of Rabbi Harold Schulweis, who is regarded as a contemporary prophetic voice within the Conservative Jewish community. Rabbi Schulweis, now eighty-five, studied under Abraham Joshua Heschel and is the longtime spiritual leader of Valley Beth Shalom in Encino, California. Following the Rwandan genocide, Rabbi Schulweis had an epiphany, realizing that the Jewish vow, "Never Again," made in response to the Holocaust, charged people of conscience with the responsibility to never stand by idly in the face of genocide. This position, grounded in the biblical understanding that we are our brother's keeper, led Schulweis to start JWW in response to the crisis in Darfur. According to Janice Kamenir-Reznik, the organization's co-founder and president of its board of directors, JWW is a form of what Heschel called "praying with our feet.[92]

JWW has a three-pronged strategy of education, advocacy, and refugee relief, which embody Judaism's concept of *tzedakah*—"justice as charity." Their staff of seven prepare presentations in synagogues, talk to campers at Jewish summer camps and to students at Jewish Day Schools, Catholic parochial schools, and public schools. They have connected to African American women's groups and law firms. As described in the introduction, every Passover, they develop materials that integrate contemporary global issues into the traditional Passover seder, thereby making the holiday more relevant to present-day realities. Their advocacy work has focused on convincing the University of California regents to vote in favor of divestment from companies doing business in Sudan; they have lobbied the California state legislature to pass a law, signed by Governor Schwarzenegger in 2009, enacting the UC divestment and requiring the same by the state's retirement funds. Additionally, the organization has raised $2 million in direct aid to Darfuri refugees and another $3 million to fund a solar cooking oven project. This action resulted in the purchase of materials to manufacture forty-six thousand solar ovens in refugee camps. Kamenir-Reznik stated that this last project demonstrated what the organization could accomplish when it focused on one single issue, namely, preventing incidences of women getting raped while searching for firewood outside the camps. The solar ovens simply eliminated the need for firewood.[93]

Now, JWW is moving into work in the Congo as well. In March 2010, Kamenir-Reznik traveled there with the newly formed Eastern Congo Initiative, whose founder is Ben Affleck, another Hollywood actor who has become an activist. Instead of relief per se, this project is focused on rebuilding civil society, reestablishing the rule of law in the war-torn regions of eastern Congo: "We can support Congolese grassroots empowerment organizations by helping their work have a broader impact. We want to support acts of courage on the ground by creating more political impact for their efforts."[94] Again, JWW is another example of the remarkable extent to which global justice organizations have the capacity to connect religious people in local U.S. congregations with people experiencing violence and genocide on the other side of the earth.

Another organization, known as Invisible Children, is organizing to end a twenty-three-year-old war in northern Uganda, one that is being waged by a rebel group called the Lord's Resistance Army (LRA). Invisible Children was co-founded by three young filmmakers from Southern California who went to Africa in 2003 with the intention of making a film on Darfur. They ended up in northern Uganda after being denied entry into the Sudan. There they were confronted with the suffering created by a war that had received virtually no attention outside of Africa. They filmed the nightly rituals in which many children leave their homes to sleep in public places as protection against being kidnapped and forced to join the LRA as child-soldiers. After returning to the United States, they produced a film titled *Invisible Children* and set up a nonprofit organization of the same name as the vehicle through which they could raise awareness of the child-soldiers.

As is the case with both ONE and the Save Darfur Coalition, Invisible Children is not a religious organization. According to Cameron Woodward, the organization's twenty-year-old manager of social media and recurring donations, the story is not exclusive—all of us can relate to this. Woodward first got involved with Invisible Children while he was a senior in high school where the film was shown at his Christian club. As a school, they raised $15,000, which placed them among the top fundraisers in the country. He was invited to travel to Uganda to see firsthand what the funds the school had raised were doing. When he returned he became a "roadie," a staff person who travels from city to city showing the film and talking about the cause. Yet, Woodward, who is a Christian, understands the work as an expression of the kingdom of God as acknowledged by the Rt. Rev. N. T. Wright, a well-known Church of England bishop. Woodward believes that Wright would understand what is occurring in Uganda as an expression of Jesus being nailed to the human condition, which in turn opens up a call to radical hospitality.[95]

Invisible Children is creating fresh, innovative forms of organizing that are also entertaining, giving it the capacity to generate both excitement and creativity from their young adult audiences. They are constructing new forms of activism geared to the YouTube generation by crossing the traditional boundaries between advocacy and humanitarian aid. Invisible Children's staff describes themselves not mainly as activists or organizers but as storytellers who seek "to inspire young people to end the longest running war in Africa." In a clear expression of their cosmopolitan identity, they go on to state, "We are young, we are citizens of the world, and we are artists, activists, and entrepreneurs."[96] Woodward described Invisible Children as a massive movement of young people committed to the story of the children in Uganda. The use of social media such as Facebook, MySpace, and Twitter plays a huge role in enabling their supporters to stay connected. According to Woodward, the effect of these new forms of social media is to render borders as imaginary. "There is an up- and a downside to globalization. Globalization can be good. If it allows humans to interact with each other, it's awesome. But, if it's about producing cheaper products, then it's detrimental."[97] Woodward's perspective is repeated in an interview with Luis Moreno Ocampo, the chief prosecutor of the ICC, featured in one of Invisible Children's videos posted on YouTube. Reflecting on the shifting meaning of globalization, Ocampo says, "It's interesting how things are changing. When Rwanda happened there was not any activism in Western countries. Now Uganda and Darfur are both creating activism. But it's not enough today to lobby one's own government—you have to go to the global system and that is something we are learning how to do. It's a new world; it's a twenty-first-century situation."[98]

As an indication of the spread of new forms of global organizing, the Invisible Children film has been seen in countries around the world. After circulating a petition, which reads "We, the citizens of the world who have witnessed the suffering of abducted child-soldiers in central Africa sign this Citizen's Arrest Warrant for Joseph Kony [the leader of the LRA]," the organization received a total of 253,000 signatures from all over the world. Those signatures were delivered to the U.S. State Department on January 11, 2010. Furthermore, the organization staged a series of "rescues" designed to imitate its goal of rescuing the child-soldiers. These events were held not only in cities throughout the United States but in ten other countries as well. In each case, groups of young people agreed to camp out in a central urban location until a media mogul or politician came "to rescue" them. According to Woodward, the "rescues" were inspired by the Freedom Rides of the 1960s when interracial groups of students rode buses throughout the South as a means of challenging racial segregation in public transportation.[99] Invisible Children works with partner organizations in Washington to secure congressional passage of "The LRA Disarmament and Northern Ugandan Recovery Act of 2009," which has received the most bipartisan support of any country-specific bill related to Africa in the last thirty years.[100] Like other groups we have already encountered, Invisible Children has also carried out what they call "hometown shakedowns" of specific senators as a means of encouraging them to vote for this bill since politicians are often moved to action after hearing from their hometown constituents.

The group is also committed to the recovery and rehabilitation of LRA affected communities in Uganda, southern Sudan, the Central African Republic, and the Democratic Republic of Congo. When they asked their Ugandan friends how they could best support them, the Ugandans responded by saying that education was the most urgent need. Ugandan kids were doing well but their schools were in deplorable shape.[101] This led to the creation of "Schools for Schools" in which American high school students raise money to rebuild schools in Uganda and its neighboring countries. At this point, they have raised $5 million to rebuild schools in Africa. Woodward emphasizes that they are intentionally not showing negative pictures in order to raise the money. That way, American kids can see themselves as standing in solidarity with the kids in Uganda. "We are trying to inspire young American high schoolers that they can make a difference."[102] Like (RED), the Invisible Children also raises humanitarian aid through the Internet and event sales of bracelets made by young people in Uganda.

In a reversal of the older WFP model of taking American delegations countries in Central America, Invisible Children has selected a group of Ugandans to visit the United States to tell their stories to audiences here. In a sad twist of fate, Nate Henn, one of Invisible Children's volunteer roadies was among the seventy-four people killed in a terrorist attack in Uganda on July 11, 2010, where he had gone to visit his friend Innocent, a young Ugandan former child soldier. Nate and Innocent had just spent three months touring the United States, speaking on behalf of Invisible Children.[103]

Concluding Remarks

We have highlighted the work of a number of very successful efforts at global organizing. The work is closely intertwined with advocacy for critically important global humanitarian needs, which resonate well with religious sensibilities. The most recently formed organizations are now moving away from specifically religious identities, even though they continue to target a portion of their organizing efforts toward religious communities. While religion does not define these organizations, it is nonetheless understood to be an important component of any successful organizing and advocacy strategy on behalf of global hunger and poverty alleviation. Thus, they are neither entirely secular nor entirely religious, making them an emerging form of hybridity. This approach gives these newly formed organizations greater flexibility in reaching the broad audiences needed to gain U.S. support for global needs, while it still allows a clear moral grounding for the work.

We have encountered not only organizations that are successfully doing outreach to young adults, but one that was actually founded by young adults. These are cosmopolitan organizations with a very different feel to them than ones we read about earlier in this book. They are adept at integrating issues with popular culture through featuring well-known personalities and interweaving popular music with activism. Perhaps more importantly, however, their use of new media, especially Facebook and YouTube allows for a great deal of local initiative and creativity. Young people who have become connected to the issues in Darfur or Uganda through the Internet can create activities independently of national organizations. In fact, these forms of local spontaneity are encouraged and valued by the national organizations. This, effectively, creates new, less hierarchical forms of organizing less dependent on large staffs or major national leaders. The use of the Internet has also made building global connections far easier than in the past. Indeed, the Internet may in part explain why Darfurian genocide has led to the formation of a global response, while that in Rwanda did not. The result of this new interconnectedness is a reconstruction of the *other*. As is being articulated by Invisible Children, no longer are children in Uganda perceived as the *other*. Instead, they have become just like us.

Our exploration has also hinted at the emergence of new marketing and fund-raising techniques within justice organizing. Both Invisible Children and (ONE) are selling products as a means of raising humanitarian aid. They are drawing on popular youth culture's embrace of trendy fashion labels and rock concerts to raise money for global health and education projects.

8

Conclusions

By taking a broad comparative approach to the study of religious activism, this book greatly expands our understanding beyond earlier research that either focused on individual movements or was situated in specific social locations. It provides readers with a fuller sense of the richness and diversity of religious activism as a very significant and distinctive presence in American public life. The organizations we have examined represent a wide spectrum of religious activism, yet, in every case, they seek to ameliorate the most negative consequences of economic globalization and the politics of empire upon highly vulnerable populations. In some cases, they are simultaneously using new information and social networking technologies to nurture coordinated global responses to injustice in regions of the world that previously remained "hidden" from U.S. religious audiences. Despite the scope of this work, much of the broader American public remains largely unaware of its presence. Indeed, many activists are unaware of its scope, especially when it occurs in social locations outside their own.

While earlier case studies that focused on religious solidarity work found that it typically mobilizes white, middle-class professionals, the use of multiple case studies situated in distinct social locations provides a fuller picture of contemporary religious activism's capacity to also engage marginalized people in organizing. Both congregational-based community organizing and worker-justice activism demonstrate religious activism's ability to empower marginalized people to construct new forms of citizenship from the bottom up. Their successes represent small, but important victories for people who are experiencing the harshest consequences of the globalized economy.

As long as comprehensive immigration reform that includes a pathway to citizenship for the undocumented is delayed, insurgent citizenship will not resolve the basic fragility of many immigrants' lives in the United States. At the same time, in the absence of access to full citizenship, insurgent citizenship does strengthen families' capacity to improve their well-being, which in turn creates greater opportunities for their children, especially those born in this country. Thus, in many immigrant contexts, the creation of rights from the bottom-up will ultimately benefit the life chances of the second generation and therefore citizens of the United States.

Our case studies have shown that borderlands activism is far more likely to consist of face-to-face organizing than is true of the cosmopolitan organizations, which frequently make extensive use of email updates and social media to connect to their supporters. Especially congregational-based community organizing and worker-justice centers emphasize the creation of community among immigrants from diverse ethnic and cultural backgrounds. Successful borderlands work requires the conscious creation of bonds of solidarity among its participants. Ordinary community members and workers must learn to work together in their fight for justice. In contrast, cosmopolitan organizing can be much more individualized. This is particularly true of groups that primarily rely on email, which often asks individuals to act autonomously from others. While cosmopolitan activism may bring supporters together for rallies or other mass events, it does not necessarily expect them to learn to work collectively.

Consistently, our case studies have shown that religious commitments to justice create new possibilities of engaging in other-regarding political behavior. This is especially true among cosmopolitans who have either had transformative experiences or been exposed to various forms of liberative pedagogy. Until recently, the creation of multi-ethnic and class coalitions primarily occurred at the local and state levels. However, as borderlands organizations, including several congregational-based community organizing networks, immigrant rights organizations, and Interfaith Worker Justice, become increasingly engaged in national legislative lobbying, we might see increased *other*-regarding behavior on national policy issues. Given these organizations' strong roots in borderlands communities, they can potentially establish a presence in Washington for a new generation of broad-based constituency organizations (see chap. 1).To the extent that they build inter-class and inter-ethnic cooperation wherein common religious commitments to justice bring more privileged Americans into solidarity around issues affecting marginalized people living in the United States, these organizations represent a very important alternative to the normally self-interested nature of American politics.

In both borderlands and cosmopolitan contexts, religious activism demonstrates a significant ability to build solidarity between the *other* and those who are privileged. It does this by its deep-seated commitment to nonviolent social change and its widespread use of popular education, both of which seek the transformation of the oppressed and the oppressors. Over and over again, we saw the importance placed on narrative, especially on enabling marginalized people to tell their stories. Clearly sharing people's own stories of suffering is transformative for those telling them and for those listening. They confirm Levinas's assertion that a commitment to human rights must be grounded to face-to-face encounters with the *other*.

We also found a number of significant efforts to build solidarity between African Americans and Latinos through the mutual sharing of their stories of suffering and commonly held religious beliefs. These efforts hold great potential for creating common ground between two groups of people who have both suffered enormously and yet today often find themselves in contention with one another.

This book has also sought to highlight the expanded interreligious nature of prophetic activism, which is also a consequence of globalization's transformation of the United States into a multireligious society. The extent to which activists from within varied religious traditions are now building their own activist religious organizations, while also collaborating with each other, can be understood as still another form of religious solidarity. Religious justice activism is enriched through the growing presence of diverse religions, each engaged in the task of developing a religious scaffolding to support justice activism within their own religion. In the twenty-first century, religious activism will become more interreligious, which simultaneously widens the spaces in which activists of varied traditions can learn from each other's religious traditions.

At a time of increasingly divisive politics, this book has demonstrated that religion actually has the ability to heal divisions by building solidarity between marginalized and privileged communities, between people of different racial and ethnic identities, and between the world's religions. The fact that religion has the capacity to build multiple forms of solidarity may seem almost counterintuitive since religion is so often perceived as either the cause of conflict or simply as irrelevant.

In deepening our understanding of both the distinctiveness of religious activism as well as the similarities it shares with a broader array of justice organizations, there is clear evidence of emerging synergies between secular and religious justice activism. Religious activism is distinguished by its ongoing efforts to construct the religious scaffolding needed to support justice activism. This work continues to occur within Christianity, where biblical passages that support peace and justice are still in contention with others that support war and the status quo. Textual interpretation is an ongoing process as new issues arise. For example, following revelations of torture at Abu Ghraib and other secret U.S. detention centers, emerging religious human rights organizations conducted extensive new textual analysis within both Christianity and Judaism. Evangelicals who have become increasingly active on peacemaking, human rights, and nuclear weapons have developed textual interpretations better suited to their biblically more conservative audiences. Muslims and Buddhists are engaged in similar textual interpretation within their religious traditions. This interpretative work is consistently one of the significant roles played by the theologians involved in these movements since they are trained to do such textual analysis.

Religious activists also draw on a variety of religious symbols to imbue their public actions and events with a sense of the sacred. These symbols resonant with many participants' sense of spirituality, while serving as reminders for their supporters and opponents alike of the deeper meaning of the campaigns in which they are involved.

At the same time, other elements of religious activists' work is often quite similar to that of secular justice organizations with whom they frequently collaborate. We have seen that within the broader arena of borderlands activism, other organizations such as IDEPSCA and the NNIRR also ground their organizing praxis in the use of popular education. In fact, both organizations are excellent examples of these liberative pedagogies' use in empowering marginalized groups of people. On the other hand, the basic organizing methodologies used by religious organizations engaged in legislative lobbying are much like those used by nonreligious legislative lobbying groups. In both cases, the most effective justice lobbying is rooted in the development of a strong grassroots presence in congressional districts. Even the use of narrative is not distinct to religious activists. The Gates Foundation uses personal narratives to tell their stories of the successes of various global anti-poverty initiatives, which they have supported. Thus, while religious activists have distinctive messages and symbols grounded in their religious traditions, their basic organizing methods are often quite similar to those used by secular justice activists.

Given these similarities, it is not surprising to see the emergence of various hybrid justice organizations that are secular, yet purposefully create space for religious activists to participate from the vantage point of their religious traditions. This was much in evidence at the NNIRR conference (chap. 5), in the work of organizations such as the Save Darfur Coalition, which includes both religious and secular member organizations, and the ONE organization, which makes worship and study materials available on their Web site for use by the four major global religions. Even Invisible Children has supporters and staff who are active out of clearly articulated religious beliefs. These organizations certainly understand that religious adherents who are motivated to act at least partly based on their religious understandings of justice are a constituency they must reach.

Justice activists are continuously evolving and innovating as they respond to the shifting realities of their contexts as well as new opportunities. For example, we saw how IWJ developed a whole new area of work in building their worker centers. This is no doubt a result of the instability of some of their allies in organized labor coupled with their growing interactions with workers in whom unions were simply not interested. Innovation was also evident among the youngest global justice organizations formed since 9/11. They rapidly incorporated the use of new media tools such as YouTube, Facebook, and Twitter into their organizing, which allow their supporters to build interactive relationships not only with staff but with each other. This opens up new spaces of innovation and collaboration at the grassroots. They also allow for the creation of broader global interactions among activists located in different parts of the world. This interconnectedness not only strengthens the possibilities of global solidarity, it also democratizes global organizing since people can be in conversation with each other without paying the high costs of overseas phone calls or air travel. The result is that activists in new groups such as Invisible Children view Ugandan youths as more like themselves rather than as the *other*. There has also been an unprecedented level of political engagement by media personalities, including rock musicians and movie stars, on behalf of various global justice and humanitarian causes. Their presence has brought these global issues much more directly into the popular media than was the case in the past.

Finally, our various case studies demonstrate that prophetic activism greatly enriches religious life in America by creating meaningful opportunities for religious people to connect their spirituality to a variety of justice causes. By creating new understandings and perspectives on traditional religious ideas, prophetic social justice work enhances the significance of religious identity for those who embrace these forms of activism. In fact, for some people, religious activism may be more meaningful spiritually than regular participation in more traditional places of worship. This may be especially true of young adults for whom hybrid organizations create spaces in which they can engage in humanitarian work alongside advocating for a cause. It also suggests that rather than shying away from justice activism, denominations might indeed do more to encourage their members' connections to the myriad forms of activism.

Notes

NOTES TO CHAPTER 1

1. *Holy Family Asks for Lodging Today at Disneyland.*" Script for the Stations, provided by Wendy Tarr, executive director, CLUE Orange County, April 22, 2010.

2. David Sanchez, *From Patmos to the Barrio: Subverting Imperial Myths* (Minneapolis: Fortress Press, 2008), 85.

3. William Stringfellow, *An Ethic for Christians and Other Aliens in a Strange Land* (Waco, TX: Word Books,1973), 14.

4. Howard Thurman, *Jesus and the Disinherited* (Boston: Beacon Press, 1996), 13.

5. See Sudarshan Kapur, *Raising up a Prophet: The African-American Encounter with Gandhi* (Boston: Beacon Press, 1992) for a complete history of this transmission.

6. "Religion Among Millennials: Less Religiously Active than Older Americans, but Fairly Traditional in Other Ways," Pew Forum on Religion and Public Life Report, February 2010.

7. Jaime Rapaport, executive director of the Progressive Jewish Alliance, Los Angeles, phone interview, August 12, 2009.

8. This basic premise of human rights is affirmed in article 1 of the Universal Declaration of Human Rights (UDHR) adopted by the General Assembly of the United Nations, December 10, 1948.

9. Article 23, UDHR.

10. Michael Hardt and Antonio Negri, *Multitude: War and Democracy in the Age of Empire* (New York: Penguin Press, 2004).

11. See David Bacon, *Illegal People: How Globalization Creates Migration and Criminalizes Immigrants* (Boston: Beacon Press, 2008) for an straightforward description of how this process of globalization has affected the Mexican economy.

12. Lawrence R. Jacobs and Theda Skocpol, eds., *Inequality and American Democracy: What We Know and What We Need to Learn* (New York: Russell Sage Foundation, 2005), 9.

13. Ibid, 12.

14. Theda Skocpol, "How America Became Civic" in *Civic Engagement in American Democracy,* ed. Theda Skocpol and Morris P. Fiorina, 69 (Washington DC: Brookings Institution and New York: Russell Sage Foundation, 1999).

15. James F. Findlay Jr., *Church People in the Struggle* (Oxford: Oxford University Press, 1993), 20.

16. Ibid., 50.

17. Robert Wuthnow, *The Restructuring of American Religion: Society and Faith since World War II* (Princeton, NJ: Princeton University Press, 1988), 145.

18. Findlay, *Church People*, 58.

19. Alan Wolf. *Transformation of American Religion: How We Actually Live Our Faith* (New York: Free Press, 2003), 41.

20. Analysis of the United Methodist Church General Agency Budgets, 1969–2008. The UMC is the only mainline Protestant denomination that has a complete record of its agencies budgets.

21. John M. Hobson, *The Eastern Origins of Western Civilization* (Cambridge: Cambridge University Press, 2004), 107–14.

22. Rabbi Jonah Pesner, executive director of Just Congregations, phone interview, March 16, 2010.

23. Richard A. Horsley, *Jesus and Empire: The Kingdom of God and the New World Disorder* (Minneapolis: Fortress Press, 2003), 79.

24. Hardt and Negri, *Multitude*, 2004, 351.

25. See Mark Chaves, *Congregations in America*, (Cambridge MA: Harvard University Press, 2004) and Wuthnow, *Restructuring of American Religion*, for examples.

26. See Albert J. Raboteau, *A Fire in the Bones: Reflections on African-American Religious History* (Boston: Beacon Press, 1995).

27. R. S. Sugirtharajah *Postcolonial Criticism and Biblical Interpretation* (Oxford: Oxford University Press, 2002), 101.

28. Ibid.

29. See Philip Jenkins, *The New Faces of Christianity: Believing the Bible in the Global South* (Oxford: Oxford University Press, 2006).

30. R. S. Sugirtharajah, "Complacencies and Cul-de Sacs: Christian Theologies and Colonialism," in *Postcolonial Theologies: Divinty and Empire,* ed. Catherine Keller, Michael Nausner, and Mayra Rivera (St. Louis, MO: Chalice Press, 2004), 36.

31. Jenkins, *New Faces of Christianity*, 13.

32. Gloria Anzaldúa, *Borderlands, La Frontera: The New Mestiza*, 3rd ed. (San Francisco: Aunt Lute Books, 2007).

33. William H. Frey, "America's New Demographics: Regions, Metros, Cities, Suburbs and Exurbs," http://www.brook.edu/metro/speeches/frey20070212_demographics.htm.

34. R. Stephen Warner and Judith Wittner, eds., *Gatherings in the Diaspora: Religious Communities and the New Immigration* (Philadelphia: Temple University Press, 1998).

35. See Anzaldúa, *Borderlands,* and Néstor, *Mestizaje: (Re)mapping Race, Culture, and Faith with Latino Catholicism* (Maryknoll, NY: Orbis Books, 2009).

36. The Sentencing Project, "Felony Disenfranchisement," http://www.sentencingproject.org/IssueAreaHome.aspx?IssueID=4.

37. http://gaylife.about.com/od/samesexmarriage/a/legalgaymarriag.htm (accessed August 13, 2010).

38. James Holston, "Spaces of Insurgent Citizenship," *Planning Theory* 13 (1995).

39. Ibid., 47.

40. Selya Benhabib, *The Rights of Others: Aliens, Residents and Citizens* (Cambridge: Cambridge University Press, 2004), 110–11.

41. Amartya Sen, *Development as Freedom* (Oxford: Oxford University Press, 2001).

42. Daniel J. Tichenor, *The Politics of Immigration Control in America* (Princeton, NJ: Princeton University Press, 2002).

43. Kwame Anthony Appiah, *Cosmopolitanism: Ethics in a World of Strangers* (New York: W. W. Norton, 2006), xv.

44. Ibid.

45. Clare Weber, *Visions of Solidarity: U.S. Peace Activists in Nicaragua from War to Women's Activism and Globalization* (Lanham, MD: Lexington Books, 2006), 54.

NOTES TO CHAPTER 2

1. This is how the American Baptist missionaries translated the meaning of "prophetic" from English into the language of the Aos, a tribal people in northeast India.

2. Michael Lerner, *Jewish Renewal: A Path to Healing and Transformation* (New York: G. P. Putnam's Sons, 1994), 26.

3. David Gutterman, *Prophetic Politics: Christian Social Movements and American Democracy* (Ithaca, NY: Cornell University Press, 2005) 32.

4. Ibid., 88.

5. Frantz Fanon, *The Wretched of the Earth* (New York: Grove Press, 1968), 67.

6. Heschel accompanied King on the third attempt to march from Selma to Montgomery in 1965 in support of African American voting rights.

7. Marvin Sweeney, *The Prophetic Literature* (Nashville: Abingdon Press, 2005) 29.

8. Ehud Ben Zvi, "De-historicizing and Historicizing Tendencies in the Twelve Prophetic Books" in *Israel's Prophets and Israel's Past: Essays on the Relationships of the Prophetic Texts and Israelite History in Honor of John H. Hayes,* ed. Brad Kelle and Megan Bishop Moore, 42 (New York: T & T Clark, 2006).

9. Sweeney, *Prophetic Literature,* 47.

10. Marvin Sweeney, *Form and Intertextuality in Prophetic and Apocalyptic Literature* (Tübingen: Mohr Siebeck, 2005), 81.

11. Seyyed Hossein Nasr, "Islam," in *Our Religions,* ed. Arvind Sharma, 453 (New York: HarperCollins, 1993).

12. Ben Zvi, "De-historicizing and Historicizing Tendencies," 44.

13. Abraham J. Heschel, *The Prophets* (New York: Harper Perennial Classics, 2001), 242.

14. Rabbi Jonathan Sacks, *To Heal a Fractured World: The Ethics of Responsibility* (New York: Schocken Books, 2005), 12.

15. Heschel, *Prophets,* 255.

16. Ibid., 254.

17. Ibid., 251.

18. Ibid., 253.

19. Roger Burgraeve, *The Wisdom of Love in the Service of Love: Emmanuel Levinas on Justice, Peace, and Human Rights* (Milwaukee, WI: Marquette University Press. 2002), 59.

20. Ibid., 103.

21. Ibid., 104.

22. Ibid., 119.

23. Leslie J. Hoppe, O.F.M., *There Shall be No Poor Among You: Poverty in the Bible* (Nashville: Abingdon, 2004), 10–11.

24. Jonathan Sacks argues that these passages should more accurately be understood as "responsibilities and duties," in place of the more familiar term of rights. See Sacks, *To Heal a Fractured World*, 101.

25. Walter Brueggemann, *A Commentary on Jeremiah: Exile and Homecoming* (Grand Rapids, MI: Eerdmanns, 1998), 257–58.

26. Daniel Smith-Christopher, "The Quiet Words of the Wise: Biblical Developments Toward Nonviolence as a Diaspora Ethic" in *Character Ethics and the Old Testament: Moral Dimensions of Scripture,* ed. M. Daniel Carroll R. and Jacqueline E. Lapsley, 147 (Louisville, KY: Westminster Jon Knox Press, 2007).

27. Sacks, *To Heal a Fractured World*, 98.

28. Ibid., 101.

29. Smith-Christopher, "Quiet Words of the Wise," 59–60.

30. See Ched Myers, *Binding the Strong Man: A Political Reading of Mark's Story of Jesus* (Maryknoll, NY: Orbis Books, 1994), chap. 2.

31. Bruce J. Malina, *The Social Gospel of Jesus: The Kingdom of God in Mediterranean Perspective* (Minneapolis: Fortress Press, 2001), 26–27.

32. Walter Wink, *The Powers That Be: Theology for a New Millennium* (New York: Doubleday, 1998), 69.

33. Henry David Thoreau, *Civil Disobedience* (New York: Book of the Month Club, 1996).

34. Ibid., 21.

35. Terrence J. Rynne, *Gandhi and Jesus: The Saving Power of Nonviolence* (Maryknoll, NY: Orbis Books, 2008), 42.

36. Krishnalal Shridharani, *War Without Violence: A Study of Gandhi's Method and Its Accomplishments* (New York: Harcourt, Brace, 1939), 36.

37. Reinhold Niebuhr, *Moral Man and Immoral Society* (New York: Charles Scribner's Sons, 1960), 247.

38. Ibid., 254.

39. I first became aware of this connection during an informal talk given by Lawrence Edward Carter Sr., dean of the Martin Luther King Chapel at Morehouse College, Atlanta, Georgia, while speaking on a panel on "Ecumenism from the Margins: Christian Unity in the Quest for Justice," April 2–3, 2008.

40. Sudarshan Kapur, *Raising Up a Prophet* (Boston: Beacon Press, 1992), 45.

41. Ibid., 50.

42. Joseph Kip Kosek, *Acts of Conscience: Christian Nonviolence and Modern American Democracy* (New York: Columbia University Press, 2009), 86.

43. Ibid., 98.

44. Ibid., 178.

45. David Cortright, *Gandhi and Beyond: Nonviolence for an Age of Terrorism* (Boulder, CO: Paradigm Publishers, 2006), 43.

46. Kapur, *Raising Up a Prophet*, 119.

47. August Meier and Elliot Rudwick, *CORE: A Study in the Civil Rights Movement 1942–1968* (Urbana: University of Illinois Press, 1975), 9.

48. Ibid., 144.

49. Rev. James Lawson, pastor emeritus, Holman United Methodist Church, Los Angeles, CA, phone interview, June 23, 2009.

50. Sudarshan Kapur, *Raising Up a Prophet*, 159.

51. John Dear, *Put Down Your Sword: Answering the Gospel Call to Creative Nonviolence* (Grand Rapids, MI: Eerdmanns, 2008), 118.

52. Marvin L. Krier Mich, *Catholic Social Teaching and Movements* (Mystic, CT: Twenty-Third Publications, 1998), 120.

53. Donal Dorr, *Option for the Poor: A Hundred Years of Catholic Social Teaching* (Maryknoll NY: Orbis Books, 1983), 152.

54. Gustavo Gutiérrez, *A Theology of Liberation* (Maryknoll, NY: Orbis Books, 1988), 63.

55. Ibid., 69.

56. Christian Smith, *Resisting Reagan: The U.S. Central America Peace Movement* (Chicago: University of Chicago Press, 1996), 148.

57. Paulo Freire, *Pedagogy of the Oppressed*, 30th anniversary ed. (New York: Continuum International, 2008), 47.

58. Ibid.

59. Aldon D. Morris, *The Origins of the Civil Rights Movement: Black Communities Organizing for Change* (New York: Free Press, 1984), 146.

60. Ibid., 142.

61. Freire, *Pedagogy of the Oppressed*, 50. (Italics added by this author.)

62. Clare Weber, *Visions of Solidarity: U.S. Peace Activists in Nicaragua From War to Women's Activism ad Globalization* (Lanham, MD: Lexington Books, 2006), 56.

NOTES TO CHAPTER 3

1. Kathy Partridge, executive director of Interfaith Funders, email correspondence, July 5, 2008.

2. Mark Naison, *Communists in Harlem during the Depression* (New York: Grove Press, 1984), 51.

3. Mark Warren, *Dry Bones Rattling: Community Building to Revitalize American Democracy* (Princeton, NJ: Princeton University Press, 2001), 42.

4. Mark R. Warren and Richard L. Wood, *Faith-Based Community Organizing: The State of the Field* (Jericho, NY: Interfaith Funders, 2001).

5. John Carr, interview, Washington DC, April 5, 2001.

6. "Religious Composition of the U.S.," Appendix to the U.S. Religious Landscape Survey published by the Pew Forum on Religion and Public Life, http://religions.pewforum.org/pdf/affiliations-all-traditions.pdf (accessed July 8, 2008).

7. Robert P. Swierenga, "Ethnoreligious Political Behavior in the Mid-Nineteenth Century: Voting, Values, Cultures" in *Religion and American Politics: From the Colonial Period to the Present*, ed. Mark A. Noll and Luke E. Harlow, 152 (New York: Oxford University Press, 2007).

8. Daniel J. Tichenor, *Dividing Lines: The Politics of Immigration Control in America* (Princeton, NJ: Princeton University Press, 2002), 56–57.

9. Peter Steinfels, "Roman Catholics and American Politics, 1960–2004," in Noll and Harlow, *Religion and American Politic,* 345–49.

10. William Purcell, associate director, Center for Social Concerns, University of Notre Dame, South Bend, IN, interview, July 8, 2008.

11. Marvin L. Krier Mich, *Catholic Social Teaching and Movements* (Mystic, CT: Twenty-Third Publications, 1998), chap. 1.

12. Mark Zwick and Louise Zwick, *The Catholic Worker Movement: Intellectual and Spiritual Origins* (New York: Paulist Press, 2005), 31.

13. James Allaire and Rosemary Broughton, "An Introduction to the Life and Spirituality of Dorothy Day," http://www.catholicworker.org/roundtable/pddintro.htm (accessed February 22, 2000), 6.

14. http://www.catholicworker.org/communities/commlistall.cfm (accessed July 14, 2008).

15. Mich, *Catholic Social Teaching*, 142.

16. Ibid., 143.

17. Allaire and Broughton, "Introduction to the Life and Spirituality of Dorothy Day," 9.

18. "Msgr. Jack Egan: Activist, Reformer, a City's Conscience," *National Catholic Reporter*, June 1, 2001, 6.

19. John Bauman, PICO executive director, interview, July 5, 2000.

20. United States Catholic Conference, *Catholic Campaign for Human Development: 1997–98 Annual Report* (Washington DC: U.S. Catholic Conference, 1998), 4.

21. Purcell interview, July 8. 2008.

22. "CCHD Continues Tradition of Empowering Those in Need," *Denver Catholic Register*, November 10, 1999, 5.

23. "The Campaign in Brief," http://usccb.org/cchd/inbrief.shtml (accessed March 14, 2010).

24. Taken from copy of a CCHD document titled "Brief History of CCHD Funding of Congregational-based Organizations" given to the author by Doug Lawson, former director of the CCHD, April 2, 2001.

25. Doug Lawson, interview, April 2, 2001.

26. John Carr, executive director, Department of Justice, Peace, and Human Development, U.S. Conference of Catholic Bishops, interview, February 26. 2001.

27. Purcell interview, July 8, 2008.

28. Kathy Partridge, interview, July 2, 2008.

29. Purcell interview, July 8, 2008.

30. Rev. Dennis Jacobson, president of the Gamaliel Clergy Caucus, interview, July 17, 2008.

31. Ibid.

32. Rabbi Jonah Pesner, interview, March 16, 2010.

33. "Reform Rabbis Teach and Preach Organizing," http://urj.org/socialaction/training/justcongregations/teachpreach/, (accessed April 11, 2010).

34. Rabbi Jonah Pesner, "Redemption for Radicals: A Call for Jewish Engagement in Congregation-Based Community Organizing," in *Righteous Indignation: A Jewish Call for Justice,* ed. Rabbi Or N. Rose, Jo Ellen Green Kaiser, and Margie Klein (Woodstock, VT: Jewish Lights).

35. Pesner interview, March 16, 2010.

36. Warren, *Dry Bones Rattling*, 2001, 42-43.

37. Meredith Ramsay, "Redeeming the City: Exploring the Relationship Between Church and Metropolis" *Urban Affairs Review* (Thousand Oaks, CA, May 1998), http://

proquest.uni.com/pqdweb?TS=9...p=1&Did=000000029091348&Mtd=1&Fmt=3, (accessed October 3, 1998).

38. See Jennifer Frost, *"An Interracial Movement of the Poor": Community Organizing and the New Left in the 1960s* (New York: New York University Press, 2001), chap. 1.

39. Rev. Don Elmer, email correspondence, July 9, 2008.

40. Timothy Matovina, "Conquest, Faith, and Resistance in the Southwest," in *Latino Religions and Civic Activism in the United States,* ed. Gastón Espinoza, Virgilio Elizondo, and Jesse Miranda, 28 (New York: Oxford University Press, 2005).

41. Mario T. García, "PADRES: Latino Community Priests and Social Action" in Espinoza, Elizondo, and Miranda, *Latino Religions*, 82.

42. Gastón Espinoza, Virgilio Elizondo, and Jesse Miranda, "Introduction: U.S. Latino Religions and faith-Based Political, Civic, and Social Action" in Espinoza, Elizondo, and Miranda, *Latino Religions,* 6.

43. García, "PADRES," 91.

44. Medina, *Mestizaje*, 28.

45. Ibid.

46. Socorro Castañeda-Liles, "Spiritual Affirmation and Empowerment: The Mexican American Cultural Center," in Espinoza, Elizondo, and Miranda, *Latino Religions*, 119.

47. Ernesto Cortes, Pasadena CA, interview, August 3, 2008.

48. García, "PADRES," 82–83.

49. Cortes, interview, August 3, 2008.

50. Warren, *Dry Bones Rattling,* 48–49.

51. García, "PADRES," 83.

52. Warren, *Dry Bones Rattling,* 47.

53. Harry Boyte, *CommonWealth: A Return to Citizen Politics* (New York: Free Press, 1989), 94–95.

54. Rev. Don Elmer, email correspondence, July 9, 2008.

55. http://www.industrialareasfoundation.org/iafabout/about.htm (accessed July 19, 2008).

56. http://www.piconetwork.org/ab_history.html (accessed July 19, 2008).

57. http://www.gamaliel.org/NewsRoom/NewsGamalielToday.htm (accessed July 19, 2008).

58. http://www.thedartcenter.org/about_dart.html (accessed July 19, 2008).

59. http://www.rcno.org/contact_us.php (accessed July 19, 2008).

60. Warren and Wood, *Faith-Based Community Organizing,* 6.

61. Ibid., 7.

62. Partridge interview, July 2, 2008.

63. Warren and Wood, *Faith-Based Community Organizing,* 19.

64. Kathy Partridge, email correspondence, July 24, 2008.

65. Corey Timson, organizer with Inland Congregations United for Change, interview by Ivy Melgar, February 5. 2008.

66. Jared Rivera, organizer with L.A. Voices, interview by Ivy Melgar, February 22, 2008.

67. Paula Cripps, organizer with Clergy and Laity United for Economic Justice, interview by Ivy Melgar, April 21, 2008.

68. Cortes interview, August 3, 2008.

69. Regina Martinez, then lead organizer for Orange County Congregation Community Organization (OCCCO), interview by Ivy Melgar, March 18, 2008.

70. Timson interview, February 5, 2008.

71. Pat Kennedy, lead organizer for Greater Long Beach Interfaith Committee, interview by Ivy Melgar, April 1, 2008.

72. Interviews were conducted in preparation of Helene Slessarev-Jamir, "Exploring the Attraction of Local Congregations to Community Organizing," *Nonprofit and Voluntary Sector Quarterly* 33, no. 4 (December 2004): 1–21.

73. Ibid.

74. Fr. David O'Connell, pastor, St. Frances X. Cabrini Church, Los Angeles, CA, interview, April 4, 2001.

75. Renee Wizig-Barrios, lead organizer, Metropolitan Organization, Houston, TX, phone interview, August 7, 2008.

76. Rebecca Gifford, then an organizer with IAF in Los Angeles, interview, April 30, 2001.

77. See Robert Fisher, "Neighborhood Organizing: The Importance of Historical Context" in *Revitalizing Urban Neighborhoods,* ed. W. Dennis Keating, Norman Krumholz, and Philip Star, 47 (Lawrence: University of Kansas Press, 1996).

78. Samuel G. Freedman, *Upon This Rock: The Miracles of a Black Church* (New York: HarperCollins, 1993), 334.

79. Jonathan Lange, BUILD lead organizer, interview, July 7, 1999.

80. Statistics from the Living Wage Resource Center, http://www.livingwagecampaign.org/index.php?id=1957 (assessed August 5, 2008).

81. Lange interview, June 29, 1998.

82. Mark Warren, *Dry Bones Rattling,* 2001, 84.

83. Pesner, "Redemption for Radicals."

84. David Liners, lead organizer for MICAH, Milwaukee, WI, interview, August 1, 2000.

85. Marilyn Stranske, PICO organizer, Denver, CO, phone interview, July 20, 2008.

86. Ibid.

87. Marissa Graciosa, co-director of FIRM, phone interview, August 7, 2008.

88. Ana Garcia-Ashley, co-chair of Gamaliel's Civil Rights of Immigrants campaign, phone interview, August 23, 2008.

89. Eugene Williams, executive director of L.A. Metro, interview, November 6, 2001.

90. Ibid.

91. Cortes interview, August 3, 2008.

NOTES TO CHAPTER 4

1. Rev. Bridie Roberts, program director of CLUE-LA, interview, June 8, 2009.

2. David Bacon, *Illegal People: How Globalization Creates Migration and Criminalizes Immigrants* (Boston: Beacon Press, 2008), 26.

3. Patricia Grogg "Remittance Drop Will Hurt Poor in Latin America," daily email bulletin, Latin America and Caribbean Communication Agency, Havana, Cuba, June 1, 2009.

4. Rev. James Lawson, pastor emeritus, Holman United Methodist Church, Los Angeles, CA, phone interview, June 23, 2009.

5. Gwendolyn Mink, *Old Labor and New Immigrants in American Political Development* (Ithaca, NY: Cornell University Press, 1986), 47.

6. Ibid, 48–51.

7. Neil Betten, *Catholic Activism and the Industrial Worker* (Gainesville: University Presses of Florida, 1976), 108.

8. Jaime Rapaport, Progressive Jewish Alliance, phone interview, August 12, 2009.

9. Betten, *Catholic Activism*, 1976, 74.

10. Ibid., 110.

11. Thomas Balanoff, president of SEIU Local 73, "This Land is Made for You and Me," presentation made to the Chicago Methodist Temple as part of "Labor in the Pulpit," 1997, reprinted in *Labor in the Pulpits: Labor Day Organizing Kit,* a joint project of National Interfaith Committee for Worker Justice and the AFL-CIO.

12. "U.S. Union Membership, 1948–2003," (New York: Labor Research Association).

13. William B. Gould IV, "Some Reflections of Fifty Years of the National Labor Relations Act: The Need for Labor Board and Labor Law Reform," *Stanford Law Review* 38 (April 1986): 937.

14. Ruth Milkman, *L.A. Story: Immigrant Workers and the Future of the U.S. Labor Movement* (New York: Russell Sage Foundation, 2006), 13.

15. Linda Chavez-Thompson, "Communities at Work: How Alliances Are Restoring our Right to Organize," *New Labor Forum* 3 (Fall/Winter 1998).

16. Kate Bronfenbrenner and Tom Juravich, "It Takes More Than House Calls: Organizing to Win with a Comprehensive Union-Building Strategy" in *Organizing to Win: New Research on Union Strategies,* ed. Kate Bronfenbrenner, Sheldon Friedman, Richard W. Hurd, Rudolph A. Oswald, and Ronald L. Seeber, 27 (Ithaca: Cornell University Press, 1998).

17. Ibid., 19–25.

18. Kate Bronfenbrenner, "Changing to Organize: Unions Know What Has To Be Done. Now They Have To Do it," *Nation*, September 3, 2001.

19. Nelson Lichtenstein, *State of the Union: A Century of American Labor* (Princeton: Princeton University Press, 2002), 187–88.

20. Eve S. Weinbaum, "Organizing Labor in an Era of Contingent Work and Globalization" in *Which Direction for Organized Labor: Essays on Organizing, Outreach, and Internal Transformations,* ed. Bruce Nissen, 40 (Detroit: Wayne State University Press, 1999).

21. "Thou Shalt Not Steal: IWJ Takes Wage Theft Campaign to Washington and Gets a Hearing," *Faith Works,* Interfaith Worker Justice newsletter, summer 2008, 1.

22. "Creating an Atmosphere for Reform" a Jim Wallis interview with John Sweeney, *Sojourners,* September-October 1998, 22–25.

23. David Moberg, "The Six-Year Itch: John Sweeney Sees the AFL-CIO Through Some Growing Pains" *Nation*, September 2. 2001.

24. Ibid.

25. Ibid.

26. Milkman, *L.A Story*, 4.

27. Mario T. García, ed. *The Gospel of César Chávez: My Faith in Action* (Lanham, MD: Sheed and Ward, 2007), 5–6.

28. Ibid., 8.

29. Msgr. George Higgins with William Boyle, *Organized Labor and the Church* (New York: Paulist Press, 1993), 88.

30. Ibid., 94.

31. Ibid., 103.

32. Workshop presentation by Dolores Huerta, "Forging Partnerships for the New Millennium: A National Religion-Labor Conference," notes, October 8–10, 1999, Los Angeles, CA.

33. David Sanchez, *From Patmos to the Barrio: Subverting Imperial Myths* (Minneapolis: Fortress Press, 2008), 98.

34. Workshop presentation by Fr. William Boyle, "Forging Partnerships for the New Millennium," notes.

35. Higgins, *Organized Labor*, 1993, 63.

36. Huerta workshop notes.

37. Luís D. León, "César Chávez and Mexican American Civil Religion" in *Latino Religions and Civic Activism in the United States,* ed. Gastón Espinosa, Virgilio Elizondo, and Jesse Miranda, 61 (New York: Oxford University Press, 2005).

38. Kim Bobo, IWJ's executive director, interview, Chicago, IL, May 21, 2009.

39. Joseph A. McCartin, "Building the Interfaith Worker Justice Movement: Kim Bobo's Story," *Labor: Studies in Working-Class History of the Americas* 6, no. 1 (Spring 2009): 91–94.

40. Rev. James Lawson, phone interview, June 23, 2009.

41. "A Track Record of Success" on LAANE's Web site, http://74.10.59.52/laane/victories.html (accessed June 19, 2009).

42. Lawson interview, June, 23, 2009.

43. Alexia Salvatierra's plenary address at the SCUPE Congress, April 2008, Chicago, IL.

44. Alexia Salvatierra, executive director of CLUE California, interview, June 18, 2009.

45. Ibid.

46. "The Qur'an and Worker Justice," *Faith Works*, March 2002.

47. Bobo interview, May 21, 2009.

48. This was Kim's conclusion in my interview with her. Bobo interview, May 21, 2009.

49. Rev. David Farley, senior pastor, Echo Park United Methodist Church, Los Angeles, CA, interview, June 20, 2009.

50. Rev. Bridie Roberts, interview June 6, 2009.

51. "Labor in the Pulpit Services Held in 37 States," *Faith Works*, December 2000, 5.

52. Taken from my personal notes from the conference.

53. Bobo interview, May 21, 2009.

54. "Northern Lights for Immigrant Workers," *Faith Works,* December 2000, 1–2.

55. "Goldman-Sachs Invests in New York Workers; Metropolitan Opera Won't Change Tune," *Faith Works,* April 2001, 3.

56. Poultry Back Pay in Motion: DOL, Perdue Farms Inc. Reach Historic Agreement," *Faith Works,* June, 2002, 1–2, 8.

57. No Quiero Taco Bell: Tomato Picker Boycott Taco Bell," *Faith Works,* July 2001, 6.

58. "NY Activists, Leaders Join 330 Mile March for Justice," *Faith Works,* July 2003, 4.

59. "Pickle Boycott Picks Up," *Faith Works,* January 2004, 12.

60. Janice Fine, *Worker Centers: Organizing Communities on the Edge of the Dream* (Ithaca, NY: Cornell University Press, 2006), 11.

61. Ibid.

62. Vanessa Tait, *Poor Workers' Unions: Rebuilding Labor from Below* (Cambridge, MA: South End Press, 2005), 130.

63. Raul Arnova, executive director of IDEPSCA, Los Angeles, interview, June 18, 2009.

64. Ibid.

65. Bobo interview, May 21, 2009.

66. Kristi Sanford and Paul Graham, *Workers Rights Manual* (Chicago: Chicago Interfaith Committee on Worker Issues, 1998).

67. Jose Oliva, director of IWJ's network of worker centers, interview, March 11, 2006.

68. Ibid.

69. "An Interfaith Workers' Rights Center: A Project of the Chicago Interfaith Committee on Worker Issues," a proposal drafted by the Chicago Interfaith Committee on Worker Justice, n.d.

70. Oliva interview, March 11, 2006.

71. http://arisechicago.org/worker-center/iwrc-achievements-2007 (accessed June 29, 2009).

72. Presentation by Kristi Sanford, Workers' Center Organizer Training, notes, March 4, 2005.

73. Oliva,, conversation, April 2005.

74. Presentation by Rich Cunningham, Workers' Center Organizer Training, notes, March 6, 2005.

75. Jeanne Geraci, staff person, *Voces de la Frontera* Workers' Center, Milwaukee, WI, phone interview, May 2006.

76. Emily Timm, staff person, Workers Defense Project, Austin, TX, phone interview, May 2006.

77. http://www.mpowercenter.org/solidarity (accessed June 29, 2009).

78. Ibid.

79. Rev. Nelson Johnson, executive director, The Beloved Community Center, Greensboro, NC, phone interview, June 23, 2009.

80. Ibid.

81. Teresa Watanabe "Goal of Foundation's Grants Is Integrating Immigrants into Southern California Life" *Los Angeles Times,* June 18, 2009, http://www.latimes.com/news/local/la-me-immigrant19-2009jun19,0,1602810.story.

82. Pierrette Hondagneu-Soleto, *God's Heart Has No Borders: How Religious Activists are Working for Immigrants' Rights* (Berkeley: University of California Press, 2008), 95.

83. Bridie Roberts interview, June 6, 2009.

84. Ibid.

85. "Reflections for Labor in the Pulpits Speakers," *Faith Works,* July 2001, special insert.

86. Kim Bobo, *Wage Theft in America: Why Millions of Working Americans Are Not Getting Paid and What We Can Do About It* (New York: The New Press, 2009).

87. Ibid., xii.

88. Bobo interview, May 21, 2009.

89. Bobo, *Wage Theft in America,* xiii.

90. Rev. Andrew Schwiebert, admissions recruiter at the Claremont School of Theology, interview, June, 23, 3009.

NOTES TO CHAPTER 5

1. Personal notes from the discussion at the NNIRR national conference, Houston TX, January 18, 2008.

2. Paul Waldman, Elbert Ventura, Robert Savillo, Susan Lin, and Greg Lewis, "Fear and Loathing in Prime Time: Immigration Myths and Cable News," report by the Media Matters Action Network, May 21, 2008, http://mediamattersaction.org/static/pdfs/fear-and-loathing.pdf (accessed July 15, 2009).

3. John M. Broder, "Immigration, From a Simmer to a Scream," *New York Times,* May 21, 2006, sec. 4, 4.

4. Nina Bernstein, "Groundswell of Protests Back Illegal Immigrants," *New York Times,* March 27, 2006.

5. Fr. Brendan Curran, pastor, Pius V Catholic Church, Chicago, phone interview, February, 2006.

6. Oscar Avila and Michael Martinez, "Immigrants at Crossroads: Stakes are High For Legalization Campaign," *Chicago Tribune,* May 1, 2006.

7. Arnoldo Garcia, communications director, NNIRR, phone interview, July 28, 2009.

8. "Rallies Across U.S. Call for Illegal Immigrant Rights" CNN, April 10, 2006, http://www.cnn.com/2006/POLITICS/04/10/immigration/index.html (accessed July 22, 2009).

9. Conversations with migrants who had just been deported at a *comidor* in Nogales, Mexico, January 15, 2009.

10. Adam Liptak and Julia Preston, "Justices Limit Use of Identity Theft Law in Immigration Cases," *New York Times,* May 5, 2009.

11. TRAC Immigration, "Immigration Prosecution for March 2009, http://trac.syr.edu/tracreports/bulletins/immigration/monthlymar09/fil/ (accessed July 15, 2009).

12. Liptak and Preston, "Justices Limit Use."

13. Universal Declaration of Human Rights, articles 13, 14, and 15.

14. Seyla Benhabib, *The Rights of Others: Aliens, Residents, and Citizens* (Cambridge: Cambridge University Press, 2004), 104.

15. Ibid., 140–41.

16. Mai Ngai, *Impossible Subjects: Illegal Aliens and the Making of Modern America* (Princeton: Princeton University Press, 2004), 60.

17. Ibid., 63.

18. Daniel J. Tichenor, *Dividing Lines: The Politics of Immigration Control in America,* (Princeton, NJ: Princeton University Press, 2002), 145–46.

19. Ngai, *Impossible Subjects,* 67.

20. Ibid., 68–69.

21. Bill Ong Hing, *Defining America through Immigration Policy,* (Philadelphia: Temple University Press, 2004), 95.

22.Tichenor, *Dividing Lines,* 213.

23. Ngai, *Impossible Subjects,* 261.

24. Don T. Nakanishi, "Political and Electoral Issues of the Asian Pacific American Population," in *America Becoming: Racial Trends and Their Consequences,* vol.1, ed. Neil J. Smelser, William Julius Wilson, and Faith Mitchell (Washington DC: National Academy Press, 2001), 175.

25. Helene Slessarev-Jamir, *A Place of Refuge and Sustenance: How Faith Institutions Strengthen the Families of Poor Asian Immigrants,* (Baltimore, MD: Annie E. Casey Foundation, 2003), 6.

26. "Separated Brothers: Latinos are Changing the Nature of American Religion," *Economist,* July 16, 2009.

27. Ibid.

28. Rev. Gabriel Salguero, executive, the Latino Leadership Circle, pastor of Lamb's Church, and executive director of the Hispanic Leadership Program, Princeton Theological Seminary, phone interview, July 22, 2009.

29. Norman Ospina, American Friends Services Committee community organizer, Chicago, IL, interview, February 15, 2002.

30. Salguero interview, July 22, 2009.

31. "Immigration, 2009," statement by the National Association of Evangelicals, http://www.nae.net/resolutions/347-immigration-200 (accessed on 03/18/2010).

32. Jonathan Treat, "Activists: Deaths in Arizona Desert Could Have Been Avoided," *Borderlines,* July 1, 2001.

33. Ernesto Trevino, pastor, *El Mesias* United Methodist Church, Nogales, AZ, interview, January 15, 2009.

34. Rev. Randy Mayer, pastor, Good Shepherd United Church of Christ, Sahuarita, AZ, conversation, January 13, 2009.

35. Ann Crittenden, *Sanctuary: A Story of American Conscience and the Law in Collision* (New York: Weidenfeld and Nicolson, 1988), xvi.

36. Hilary Cunningham, *God and Caesar at the Rio Grande: Sanctuary and the Politics of Religion* (Minneapolis: University of Minnesota Press, 1995), 21.

37. Treat, "Activists: Deaths in Arizona Desert."

38. Rev. Robin Hoover, remarks at the 7th annual Memorial and March for Migrants, First Christian Church, Tucson, AZ, September 30, 2007, reprinted in *Desert Fountain,* September-October, 2007.

39. "A Message from Rev. Robin Hoover, PhD" *Desert Fountain,* September-October, 2007, 1.

40. Rev. Robin Hoover, "Realistic Employment an Legalization: A Real Plan"

41. Hoover, remarks, September, 30, 2007.

42. Quoted from Samaritans' guiding principles found on their Web site, http://www.samaritanpatrol.org/guidingprinciples.html, (accessed on July 25, 2009).

43. Maryada Vallet, volunteer for No More Deaths, Tucson AZ, interview, January 13, 2009.

44. Harry Smith, Samaritans activist, phone conversation, July 29, 2009.

45. "Border Volunteers Cleared," *National Catholic Reporter,* September 15, 2006, http://findarticles.com/p/articles/mi_m1141/is_40_42/ai_n17113275/ (accessed July 25, 2009).

46. Stephanie Innes, "Volunteers to Work with Border Patrol," *Arizona Daily Star,* May 20, 2006, http://www.azstarnet.com/sn/printDS/130016 (accessed July 25, 2009).

47. Rev. Randy Mayer, conversation, January 13, 2009.

48. Maryada Vallet, phone conversation, August 12, 2009.

49. Hunter Jackson, "*Ya Van Muchos Hermanos Muertos:* Six Weeks at the U.S. Mexico Border," No More Deaths Web site, BorderReadSmall-1.pdf (accessed July 25, 2009).

50. Vallet, phone conversation, August 12, 2009.

51. Emrys Staton, volunteer with No More Deaths, phone interview, August 5, 2009.

52. "Trial for Border Volunteer, Cited while Picking Up Trash," No More Deaths, press release, July 22, 2008.

53. Staton, phone interview, August 5, 2009.

54. Ibid.

55. This description is based on a personal visit to the Mariposa aid station on January 14, 2009.

56. *Crossing the Line: Human Rights Abuses of Migrants in Short-Term Custody on the Arizona/Sonora Border,*(report, September 2008), 7.

57. Jackson, "*Ya Van Muchos Hermanos Muertos.*

58. Minerva Carcaño, Presiding Bishop of the Desert Southwest Annual Conference, United Methodist Church, Des Moines, IA, interview, July 20, 2009.

59. See Ignatius Bau, *This Ground is Holy: Church Sanctuary and Central American Refugees* (Mahwah, NJ: Paulist Press, 1985), 124–57; Hilary Cunningham, *God and Caesar at the Rio Grande: Sanctuary and the Politics of Religion* (Minneapolis: University of Minnesota Press, 1995), 68–101.

60. Juan Carlos Ruiz, deputy director, Youth Ministries for Peace and Justice, South Bronx, phone interview, August 3, 2009.

61. Alexia Salvatierra, "The New Sanctuary Movement," email text sent November 23, 2006.

62. Taken from the New Sanctuary Movement's Web site, http://www.newsanctuary-movement.org/the-convening.htm (accessed July 30, 2009).

63. Peter Prengaman, "Churches to Provide Immigrants Sanctuary," Associated Press, May 10, 2007.

64. Amy Dalton, phone interview, August 5, 2009.

65. Judson Memorial United Church of Christ, New York City, http://www.judson.org/peaceandjustice.html (accessed July 30, 2009).

66. Ruiz, phone interview, August 3, 2009.

67. Jan Snider, "Information regarding the expected Human Rights Abuse case of Juana Villegas," Memo to the United Methodist Immigration Task Force, February 11, 2008.

68. Arnoldo Garcia and Laura Rivas, "The U.S. Immigration Control Regime Destroys the Rights of Immigrants," *NNIRR Network News,* winter 2008–9, 10.

69. Garcia, phone interview, July 28, 2009.

70. "National Conference for Immigrant and Refugee Rights: 2008 National Conference Report", http://nnirr.org/events/conference/2008/NationalConferenceReport.pdf (accessed July 11, 2009).

71. Rev. Walter Coleman, "Social Evangelism in 2009," email, May 23, 2009.

72. Rev. Walter Coleman, phone interview, July 22, 2009.

73. Rev. Gabriel Salguero, phone interview, July 22, 2009.

74. Emma Lozano, president of La Latin Familia Sin Fronteras, "Speech in Springfield IL, on Friday, May 12, 2009, email, May 23, 2009.

75. Ibid.

76. Rev. Jim Perdue, United Methodist missionary for immigration, Sioux City, IA, phone interview, July 13, 2009.

77. "Postville Community Needs Your Support—End ICE Raids/Stop Detentions & Deportations!," email appeal sent by NNIRR.org on Friday, July 11, 2008.

78. "Thoughts on the first anniversary of the 2008 ICE raid at Postville, Iowa," email from Rev. Jim Perdue.

79. Shalom Center, "Summary, Jewish action about Unkosher Postville," email from office@shalomctr.org, July 27, 2008.

80. Chris West, director of Field Operations, Justice for Immigrants, phone interview, August 5, 2009.

81. Casey Sanchez, "Chained Immigrants on Parade: Who will Stand up to the Sick Antics of a Racist Sheriff?" *Southern Poverty Law Center's Hate Watch*, February 10, 2009.

82. West, phone interview, August 5, 2009.

83. Bishop Minerva Carcaño, National Faith Leaders Call on Obama to Lead Immigration Reform Press Conference, Washington DC, February 11, 2009.

84. Bill Mefford, director of Civil and Human Rights, General Board of Church and Society, United Methodist Church, Des Moines, IA, July 21, 2009.

85. Carcaño, interview, July 20, 2009.

86. Interfaith Immigration Coalition, "Interfaith Platform on Humane Immigration Reform" February 11, 2009, http://www.interfaithimmigration.org/wp-content/uploads/2009/10/interfaith-immigration-platform-2009.pdf.

87. Allison Johnson, Sojourners Community and CCIR's staffperson, interview, July 24, 2009.

88. Coleman, phone interview, July 22, 2009.

89. Mennonite Central Committee U.S. Immigration Legislation in Congress, March 25, 2006, http://www.mcc.org/us/immigration/advocacy/2006%20Immigration%20statement%20-%20short.pdf (accessed August 7, 2009).

90. West, phone interview, August 5, 2009.

91. Salguero, phone interview, July 22, 2009.

92. National Hispanic Christian Leadership Conference, "Statement on Comprehensive Immigration Reform," http://www.nhclc.org/about/immigration_reform.html (accessed August 7, 2009).

93. Mefford, interview, July 21, 2009.

94. "Esperanza's Statement of Principles: Comprehensive Immigration Reform, 2009," provided by Esperanza USA to author.

95. SBC Resolutions, "On the Crisis of Illegal Immigration," June 2006, http://www.sbc.net/resolutions/amResolution.asp?ID=1157 (accessed August 7, 2009).

96. La Familias Unidas, "We Will Never Give Up the Struggle for our Families Against the Borken Law," August 10, 2010, http://fluenglish.wordpress.com/.

NOTES TO CHAPTER 6

1. Walter Wink, *The Powers That Be: Theology for a New Millennium* (New York: First Galilee Trade, 1999), 56.

2. David Cortright, *Peace: A History of Movements and Ideas* (Cambridge: Cambridge University Press, 2008), 172.

3. Michael Hardt and Antonio Negri, *Multitude: War and Democracy in the Age of Empire* (New York: Penguin Press, 2004), 215.

4. Cortright, *Peace*, 171.

5. Ibid., 174.

6. Siri Mergerin, United for Peace and Justice, phone interview, January 12, 2010.

7. Joseph Kip Kosek, *Acts of Conscience: Christian Nonviolence and Modern American Democracy* (New York: Columbia University Press, 2009), 5.

8. See Wes Avram, ed., *Anxious about Empire: Theological Essays on the New Global Realities,* (Grand Rapids, MI: Brazos Press, 2004).

9. http://www.bpf.org/about-us/history (accessed December 23, 2009).

10. Christian Smith, *Resisting Reagan: The U.S. Central America Peace Movement* (Chicago: University of Chicago Press, 1996), 171.

11. Ibid., 173.

12. Kevin Martin, executive director of Peace Action, phone interview, December 21, 2009.

13. Glen Stassen, ed., *Just Peacemaking: Ten Practices for Abolishing War* (Cleveland: Pilgrim Press, 1998), 2. .

14. Susan Thistlethwaite and Glen Stassen, *Abrahamic Alternatives to War: Jewish, Christian and Muslim Perspectives on Just Peacemaking* (Washington DC: U.S. Institute of Peace, 2008), www.usip.org.

15. Charles DeBenedetti, *The Peace Reform in American History* (Bloomington: Indiana University Press, 1980), 35.

16. Ibid., 37.

17. Ibid., 69.

18. Cortright, *Peace*, 70.

19. Charles F. Howlett, "John Nevin Sayre and the American Fellowship of Reconciliation," *Pennsylvania Magazine of History and Biography* 114, no. 3 (July 1990): 405.

20. Ibid., 404.

21. Cortright, *Peace*, 71.

22. Peter Brock and Nigel Young, *Pacifism in the Twentieth Century* (Syracuse, NY: Syracuse University Press, 1999), 101.

23. Ibid., 369.

24. Duane Shank, senior policy advisor, Sojourners, phone interview, December 15, 2009.

25. Kosek, *Acts of Conscience*, 242.

26. Ibid., 234–35.

27. Ibid., 50.

28. Ibid., 43.

29. Ibid., 76.

30. Mark Johnson, executive director of the Fellowship of Reconciliation, phone interview, December 14, 2009.

31. Nathan Schneider, "Beginning with Witness: An Interview with Mark Johnson" Immanent Frame (an online blog on secularism, religion, and the public sphere, published by the Social Science Research Council), posted December 8, 2009, http://blogs.ssrc.org/tif/2009/12/08/beginning-with-witness-an-interview-with-mark-johnson/ (accessed December 14, 2009).

32. "The Peace Community of San José de Apartadó," http://www.forcolombia.org/node/12 (accessed December 31, 2009).

33. "Volunteer in Colombia," http://www.forcolombia.org/node/11#requirements (accessed January 1, 2010).

34. Sarah Weintraub, executive director of BPF, phone interview, January 5, 2010.

35. Ibid.

36. Ibid.

37. "Grassroots Civilian Diplomacy Trips to Iran: Why," http://www.forusa.org/programs/iran/ (accessed January 1, 2010).

38. Seema Mustafa, "Gaza Freedom March Diary," January 6, 2010, http://usa.mediamonitors.net/content/view/full/70263 (accessed January 8, 2010).

39. Mark Johnson, "A Full Moon on Tahrir Square," submitted to the FOR blog on January 1, 2010, http://forpeace.net/blog/mark-johnson/full-moon-over-tahrir-square (accessed on January 1, 2010).

40. Cortright, *Peace*, 140.

41. Shank, phone interview, December 15, 2009.

42. Cortright, *Peace*, 141–42.

43. Ibid., 142.

44. Shank, phone interview, December 15, 2009.

45. Jim Wallis, executive director of Sojourners, phone interview, November 2, 2009.

46. Cortright, *Peace*, 144.

47. Dr. Glen Stassen, professor of Christian ethics, Fuller Theological Seminary, Pasadena, CA, interview, October 29, 2009.

48. Martin, phone interview, December 21, 2009.

49. Ibid.

50. Rebecca Griffin, political director, Peace Action West, phone interview, December 11, 2009.

51. Martin, phone interview, December 21, 2009.

52. Ibid.

53. Martin, phone interview, January 8, 2010.

54. Griffin, phone interview, December 11, 2009.

55. Griffin, phone interview, January 12, 2010.

56. Griffin, phone interview, December 11, 2009.

57. Martin, phone interview, December 21, 2009.

58. Marie Denis, president, Pax Christi International, phone interview, November 23, 2009.

59. Tyler Wigg-Stevenson, founder and director, Two Futures Project, phone interview, January 14, 2010.

60. "Endorsements," http://twofuturesproject.org/endorsements (accessed January 15, 2010).

61. Wigg-Stevenson, phone interview, January 14, .

62. Ibid.

63. Smith, *Resisting Reagan,* 71.

64. Ibid., 76–77.

65. Cited in Clare Weber, *Visions of Solidarity: U.S. Peace Activists in Nicaragua from the War to Women's Activism and Globalization* (Lanham, MD: Lexington Books, 2006), 54.

66. Melinda St. Louis, "25 Years of Taking Action for Peace and Justice," http://witness-forpeace.live.radicaldesigns.org/article.php?id=501 (accessed January 13, 2010).

67. Weber, *Visions of Solidarity*, 21.

68. Smith, *Resisting Reagan*, 142.

69. Gail Phares, co-founder, WFP, phone interview, November 25, 2009.

70. Judy Coode, former Pax Christi USA president of the board, and current staff of Maryknoll Office for Global Concerns, phone interview, November 17, 2009.

71. Rose Mary Berger, associate editor, *Sojourners,* phone interview, November 13, 2009.

72. Coode phone interview, November 17, 2009.

73. Ibid.

74. James Satterwhite, "Christian Peacemaker Teams as an Alternative to 'Redemptive Violence,'" *Peace and Change* 31, no. 2 (April 2006): 222.

75. Ibid., 223.

76. Ibid., 224.

77. Carol Rose, operations co-director, CPT, phone interview, November 20, 2009.

78. Doug Pritchard and Carol Rose, "Iraq Journal: CPT Rejoices in the Rescue of our Peacemakers," www.sojo.net (accessed March 23, 2006).

79. Rose Marie Berger, "Faith in Action: Free at Last," www.sojo.net (accessed March 26, 2006).

80. Rose, phone interview, November 20, 2009.

81. Ibid.

82. Ibid.

83. Ibid.

84. Richard Killmer, executive director, NRCAT, phone interview, November 20, 2009.

85. "NRCAT's History," http://www.nrcat.org/index.php?option=com_content&task=view&id=36&Itemid=65 (accessed January 15, 2010).

86. Ibid.

87. Killmer, phone interview, November 20, 2009.

88. Bill Mefford, staff for the General Board of Church and Society, United Methodist Church, phone interview, November 30, 2009.

89. "An Evangelical Declaration Against Torture: Protecting Human Rights in an Age of Terror," http://www.evangelicalsforhumanrights.org/storage/mhead/fullstatement.pdf (accessed January 15, 2010).

90. David Gushee, professor of ethics, Mercer University and president of the board of directors for Evangelicals for Human Rights, phone interview, January 5, 2010.

91. "The Religious Dimensions of the Torture Debate," *Pew Forum on Religion and Public Life,* April 29, 2009, http://pewforum.org/docs/?DocID=156 (accessed January 15, 2010).

92. "About RHR-NA," http://www.rhr-na.org/about (accessed January 24, 2010).

93. See Wink, *Powers That Be.*

94. "About the Jewish Peace Fellowship," http://www.jewishpeacefellowship.org/index.php?p=about (accessed December 31, 2009).

95. Rabbi Gerald Serotta, former member of Breira and founding member of Rabbis for Human Rights, phone interview, February 3, 2010.

96. Evelyn Wilcock, "Impossible Pacifism: Jews, the Holocaust and Nonviolence" in *The Challenge of Shalom: The Jewish Tradition of Peace and Justice,* ed. Murray Polner and Naomi Goodman, 60 (Philadelphia: New Society Publishers, 1994).

97. Helen Fein, "Reading the Second Text: Meaning and Misuses of the Holocaust" in Polner and Goodman, *Challenge of Shalom,* 75–77.

98. Ibid., 80.

99. Serotta, phone interview, February 3, 2010.

100. Stefan Merken, "Notes From Where I Sit," *Shalom: Jewish Peace Letter* 39, no. 2, March 2010, 2.

101. Michael E. Staub, *Torn at the Roots: The Crisis of Jewish Liberalism in Postwar America* (New York: Columbia University Press, 2002), 158.

102. Ibid., 164.

103. Rabbi Arthur Waskow, founder and director, Shalom Center, phone interview, December 30, 2009.

104. "The Shalom Center's Mission in Detail," http://www.theshalomcenter.org/node/1496 (accessed January 24, 2010).

105. Waskow, phone interview, December 30, 2009.

106. Ibid.

107. "Shalom Center's Mission in Detail."

108. Waskow, phone interview, December 30, 2009.

109. "Shalom Center's Mission in Detail."

110. "About RHR-NA," http://www.rhr-na.org/about.

111. Serotta, phone interview, February 3, 2010.

112. Rabbi Melissa Weintraub, "Kvod Ha-Briot: Human Dignity in Jewish Sources, Human Degradation in American Military Custody," http://www.rhr-na.org/kvod_habriot/treatise (accessed January 25, 2010).

113. Rabbi Melissa Weintraub, "The Bar against Self-Incrimination as a Protection against Torture in Jewish and American Law," http://www.rhr-na.org/files/no%20self%20incrimination_short_o.pdf (accessed January 25, 2010).

114. "About Us," http://jstreet.org/about/about-us (accessed January 25, 2010.

115. Serotta, phone interview, February 3, 2010.

116. Amy Spitalnick, spokesperson, J Street, phone interview, January 22, 2010.

117. Ibid.

118. Ibid.

119. Ibid.

120. David N. Myers, "New Israel Fund Holds Country to Founders' Standards," *Jewish Journal,* February 9, 2010, http://www.jewishjournal.com/articles/print/new_israel_fund_holds_country_to_founders_standards_20100209/ (accessed February 12, 2010).

121. Samina Sunda, founder and executive director, American Muslim Voice, phone interview, January 5, 2010.

122. Ibid.

123. Ibid.

124. Donald Rothberg and Hozan Alan Senauke, "Active Visions: Four Sources of Socially Engaged Buddhism," *Turning Wheel: The Journal of Socially Engaged Buddhism* (Summer/Fall 2008):24–25.

125. Allen Senauke, former executive director and senior advisor, BPF, phone interview, January 5, 2010.

126. Ibid.

127. Claude AnShin Thomas, "Finding Clarity: Tapping into Places that were Centers of Pain," *Turning Wheel* (Summer/Fall 2008):36–37.

128. Sarah Weintraub, phone interview, January 5, 2010.

NOTES TO CHAPTER 7

1. "Pat Robertson Says Haiti Paying for 'Pact to the Devil,'" CNN U.S., January 13, 2010, http://www.cnn.com/2010/US/01/13/haiti.pat.robertson/index.html (accessed February 1, 2010).

2. Stephanie Condon. "Pat Robertson Haiti Comments Spark Uproar," *Political Hotsheet*, January 14, 2010, http://www.cbsnews.com/blogs/2010/01/14/politics/political-hotsheet/entry6096806.shtml?tag=contentMain;contentBody (accessed February 1, 2010).

3. A. D. McKenzie, "Time to Pay Haiti Back," Latin American and Caribbean Communication Agency, January 17, 2010.

4. Alex Dupuy, "Analysis: Haiti-Earthquake: A Wake up Call," Latin America and Caribbean Communication Agency, January 24, 2010.

5. Neil MacFarquhar, "Haiti is Again a Canvas for Approaches to Aid," *New York Times*, January 31, 2010.

6. See David Bacon, *Illegal People: How Globalization Creates Migration and Criminalizes Immigrants* (Boston: Beacon Press, 2009).

7. McKenzie, "Time to Pay Haiti Back."

8. "Haitian Ambassador to US, Raymond Joseph, Thanks ONE," http://www.one.org/us/actnow/drophaitiandebt/ambassador.html (accessed February 5, 2010).

9. David Beckman, executive director of Bread for the World, March 12, 2010.

10. Ibid.; Bobby Shriver, ONE board member and co-founder of Product (RED), phone interview, March 22, 2010.

11. Bread for the World Institute, *Foreign Aid to End Hunger* (Washington DC: BWI, 2001), 50.

12. Ibid., 45.

13. Jeffrey Sachs, *The End of Poverty: Economic Possibilities for our Time* (New York: Penguin Press, 2005), 189–90.

14. Ibid., 194.

15. Ibid.

16. Arthur Simon, *The Rising of Bread for the World: An Outcry of Citizens Against Hunger* (New York: Paulist Press, 2009), 73.

17. Ibid., 75.

18. Ibid., 77.

19. Ibid., 95.

20. Beckman, phone interview, March 12, 2010.

21. "Lee de Leon (Español): Offering of Letters," http://www.youtube.com/breadfortheworld#p/u/4/TTwBlscSzno (accessed on February 14, 2010).

22. Beckman, phone interview, March 12, 2010.

23. Bread for the World, *African: Hunger to Harvest: 2001 Offering of Letters* (Washington DC: BFW, 2001), 9.

24. Bread for the World Annual Gathering, Washington DC, notes, June 25, 2010.

25. Joseph A. McCartin, "Building the Interfaith Worker Justice Movement: Kim Bobo's Story," *Labor: Studies in Working-Class History of the Americas* 6, no. 1 (Spring 2009): 90–91.

26. "Get Involved: On Campus," http://www.bread.org/get-involved/on-campus/ (accessed February 13, 2010).

27. "Bread for the World's 2010 Offering of Letters," http://www.youtube.com/breadfortheworld (accessed on February 13, 2010).

28. Simon, *Rising of Bread for the World*, 143.

29. Clare Weber, *Visions of Solidarity: U.S. Peace Activists in Nicaragua from the War to Women's Activism and Globalization* (Lanham, MD: Lexington Books, 2006), 107.

30. Ibid., 72.

31. Ibid., 79.

32. Ibid., 112–16.

33. Ibid.

34. St. Louis, "25 Years of Taking Action for Peace and Justice," http://witnessforpeace.live.radicaldesigns.org/article.php?id=501 (accessed January 13, 2010).

35. Gail Phares, co-founder, WFP, phone interview, November 25, 2009.

36. Ibid.

37. Ibid.

38. Joshua William Busby, "Bono Made Jesse Helms Cry: Jubilee 2000, Debt Relief, and Moral Action in International Politics," *International Studies Quarterly* 51 (2007): 257.

39. David Beckman, "Debt Relief at the Millennium: This Could Be the Start of Something Big." *Commonweal,* December 15, 2000, 13.

40. Ibid., 12.

41. Marjorie Mayo, *Global Citizens: Social Movements and the Challenge of Globalization* (London: Zed Books, 2005), 174.

42. Ibid., 188.

43. "Jubilee Plus Gets off to Flying Start," *Jubilee+News,* June 2001, 2.

44. Daniel Driscoll-Shaw, national coordinator of Jubilee2000 USA, interview, April 10, 2001.

45. Shriver, phone interview, February 22, 2010.

46. Beckman, phone interview, March 12, 2010.

47. Mayo, *Global Citizens,* 173.

48. Rev. Bernardino Mandiate, keynote speaker, "Debt Cancellation Workshop," World Methodist Conference, Brighton, UK, August 2001.

49. Driscoll-Shaw, interview, April 10, 2010.

50. Ibid.

51. Busby, "Bono Made Jesse Helms Cry," 264.

52. "Jubilee Is Proclaimed!" *Bread: The Bread for the World Newsletter,* November/December 2000, 2.

53. "Message to Congress," *Jubilee 2000 USA,* April 10, 2000.

54. Beckman, interview, Washington DC, June 2001.

55. "BFW Members Help Break the Chains of Debt," *Bread: The Bread for the World Newsletter,* November/December 2000, 1.

56. Elena McCollim, "Beyond Jubilee 2000: National Plans to Fight Poverty," *Foreign Aid to End Hunger* (Washington DC: BFW Institute, 2001), 70.

57. Elena McCollim, ed., *Debt and Development Dossier,*no. 6 (Washington DC: BFW Institute, June 2001), 1.

58. Mayo, *Global Citizens,* 182.

59. Beckman, interview, June 2001.

60. Social Democratic Party member of Parliament, Nairobi Kenya, interview, August 21, 2001.

61. Rev. Ochola Chalton, theological programme director, National Council of Churches of Kenya, Nairobi Kenya, interview, August 16, 2001.

62. Melinda St. Louis, deputy director, Jubilee USA Network, phone interview, March 10, 2010.

63. Ibid.

64. Ibid.

65. "Strategic Plan: 2009–2012," http://www.jubileeusa.org/de/about-us/strategicplan.html (accessed on March 12, 2010).

66. "Moral and Strategic Imperative on Race," http://www.jubileeusa.org/about-us/diversity.html (accessed March 12, 2010).

67. The bill is HR 4405, titled The Jubilee Act for Responsible Lending and Expanded Debt Cancellation of 2009, http://thomas.loc.gov/cgi-bin/query/F?c111:1:./temp/~c111xsHGWv:e8062 (accessed March 12, 2010).

68. St. Louis, phone interview, March 10, 2010.

69. Shriver, phone interview, March 22, 2010.

70. Beckman, phone interview, March 12, 2010.

71. Rev. Adam Phillips, faith relations manager, ONE.org., phone interview, March 1, 2010.

72. Beckman, phone interview, March 12, 2010.

73. "Search Past Grants," http://www.gatesfoundation.org/grants/Pages/search.aspx?meta=MDProgram%3aGlobal+Development (accessed on March 6, 2010).

74. Ibid.

75. "Living Proof Project: Videos," http://www.gatesfoundation.org/livingproofproject/Pages/video-gallery.aspx (accessed on March 6, 2010).

76. Shriver, phone interview, March 22, 2010.

77. "Global Progress: Are We on Track to Meet the MDGs by 2015?" *United Nations Development Programme,* http://www.undp.org/mdg/basics_ontrack.shtml (accessed March 5, 2010).

78. "United Nations Millennium Declaration," Resolution Adopted by the General Assembly, September 8, 2000, http://www.un.org/millennium/declaration/ares552e.htm (accessed August 27, 2010).

79. Phillips, phone interview, March 1, 2010.

80. "ONE Sadaqa Masjid Guide," http://www.one.org/us/onesabbath/muslims.html (accessed March 6, 2010).

81. Phillips, phone interview, March 1, 2010.

82. For a full account of this genocide, see Adam Hochschild, *King Leopold's Ghost: A Story of Greed, Terror, and Heroism in Colonial Africa* (Boston: Houghton Mifflin, 1998).

83. "Sudan Aid Group Halts Activity," February 25, http://www.savedarfur.org/pages/clips/sudan-aid-group-halts-activity/ (accessed February 28, 2010).

84. Phone interview with Will Fisher, campaign field organizer, Save Darfur Coalition, phone interview, November 30, 2009.

85. Jerry Fowler, "On the Ground Update from Sudan," http://blogfordarfur.org/ (accessed February 28, 2010).

86. "Voices for Darfur: 5 Years of Advocacy," http://www.youtube.com/watch?v=Fmo Dq87wtRE&feature=player_embedded# (accessed February 28, 2010).

87. "Idaho Activist Passionate about Sudan," February 3, 2010, http://blogfordarfur.org/archives/category/activist-stories (accessed February 28, 2010).

88. "Why Target These Five Companies?" *Divest for Darfur: The Save Darfur Coalition's Divestment Campaign.* PDF files, http://www.savedarfur.org/page/content/other_resources/ (accessed February 28, 2010).

89. Fisher, phone interview, November 30, 2009.

90. Janice Kamenir-Reznik, co-founder and chair of the board of Jewish World Watch, phone interview, March 23, 2010.

91. "Accomplishments: JWW Progress Report as of October 2009," http://www.jewishworldwatch.org/aboutjww/accomplishments.html (accessed March 27, 2010).

92. Kamenir-Reznik, phone interview, March 23, 2010.

93. Ibid.

94. Ibid.

95. Cameron Woodward, social media and recurring donations manager, Invisible Children, phone interview, February 5, 2010.

96. "We Are Story Tellers: We Make Documentaries about War-Affected Children in East Africa and Tour Them Around the World,"http://www.invisiblechildren.com/about/ourStory (accessed March 1, 2010).

97. Woodward, phone interview, February 5, 2010.

98. "The Rescue Update," http://www.youtube.com/watch?v=feJm2G-kPXY&feature=channel (accessed March 1, 2010).

99. Woodward, phone interview, February 5, 2010.

100. Ibid.

101. Ibid.

102. Ibid.

103. Nate's tragic death is unfortunately the risk taken on by young Americans who chose to stand in solidarity with people in war torn regions of the world. See "In Loving Memory of Nate," at http://www.invisiblechildren.com/media/videos/detail.php?id=1811646433&utm_source=Email+Newsletter+Sign+Ups&utm_campaign=62c99e7733-in_loving_memory_nate_henn_7_16_2010&utm_medium=email (accessed August 27, 2010).

Index

Accompaniment, 38, 63–64, 150, 175–76, 183, 198

ACORN. *See* Association of Community Organizations for Reform Now

Activism. *See* Anti-poverty advocacy; Borderlands; Community activism, emergence of; Congregation-based activism; Immigrant rights activism; Peace activism; Prophetic activism; Worker rights activism

Activists, justice: borderlands, 38, 99, 113; cosmopolitan, 99, 113, 146, 165; cosmopolitan-borderlands, 99, 113; evolution/innovation of, 235; prophets as, 41; religious v. secular, 38; texts commonly used by, 37–38; textual use by, 115, 160–61; training, 82, 96, 114, 146–47, 207; younger generation of, 77–78, 84, 85, 129–30, 201, 207, 211. *See also* Borderlands; Cosmopolitans; Peace activism; Prophetic activism

Afghanistan, 177

AFL-CIO, 102, 103–4, 106, 108–10, 129; scriptural texts in manuals published by, 114

Africa, 33, 222, 226–28; BFW in, 206; child soldiers in, 227–28; debt-relief program for, 215; HIV/AIDS programs in, 201–2, 219; humanitarian aid to, 201–2; poverty/colonialism in, 204. *See also* Darfur

African Americans, 85, 118; civil rights leaders, 54–55, 56; congregational-based organizing among, 82; incarceration of male, 95–96; Latinos/Latinas alliances with, 125, 155; marginalization of immigrant, 12; Protestant, 72; right to

vote loss by, 24; *satyagraha* embraced by, 55; urban politics involvement of, 68–69; volunteer organizations founded by, 13; young/radical, 77–78

Agricultural laborers, Mexican, 137

Agriprocessors, raid on, 153, 157–58

AIDS, 201–2, 219

Alinsky, Saul, 69, 76, 77, 81, 111; UFW model v. CSO of, 105, 106

Alliance Schools, 93

American Muslim Voice (AMV), 195

Amnesty International, 148, 154

AMV. *See* American Muslim Voice

Anti-globalization movement, 203

Anti-immigrant law, Arizona's, 164–65. *See also* Sensenbrenner bill

Anti-immigrant organizations, 133–34

Anti-poverty advocacy, 201–30; BFW's, 201, 204–9; Invisible Children, 64–65, 226–29, 234–35; Jubilee 2000 campaign, 212–18; ONE campaign, 200, 201, 219–21; overview of global, 201–4; Save Darfur Coalition for, 222–26, 234; storytelling in, 211, 227, 228; WFP's new focus on, 209–11

Anti-torture campaign, 187–89

Appiah, Kwame Anthony, 27

Arellano, Elvira, 131–32, 150

Arizona, 133, 134, 135, 140–48, 149; immigrant deaths in border/desert of, 144; SB 1070 anti-immigrant law of, 164–65

Arnova, Raul, 121

Arpaio, Joe, 158, 159

Arrests: Arellano, 132; ICE raid/sixty mothers', 157; NMD volunteers, 144, 147; Postville, 135; Villegas, 154

Central America, 141, 152, 183–84, 217; 1980s solidarity movements supporting, 63; sanctuary movement in, 150; U.S. intervention in, 182–83

Chambers, Ed, 80

Change to Win (CtW), 104, 118, 130

Chávez, César, 39–40, 76, 184; borderlands background/context for, 105; Catholicism of, 107; civil rights movement influence on, 107–8; Gandhi and, 105

Chavez-Thompson, Linda, 102

CHC. *See* Congressional Hispanic Caucus

Chicago, 2006 immigrant rallies in, 134

Chicago Area Workers Rights Initiative, 122

Chicago Interfaith Committee on Workers Issues (CICWI), 122

Chicanos, 79

Child Citizens Protection Act, 152

Child soldiers, 227–28

Chinese, exclusion of, 99

Christians: immigrant rights denied by conservative, 47; obedience to state, 163–64; pacifism of today's, 168–69; progressive, 47; text use by conservative v. progressive, 35–38

Christianity, 18–20; diversification within activist, 6; global South and, 21; IAFs blend of Judaism and, 85; IWJ integration of Hebrew/Muslim texts with, 129; in politics, 2–3; Triumphalist, 18, 36, 163, 167; Western society decline of, 21

Christian Peacemaker Teams (CPT), 29, 165, 185–87

Christian Right, on torture, 189

Churches: sanctuary provided by, 150–53. *See also* Sanctuary movement; *specific churches*

CICWI. *See* Chicago Interfaith Committee on Workers Issues

CIO. *See* Congress of Industrial Organizations

Citizenship rights, 96; African American male incarceration and, 95–96; borderlands and, 24–26; citizenship criteria and, 136; gradual advancement of U.S., 17; immigrant worker exploitation and, 98; insurgent citizenship and, 26, 67, 90–96, 105, 120, 121, 231; transnational, 24; U.S. immigrants denied, 8–9, 11, 26, 131–35. *See also* Insurgent citizenship

Civil disobedience, 38, 39, 144; Dear's activist stories on, 58; deportation and, 131; peace activism, 179–80; religion and, 133; Thoreau's, 53

Civil initiative, 144, 146

Civil rights movement, 7, 13–15, 39, 77; African American leaders of, 54–55, 56; African American Protestants in, 72; Alinsky organizations inspired by, 76; Catholic lack of involvement in, 72; Chávez influenced by, 107–8; Gandhi's influence on, 53–57; Highlander Folk School and, 62; Indian independence movement and, 54–55, 240n39; popular education methodology of, 62; worker rights and, 98

Clergy and Laity United for Economic Justice (CLUE), 1, 2, 32, 84, 150; formation of, 109; internship programs of, 129–30; methodology of, 111; union collaboration with, 29; worker rights activism of, 97, 110–13, 126

Clinton Administration, 140

CLUE. *See* Clergy and Laity United for Economic Justice

Colombia, 175–76, 184–85

Colonialism, poverty and, 199, 204, 213, 216

Colonial period, peace activism during, 172

Communities Organized for Public Service (COPS), 78–80; IAF collaboration with, 92–93

Community activism, emergence of, 68–70. *See also* Neighborhood-based activism

Community Service Organization (CSO), 105, 106

Concientización, 61

Congo, 222, 226

Congregation-based activism: border-lands, 67–96; Catholic Church, 70–76; community organizing emergence with, 68–70; grievances identified in, 88–89; immigrant rights and, 94–95; insurgent citizenship and, 90–96; narratives infused in, 86–90; neighborhood-based model preceding, 69, 77–80; prophetic tradition use in, 81, 84–86; reasons for shift to, 81; unions and, 69

Congress, debt-relief support from, 213–15

Congressional Hispanic Caucus (CHC), 155

Congress of Industrial Organizations (CIO), 69, 100

Congress of Racial Equality (CORE), 56, 174

Conservatives, 4–5, 47; de-unionization and, 101–2; progressive v., text use by, 35–38; textual basis for religious, 35–38, 163–64, 189; U.S. religious life and, 14–16

Construyendo Juntos, 84

Contract employees, unionized, 92

Contra war, 63, 182–83

COPS. *See* Communities Organized for Public Service

CORE. *See* Congress of Racial Equality

Cortes, Ernesto, 78, 79, 85

Cortright, David, 178

Cosmopolitans, 27–30, 32–33; borderlands methodologies v., 169–73, 232; defined, 22; email used by, 181, 198, 232; Hebrew Scriptures viewed by, 29; immigrant rights activists as, 146, 165; liberation theology and, 29–30, 61; methodologies of, 30, 38–39, 169–73, 232; peace activism, 169–71, 198; religious, 27–28; as social location, 22, 27–30; solidarity with borderlands low-wage workers, 99, 113; worldview of, 28, 84; youth as, 84

CPT. *See* Christian Peacemaker Teams

Creation story, Genesis, 50

Cripps, Paula, 84

Crisóstomo, Flor, 131–32

"Crossing the Line," 148

CSO. *See* Community Service Organization

CtW. *See* Change to Win

Daley, Richard J., 76

Darfur, 2, 64–65, 222–26, 234

Day, Dorothy, 39–40, 71–72, 86

DCP. *See* Developing communities Project

Dear, John, 57–58

Deaths: border-crossing migrant, 58, 140–41, 144, 145–46, 165; 2000 v. 1998 total, 140–41, 144. *See also* No More Deaths

Debt-relief, 200, 201, 215; eligibility for, 216–17; Jubilee 2000 campaign, 33, 212–18; use of savings from, 219

Delano march, UFW, 107–8

Delegations: anti-poverty solidarity work through, 211; to Iran, 176; to Nicaragua, 183, 210–11

Democracy, debt-relief focus on building, 218

Department of Homeland Security (DHS), 148–49, 152, 154, 158

Department of Labor, Perdue Farms settle-ment brokered by, 118–19

Deportation, 131, 132; ICE agents and, 108; immigrant family, 150–52, 155–57; incarceration prior to, 135; Reagan policy on, 141; Sellz/Strauss case of, 144, 145; 2007-2008 increased, 154

Deregulation, 102

Detention centers, 157, 193

De-unionization, 101–5

Deuteronomy, 45, 51

Developing communities Project (DCP), 7

DHS. *See* Department of Homeland Security

Disarmament, 177–82

Disney Corporation, 1–2

Du Bois, W. E. B., 56

Durazo, Maria Elena, 109–10

Earned Income Tax Credit (EITC), 208

Echo Park, 113

Education: JWW's methodology of, 2, 225; worker rights activism, 126–30. *See also* Popular education

Educational reform, 93
EFCA. *See* Employee-Free Choice Act
Egalitarianism, Hebrew Bible and, 45–46
Egan, Jack, 72, 109
EITC. *See* Earned Income Tax Credit
Elizondo, Virgilio, 79
Email, 181, 198, 232
Empire, 9–12; migration and, 22–23; poli-
   tics of U.S., 12–17; prophetic activism as
   resistance to, 17–20; prophetic tradition
   and, 49; Roman, 21
Employee-Free Choice Act (EFCA), 105
Employees. *See* Unions
Evangelicals, 75, 234; Latino/a, 130, 162–63;
   torture record of white, 189
Exclusion, Chinese worker, 99
Executive Order, against torture, 188
Exile, prophetic readings of, 40–41
Exodus, book of, 48, 76
Ezekiel, 46

Fair Labor Standards Act, 103
Faith Works, 117, 119, 128
Families: Catholic/Protestant focus on
   unity of, 155; deportation of migrant,
   150–52, 155–57
Fanon, Franz, 37
Farley, David, 113
Farmer, James, 56
Farm workers, 119
Fein, Helen, 191
Fellowship of Reconciliation (FOR), 55,
   173–77, 197–98; diverse membership of,
   175; founding of, 172
Field, Marshall, III, 69
Fife, John, 141
Fine, Janice, 108–9, 120
Fisher, Will, 222–23, 224
FOR. *See* Fellowship of Reconciliation
Freedom, prophetic activism as means to,
   90–91
Freedom Rides, 56, 64, 128, 228
Freire, Paulo, 61–62, 81
Funding: Darfur genocide, 224; decline
   in CCHD, 74–75; IWJ, *116*, 116–17; NYC
   Nehemia Plan, 91; Reagan's cuts in

federal, 81; state, 92–93; WFP's interreligious, 182–83

Gamaliel Foundation, 7, 82, 93, 94–95
Gandhi, Mahatma, 5, 28–29, 55, 174;
   Chávez and, 105; civil rights movement
   influenced by, 53–57; Gregg as translator
   of, 55–56; Sermon on the Mount and, 57
Garvey, Marcus, 13
Gates, Bill, 201, 219
Gates Foundation, 62, 220, 234
Gaudium et Spes (Joy and Hope), 58
GED program, 96
Geldof, Bob, 201
Genesis, 36, 42; creation story, 50
Genocide, 2, 222, 223, 224; anti-, 33; against
   Canaanites, 50; companies funding
   Darfur, 224; Judaism and, 2, 190–91
German peace sects, colonial, 172
Global activism, 199–230; religion's role
   in, 229. *See also* Anti-poverty advocacy;
   Peace activism
Global Empire: prophetic activism in
   context of, 9–12. *See also* Empire
Globalization, 231; human rights movement,
   132; manufacturing, 92; migration and,
   136–39; movement for anti-, 203; poverty
   deepened by, 9–10, 203, 216; prophetic
   activism as response to, 5, 9–12
Global South, 27; Christianity in, 21;
   immigrants from, 23; liberation theology
   and, 59
Good Samaritan story, 140. *See also*
   Samaritans
Grassroots networks, 39, 64–65, 67, 198;
   CLUE as worker rights, 110; congrega-
   tion-based, 82–83
Great Depression, 71–72
Gregg, Richard Bartlett, 55–56
Grievances, congregation-based activism
   primary, 88–89
Guest-worker program, 143
Gutterman, David, 36

Haiti, 199–200
Hancock, Gordon, 55

Hardt, Michael, 9, 17, 19, 167–68
Health care insurance, 92, 93–94
Heavily Indebted Poor Countries (HIPC), 215
Hebrew Bible, 44–51, 115, 160–61; centrality of justice in, 42–43; as foreshadowing of New Testament, 128; hegemony justified by, 37; historicity of narratives in, 40; immigrant rights and, 240n24; liberation theology and, 60; Nehemiah Plan and, 91; peace activism in, 50–51; prophetic tradition within, 40–44; as story of oppressed, 84; version of, 33; warfare in, 50; worker rights and, 115
Hebrew Scriptures: cosmopolitan view of, 29; Muslim/Christian texts integrated with, 129
Hegemony: textual justification of, 37; U.S., 3
Helms, Jesse, 219
HERE. *See* Hotel Employers and Restaurant Employees
Heritage Foundation, 74
Heschel, Abraham Joshua (rabbi), 29, 42–43, 225
HIPC. *See* Heavily Indebted Poor Countries
Historical legacy, prophetic activism, 6–7
Historicity, Hebrew Bible narrative, 40
HIV/AIDS, 201–2, 219
Hog growers, 126
Holston, James, 25, 26
Horton, Myles, 62
Hotel Employers and Restaurant Employees (HERE) union, 1, 109–10, 118
HR 4437. *See* Sensenbrenner bill
Humane Borders, 141–43, 145, 147–48
Humanitarian aid, 145; to Africa, 201–2; RED label product selling for, 219, 228, 230
"Humanitarian Aid is never a Crime" campaign, 145
Human rights, 8, 154, 237n8; accompaniment, 63–64; global movement for, 132; local/state jurisdiction over, 25; nation-states' enforcement of, 224; universal

declaration of, 136, 162, 205; U.S. border policies and, 144; U.S.-sponsored torture issue of, 193; violations, 144, 148
Hunter, Duncan, 133
Hurricane Katrina, 119
Hybridity, 235; borderlands activism, 120, 130; identity, 88–89, 132; immigrants' religion, 23–24; worker rights activism, 108–13

IAF. *See* Industrial Areas Foundation
ICE. *See* Immigration Control and Enforcement
Identity, hybridized, 88–89, 132
IDEPCSA. See *Instituto de Educacion Popular del Sur de California*
IIC. *See* Interreligious Immigration Coalition
IMF. *See* International Monetary Fund
Immigrant rights, 69, 94–95; conservative Christians' denial of, 47; opponents of, 159; prophetic tradition and, 47–50, 240n24; Sensenbrenner bill, 125, 134, 154, 155, 158, 164; worker rights activism intertwined with, 117–18, 123–24
Immigrant rights activism, 131–65; Borderlands setting for, 165; guest-worker program, 143; history of U.S. policy and, 137–38; Humane Borders/water in desert, 141–43, 145, 147–48; immigration reform, 123, 153–56, 159, 160–64; migration in globalized context, 136–39; religiously grounded, 132–33, 145; religious support for, broadening of, 153–60; Samaritans, 140, 143–46; sanctuary movement in, 150–53; textual basis for, 145; 287g program triggering new, 152, 154, 155, 158, 159
Immigrants: Arizona's SB 1070 anti-immigrant law, 164–65; Asian, 83, 137–38; barring help to illegal, 125; border deaths of, 2000 v. 1998, 144; borderlands created by, 23–24; citizenship rights denied U.S., 8–9, 11, 26; congregation-based organizations with, 83; defense committees for illegal families of, 151–52; early labor

leaders as, 99–100; 1840s/1850s surge of Catholic, 70–71; from Global South, 23; Latin American, 138; marginalized, 12, 26, 120, 133; myths about threat of, 133–34; punishment of illegal, 135; quotas, 138; raids opposition, 95; remittances to families of, 97–98; 2006 march of, 134; undocumented, 125, 153–54, 155

Immigration Control and Enforcement (ICE): Arellano's arrest by, 132; detention centers, 157, 193; Postville raid/mothers arrested by, 157; raids by, 95, 108, 113, 126, 153; strike-breaking of, 117; 287g program, 152, 154, 155, 158, 159; 2005 policy, 135

Immigration reform, 123, 139, 148, 153–56, 159, 231–32; religious groups' view of, 161–64; religious lobbying for, 160–64

Immigration Reform and Control Act (IRCA), 148, 154

Incarceration: African American male, 95–96; prior to deportation, 135

Income inequality, 12–13

India, Methodist Church in, 57

Indian independence movement, 54–55, 240n39

Industrial Areas Foundation (IAF), 69, 75, 77, 78, 80, 82; Christian/Jewish traditions in, 85; COPS collaboration with, 92–93; Nehemia Plan of, 91; storytelling as central to, 89

Inheritance laws, ancient Israel's, 44–45

Instituto de Educacion Popular del Sur de California (IDEPCSA), 120–21, 234

Insurgent citizenship, 25, 26, 67, 105, 121; congregation-based activism as, 90–96

Interfaith Worker Justice (IWJ), 29, 32, 109, 151, 235; BFW similar methodologies to, 207; funding for, 116, 116–17; internship programs of, 129–30; launching of national, 109; local affiliates of, 117–19; methodology, 110–11; prophetic tradition texts in work of, 127–29; religious diversity among staff of, 112; union collaboration of, 114–17; worker centers affiliated with, 109, 120–26; worker self-organizing methodology of, 123–24

Interfaith worker-justice groups, 100; number of, 98

International Monetary Fund (IMF), 10, 199, 206, 208, 212, 213

Internship programs, IWJ/CLUE, 129–30

Interpretation. See Reinterpretation

Interreligious Immigration Coalition (IIC), 159, 160–61

Interviews, 31, 87

Invisible Children, 64–65, 226–29, 234–35

Iran, peace delegations to, 176

Iraq, U.S. invasion of, 167–69, 192

IRCA. See Immigration Reform and Control Act

Irish Catholics, 76

Isaiah, 46, 50, 75; Second, 50–51

Islam, 112, 114–15, 128, 221

"Islam and Labor: Forging Partnerships Conference," 112, 114–15

Israel, ancient, 40, 41, 44–45, 47–50

Israel-Palestine conflict, 186–87, 192, 195

IWJ. See Interfaith Worker Justice

Jacobs, Lawrence R., 12

Jeremiah, 49

Jesus: Catholic Worker movement based on life of, 72; liberation theology and, 60; NMD volunteer on, 146; prophetic tradition expanded on by, 51–53; Satyagraha and, 53–54; on visiting prisoners, 96

Jewish activists: Isaiah quoted by, 75; Postville and, 158; prophetic text use by Christian and, 44

Jewish Peace Fellowship, 190, 191

Jewish peace organizations, 170, 190; newest, 193–95

Jewish World Watch (JWW), 2, 225

John Paul, II (pope), 20, 213

Johnson, Lyndon, 138

John XXIII (pope), 183

J Street, 193–95

Jubilee (Leviticus), 45, 47

Jubilee 2000 campaign, 33, 212–18; goal of, 213; interreligious support for, 214; successor organization, 217–18

Medicaid, Social Security Act amendment for, 94
Medvedev, 180
Mennonites, 161, 172, 179
Mestizaje, 24
Methodist Church, in India, 57
Methodologies: accompaniment, 38, 63–64, 150, 175–76, 183, 198; BFW/IWJ similar, 207; civil disobedience, 38, 39; CLUE's blend of, 111; cosmopolitan, 30, 38–39, 169–73, 232; cosmopolitan v. borderlands, 169–73, 232; email, 181, 198, 232; grassroots, 39, 64–65, 67, 110, 198; immigrant law requiring new IWJ, 123–24; Immigrant rights opponents', 159; insurgent citizenship building as, 121; lobbying, 160–64, 206; neighborhood-based, 77–80; one-on-ones, 81, 92, 111, 122; origin of, 39; popular education, 81–82, 86–90, 111, 125; privilege as, 38; research, 31; social networking, 65, 181, 198, 201, 207, 218, 221. *See also* Liberation theology; Popular education; Privilege
Mexican American Cultural Center (MACC), 60, 79, 150
Mexican Americans, 76; Roman Catholic clergy, 78
Mexicans: agricultural laborer, 137; population percentage of, 138
Mexico: Arellano's deportation to, 132; -U.S. border, 133–34, 136, 140–43, 144, 210
Middle class, hybridization and, 88–89
Middle East, 186–87, 224
Migrants, death of border-crossing, 58, 140–41, 144, 145–46, 165
Migration, 71; empire and, 22–23; globalization and, 136–39; as survival strategy, 10. *See also* Immigrant rights; Immigrants
Millennium Development Goals (MDGs), 220
Mink, Gwendolyn, 99
Minutemen, 133, 142
Mohammed, 41, 55
Moral Man and Immoral Society (Niebuhr), 54

Morris, Aldon, 62
Mosaic Law, 45
Moses, sanctuary movement based on, 150
Multitude (Hardt/Negri), 19
Muslim immigrants, racial profiling of, 133, 153
Muslims, 84; CLUE's work with leadership among, 112; peace organizations, 170, 195
Muslim texts, 129

NAACP. *See* National Association for the Advancement of Colored People
NAFTA. *See* North American Free Trade Agreement
Narrative, 86–90. *See also* Storytelling
The Nation, 102
National Association for the Advancement of Colored People (NAACP), 13, 56
National Council of Churches of Kenya (NCCK), 216
National Hispanic Christian Leadership Conference (NHCLC), 162
National Labor Relations Act, 101–2
National Labor Relations Board (NLRB), 14
National Network for Immigrant and Refugee Rights (NNIRR), 131, 134, 153, 234; popular education used by, 154–55
National Religious Campaign Against Torture (NRCAT), 187–88
Nation states: border control by, 136; human rights enforced by, 224; Matthew and, 51–52
NCCK. *See* National Council of Churches of Kenya
Negri, Antonio, 9, 17, 167–68; *Multitude*, 19
Negro Improvement Association, 13
Nehemiah Plan, 91
Neighborhood-based activism, 69, 77–80, 82
New Labor Forum, 102
New Revised Standard Version (NRSV), 33
New Sanctuary Coalition of New York City, 151–52

ment, 177–82; Hebrew Bible and, 50–51; interreligious nature of, 168–69, 170, 175, 182–83, 189–97; religions in broad span of, 170; religious/secular nature of, 168; solidarity work in, 182–87

People Improving Communities through Organizing (PICO), 73

Perdue Farms, 118–19

Pesner, Jonah (rabbi), 75

Pew Charitable Trust, 6, 189

Phares, Gail, 182, 183–84, 211

Pickle growers, 126

PICO. See People Improving Communities through Organizing

Plan of Delano, 107–8

Policy. See specific legislation; specific topics

Policy analysis, 208

Politics: African American urban, 68–69; BFW's awareness of/influence on, 208; conservative, 14–16, 47, 101–2, 163–64, 189; Judaism in progressive, 4; religion used by, 2–3, 4; U.S. empire, 12–17. See also Conservatives

Poor, grievances of middle class v., 88–89

Pop culture, 220

Popular education, 38, 61–63, 111, 143, 154–55; borderlands use of, 67–68, 81–82, 143; civil rights movement use of, 62; narratives in, 86–90; storytelling as form of, 152; worker rights and, 124, 125

Population: U.S. Catholic, 70; U.S. immigrant, 138

Posada, 1

Postville, Iowa, workplace raid in, 135, 153, 156–58

Poultry workers, 118

Poverty: civil rights movement attention to, 77; colonialism and, 199, 204, 213, 216; dependency issue in addressing, 202; globalization causing deeper, 9–10, 203, 216; Haiti's, 199–200; peace activism and, 185; U.S./government policy and, 205–6. See also Anti-poverty advocacy

The Power of Nonviolence (Gregg), 55

Prayer vigils, 159–60

Prisoners, Jesus on visiting, 96

Privilege: accompaniment and, 63–64, 198; border work and, 145, 146–47, 149; as methodology, 38; peace activism and, 170

Progressive Christians, 47

Progressive Jewish Alliance, 6–7, 100

Progressive politics, 4

Property rights, Jubilee, 45

Prophetic activism: Christianity and, 6, 18–20; contours of contemporary, 4–9; freedom as goal of, 90–91; globalization and, 5, 9–12; historical legacy of, 6–7; hybrid forms of, 108–13, 120, 130, 235; immigrant rights and, 145; interreligious nature of, 18, 168–69, 170, 182–83, 189–97, 214, 221, 223, 233; as nonviolent resistance, 53–58; overview of, 31–33; "prophetic" definition, 35, 239n1; qualities of, 35–65; resistance to empire through, 17–20; social location centrality in, 20–30. See also Activists, justice; Anti-poverty advocacy; Borderlands; Community activism, emergence of; Congregation-based activism; Immigrant rights activism; Neighborhood-based activism; Peace activism; Worker rights activism; specific organizations

Prophetic tradition: borderlands and, 40–41; congregation-based activism use of, 81, 84–86; Hebrew Bible, 40–44; immigrant rights and, 47–50, 240n24; IWJ use of, 127–29; Jesus as expanding on, 51–53; otherness and, 43–44; wage theft struggle as grounded in, 129; youth activists and, 85

Prophets, as activists, 41

Protestant Church: Catholic v., 69–70, 71; U.S. empire and, 14–15

Protestants: African American, 72; anti-Catholicism of northern, 70; family unity concern in immigration issues, 155; FOR affiliation of liberal, 173; Latin American, 139; liberation theology and, 60–61; 2001 congregation assessment, 82–83; UFW's, 107

Save Darfur Coalition, 64–65, 222–26, 234; inclusivity of membership, 223
SB 1070 anti-immigrant law of, 164–65
SBC. *See* Southern Baptist Convention
SCHIP. *See* State Children's Health Insurance Program
Schwarzenegger, Arnold, 225
Second Isaiah, 50–51
Secularism/secularists, 3, 6, 38, 168; union, 114
"See, judge, act" paradigm, 95
SEIU. *See* Service Employees International Union
Sellz, Santi, 144, 145
Sen, Amartya, 25–26, 90–91, 208, 216
Sensenbrenner bill, 125, 134, 154, 155, 158
September 11, 133, 153, 167
Sermon on the Mount, 37, 52, 54, 57, 86
Service employees, 16, 114, 115, 116, 117–18
Service Employees International Union (SEIU), 114, 116
Shalom Center, 192
Sheil, Bernard J., 69
Shriver, Bobby, 201, 213, 215, 220
Simon, Arthur, 204–5
Simon, William, 74
Sins, 42; of Israel, 41
Skocpol, Theda, 12, 13
Smith, Christian, 170–71
Smith-Christopher, Daniel, 49–50
Social location: borderlands as, 22–26; centrality of, 20–30; cosmopolitan, 22, 27–30
Social networking, 65, 201, 207; ONE campaign, 218, 221; peace activism use of, 181; Save Darfur Coalition, 223–24
Social Security Act, Medicaid amendment to, 94
Social Security Administration, 123
Social Security number, false, 135
Sojourners (magazine), 20
Sojourners/Call to Renewal, 36, 94
Solidarity, 211; cosmopolitan-borderlands activist-worker, 99, 113; FOR emphasis on, 175; 1980s and, 63; with oppressed, 62; peace activism, 182–87; U.S.-Uganda children, 228–29

Southern Baptist Convention (SBC), 163–64
State: Christian obedience to, 163–64; funding by, 92–93; human/substantive rights and, 25
State Children's Health Insurance Program (SCHIP), 94
Staton, Emrys, 146–47
Storytelling, 86–90; anti-poverty advocacy attention to, 211, 227, 228; Invisible Children and, 228–29; peace activism use of personal, 184–85, 198; sanctuary families' personal, 152; worker rights activism, 127
Strauss, Daniel, 144, 145
Stringfellow, William, 3
Structural adjustment policies (SAPs), 10, 199, 209, 210
Students, 78, 223–24
Sugirtharajah, R. S., 21
Sunda, Samina, 195–96
Sunday, Billy, King, Jr., v., 36–37
Supreme Court rulings, false Social Security number, 135
Sweeney, John, 103, 115
Symbolism, religious, 214, 234

Taco Bell, 119
Tagore, Rabindranath, 55
Texts, scriptural, 86; anti-torture campaign grounding in, 188–89; Bobo's integration of Muslim/Christian/Hebrew, 129; Borderlands activist passages from, 46, 72; Christian conservatives v. progressives use of, 35–38; commonly used, 37–38; conservatives' references to, 35–38, 163–64, 189; cosmopolitans' view of, 29; immigrant rights activism basis in, 145; Jewish congregations' use of, 72; Jubilee 2000 campaign location in, 212; reinterpretation of, 53, 65, 233–34; relational approach to reading, 19; religious lobbying use of, 160–61; sanctuary movement and, 150; selective proof-texting, 18; social location and, 21; as theodicy, 41; training materials including use of specific, 114, 207; worker rights and, 115, 127–29. *See also specific texts*

Theodicy, prophetic texts as, 41
Theologians, contemporary, 86
Thoreau, Henry David, 53
Thurman, Howard, 4, 55, 174
Tichenor, Paul, 26
Tikkun olam, 4
Timson, Corey, 84, 85
Tocqueville, Alexis de, 85
Tolstoy, Leo, 53–54
Torture, 187–89, 193
TRAC. *See* Transactional Records Access Clearinghouse
Training, volunteer/activist, 82, 96, 114, 146–47, 207
Transactional Records Access Clearinghouse (TRAC), 135
Transnational citizenship rights, 24
Triumphalist Christianity, 18, 36, 163, 167
Tucson, Arizona, 135, 140–46
Tutu, Desmond (archbishop), 213
TWO. *See* The Woodlawn Organization
287g program, 152, 154, 155, 158, 159
Two Futures Project, 181–82
Tzedakah, 225

UFW. *See* United Farm Workers
Uganda, 226, 227, 228–29
UN. *See* United Nations
Unions, 75, 99–110, 192; Catholic Church organizing of, 100; CLUE collaboration with, 29; collaboration with, worker rights groups, 114–17; congregation-based activism and, 69; contract employee, 92; CtW, 118; decline of, 16, 100, 101–5; de-unionization, 101–5; early labor leaders establishing, 99; ICE raids and, 126; living wage ordinance and, 92; Obama supported by, 104–5; service worker, 114; UFW model of, 105–8, 130; worker centers as new form of, 108–9, 120–26
Union of Reform Judaism, 75, 192
United Farm Workers (UFW), 40, 106; Alinsky-style organizing v., 106; as worker rights activism model, 105–8, 130

United Methodist Church, 16, 109, 149, 178, 238n20. *See also* Methodist Church, in India
United Nations (UN), MDGs of, 220
United Neighborhoods Organization (UNO), 80
United States (U.S.): Catholic population in, 70; Central America intervention by, 182–83; children of Uganda and, solidarity between, 228–29; citizenship rights advancement in, 17; citizenship rights struggle in, 8–9; debt-relief congressional support in, 213–15; detention centers, 157, 193; empire politics of, 12–17; hegemony of, 3; immigrants denied citizenship in, 8–9, 11, 26, 131–35; immigration policy in, historical perspective on, 137–38; international human rights violations in, 144; invasion of Iraq, 167–69, 192; -Mexico border, 58, 133–34, 136, 137, 140–43, 144, 145, 148–49, 161–64, 210; ODA contributions by, 202; poverty in, 205–6; -sponsored torture, 193; voting rights loss in, 24; worker rights regional activism in, 117–19; worker rights violations in, 97
Universal Declaration of Human Rights, 136, 162, 205
UNO. *See* United Neighborhoods Organization
Urban politics, community organizing and, 68–69
U.S. *See* United States

Vallet, Maryada, 146
Vatican II, 58–59, 73
Vietnam War, church refuges for drafters of, 150
Villegas, Juana, arrest of, 154
Volunteer organizations, African American founders of, 13
Volunteer training, 82, 96, 114, 146–47, 207
Voting rights, number of U.S. citizens losing, 24

Wage Theft in America (Bobo), 129
Wallis, Jim, 20